Scot

Trail Running

 Pesda Press LTD

www.pesdapress.com

First published in Great Britain 2012 by Pesda Press

Tan y Coed Canol

Ceunant

Caernarfon

Gwynedd

LL55 4RN

Maps – Bute Cartographic

Contains Ordnance Survey data © Crown copyright and database right 2012

ISBN: 978-1-906095-39-0

Printed and bound in Poland. www.hussarbooks.pl

Introduction

"And we run because we like it
Through the broad bright land."
C. H. Sorley

This book is about running for fun in beautiful places. Each route has been selected for its inspirational scenery and runnable terrain. The range of routes is deliberately diverse – these runs follow rivers and coastlines, go up hills and through glens, cross barren Highlands and weave between Lowland trees. The selected routes come highly recommended by local runners and include many of Scotland's most enjoyable and runnable paths. But this is not a definitive collection. These runs are intended as a springboard for further personal exploration of Scotland's trails.

Glen Etive (Route 27)

Contents

Glen Affric
(Route 59)

West Highland Way
(Route 24)

Why Trail Running?

Moving fast and light through the great outdoors is what trail running is all about. Trail runners leave roads and traffic behind in search of the quieter and wilder, sometimes hidden, paths and tracks that criss-cross the country. Leafy woodland, lazily meandering riverbanks, dramatic sea cliffs, remote mountain passes: Scotland has all of these and all are fantastic places to run.

Trails are everywhere

The beauty of trail running is that it combines the speed and ease of running on roads with the fresh air and wide open spaces beloved by hill runners. Trails enable runners to move quickly over ground that would otherwise be too rough or boggy for a speedy passage. Trails enable runners to explore all over Scotland; from the inner reaches of dense suburban woodland to remote Highland glens.

Trails are for everyone

Trail running is a simple activity which is accessible to everyone willing to give it a go. Great off-road running trails are found anywhere and everywhere; in cities and towns as well as in the countryside. Anyone can take up trail running. Many trails are easily tackled by the most novice of runners and just as many trails will delight experienced runners seeking new challenges. Trail running is an activity that fits and grows with the experience and skill of the individual runner.

Definition of a Scottish running trail

A trail is simply a path or a track. This book exists because the paths and tracks found on the ground and marked on maps of Scotland are drawn from the whole spectrum of runnability. Runners exploring Scotland's trails are often thwarted by mud and bog, tussocks, deep heather or boulder fields. While these exploratory missions can be a great adventure, most of the time all a runner really wants to do is find and follow a clear, runnable trail in a beautiful place. This book is intended for that runner. The routes are based on a working definition of a Scottish running trail as a continuously visible route on the ground which is not a tarmac road and has no deep mud or bog, tussocks or boulder fields.

Guidebook scope and purpose

This guidebook sets out to describe enjoyable trail runs all over Scotland, including the islands. The routes selected for each chapter showcase the variety of trail running experiences that can be found in each of Scotland's diverse regions. Many of the routes are easily accessible trails close

Why Trail Running?

Lammer Law
(Route 13)

to towns, cities and popular holiday destinations. These runs range from short, straightforward circuits to longer, half-day outings. The remaining routes strike out into more remote terrain taking runners into the heart of Scotland's wildest and most spectacular landscapes. The selection process has inevitably required compromise as many enjoyable routes would have to be excluded in order to strictly adhere to the definition of a running trail given above. A few routes require some road running and at the other end of the spectrum a few of the most challenging circuits have short, unrunnable sections. Running on rougher trails does require skill and experience. The routes in this book have been selected to cover a wide range of running terrain so that runners can develop their ability in whichever direction they want: to run further; climb higher; tackle trickier ground; navigate more complex terrain. Developing these skills opens up a whole new world of opportunities for exploring the rich and varied Scottish landscape.

Disclaimer

Every effort has been made to ensure that the information supplied is accurate. However, mistakes happen and trails are subject to change. The author welcomes updates/ corrections.

As with any activity, trail runners must accept responsibility for their own actions, stay within their own limits and avoid harming other people or property. The author, publisher and distributor of this book do not recognise any liability for any injury or damage to person or property arising from the use of this guide.

How to Use This Book

This book is for reading in the armchair at home or for storing in the car glove box. It has been designed so that the turn-by-turn route description and map can be photocopied onto a single A4 page and taken on the run. Each route is laid out in the same format.

Quick reference

This section lists the length of the route in kilometres and miles as well as the cumulative ascent (height gain) in metres and feet. Distances are given to the nearest 0.5km for routes under 10km and to the nearest 1km for routes over 10km. Ascent is given to the nearest 25m (100ft/50ft for lower routes). A mixture of computer, GPS and paper mapping has been used to calculate distance and ascent. Although every effort has been made to supply accurate information it is inevitable that there will be inconsistencies with readers' own plots and GPS tracks. Ascent calculations are liable to vary much more than distance. Relevant maps are listed along with the start (and end) point(s) of the route with grid references and postcodes. The grid reference gives the precise location of the start of the route. The postcode is approximate and is provided to help sat-nav users reach the right general area. Rural postcodes cover a much larger area than urban postcodes. The most misleading postcodes have been omitted. Each route is rated to indicate the level of navigation required, the roughness of the terrain underfoot and the likelihood of getting wet feet.

Rating system

Three aspects of the route are rated to set appropriate expectations. The rating is based on the section of the route which requires the highest level of navigation, has the roughest terrain and the highest probability of wet feet.

Navigation •••	These routes are relatively easy to follow, usually with full or partial waymarking or sign posts.
Navigation •••	Some care is needed to stay on the described route as there are multiple junctions without waymarkers or signs. Some routes are graded 2 if they are technically easy to navigate but in a remote area where the consequences of getting lost could be serious. Map and compass are advisable.
Navigation •••	These routes cross remote regions where the consequences of getting lost are serious. A map, compass and the ability to use both are required in addition to the route description. The route may not always follow obvious land features. The path may not always be easily visible on the ground and may depend on the season and weather conditions.

How to Use This Book

Wet feet may be inevitable

Terrain ●●●	Smooth paths or tracks which are easy to run. There may be a few short rougher sections.
Terrain ●●●	Fairly easy to run but stones, tree roots or uneven path sections merit care at times.
Terrain ●●●	These routes are almost entirely runnable providing sufficient attention is paid to foot placement. They may be rocky, boggy or generally uneven. A couple of routes have sections where walking is unavoidable.
Wet feet ●●●	On a dry day wet feet are unlikely. There may be occasional and avoidable muddy puddles or patches of shallow mud.
Wet feet ●●●	Damp feet are likely, particularly in autumn and winter. During drier spells puddles and muddy patches can often be avoided. In normal conditions streams can be crossed by jumping or on stepping stones.
Wet feet ●●●	Wet feet are inevitable due to un-jumpable stream or river crossings and/or boggy areas.

How to Use This Book

Route description

The route description is divided into two parts: a scene setting preamble followed by functional, turn-by-turn instructions. The numbering in the functional part of the description matches the numbers on the route maps. Some runs follow waymarked or signed trails. Obviously these are subject to change. The description and map are intended to be sufficient to follow the route even if the waymarkers or signs have been removed.

Route map

The route maps are based on Ordnance Survey mapping with the scale varied in order to fit the whole route onto one page spread. They are intended to be complementary to, not substitutes for, Ordnance Survey or other published maps.

Trip planning

The closest public transport stops are named and included on the maps to help journey planning using websites or telephone helplines such as *www.travelinescotland.com* 0871 200 22 33 (24 hours). Brief driving directions and parking information are given. Cars should be booked onto ferries in advance to guarantee passage but foot passengers can just turn up on the day, usually half an hour before sailing. Conveniently located or personally recommended accommodation, pubs and cafés are mentioned. Inclusion of particular businesses is no guarantee of their suitability or that there is not somewhere better nearby. Tourism is rural Scotland's biggest industry so there are plenty of alternatives waiting to be found. Bear in mind that opening hours are often shorter in rural areas than in towns, and many tourism businesses only operate during the summer months, usually April to September. Phone ahead to check availability if reliant upon finding an evening meal or overnight accommodation. Useful websites for trip planning are listed in the resources section at the back of the book.

Other routes, activities and events

Every runner is different so this section aims to help those looking for longer, shorter or just plain different routes as well as runners staying in the area for more than one day. It is expected that readers will be interested in other outdoor activities so these are mentioned where appropriate. The Events section is a non-comprehensive list of trail races held on the route or in the local area. Some hill races, adventure races and road races are included too. Comprehensive events listings can be found at *www.scottishrunningguide.com* and *www.scottishhillracing.co.uk*

Getting Started

Running is one of the simplest and most satisfying activities in the world: just head out the door and put one foot in front of the other. There are just a few things it may help to think about first.

Why run?

People run for all sorts of reasons. Sometimes running is merely a means to an end: becoming physically fit; losing weight; maintaining mental health. This book focuses on the act of running itself. Running for fun. Running for the sheer joy of moving quickly through the Scottish landscape. Enjoying the runs in this book may have inadvertent side effects including stronger muscles, a healthier heart and lungs, weight loss and a greater sense of wellbeing.

First steps

All of the routes in this book are just as well walked as jogged or run, so there is no fitness barrier to getting started. Just get out there and give them a go. Start off by only running the downhills. Even the world's best hill runners walk steep uphill sections. As with any activity it is sensible to start small and gradually increase the effort required. Check the suitability of a route by looking at the distance and ascent (height gain) given in the route description.

Steady progress

Increase activity levels gradually to give both muscles and brain time to adapt to the demands of moving on trails. Running on uneven trails engages a wider range of muscles than running on smooth roads or pavement. On slippery or rocky trails the brain needs to work quickly to pick the most secure foot placements. There is an abundance of information on running-specific training and technique available from medical professionals and running coaches as well as from books and magazines.

Footwear

Well-fitting shoes suitable for the terrain are essential for enjoyable and injury-free running. The two fundamentals of choosing the right footwear are comfort and grip. Comfort depends on the way the shoe fits, stabilises, supports and cushions the runner's foot. The right shoe is a very individual decision. Shoe manufacturers use differently shaped lasts and have different ideas about the ideal amount of stability, support and cushioning. Specialist running shops can advise on these differences and suggest appropriate footwear. Road shoes usually have the most stability, support and cushioning. On uneven terrain this can make it more difficult to place feet accurately. Fell shoes have comparatively little cushioning. They can be an uncomfortable choice on anything harder than earth or grass paths, particularly during longer runs. Trail shoes are often a good compromise. Grip depends upon the sole of the shoe. Road trainers have a smooth sole which will give adequate grip in dry conditions for well-constructed paths and tracks.

Rugged soles give good grip on trails

Trail shoes have a rugged sole and are the best choice for most of the routes in this book.

The rugged sole gives better grip, particularly on wet days, and makes each step much more secure. Fell shoes have an exaggerated knobbly sole which helps runners stay secure on steep wet grass.

Clothing

There is plenty of technical clothing and advice available from specialist running shops. Synthetic materials are recommended as cotton takes a long time to dry and can rub badly when wet. Multiple thin layers are more flexible for regulating temperature than one thick layer. Zip neck tops are good for the same reason. Ankle socks are better at preventing stones and dirt entering shoes than low cut trainer liners. Well-fitting underwear is essential for both men and women: for women this means a high impact level sports bra. The Scottish weather is notoriously fickle so lightweight, breathable waterproofs are an important element of the runner's wardrobe. Hats and gloves will be needed in colder weather. Runners need to wear enough to stay warm. It can be tempting to wear less clothing on the assumption that running will help keep the body warm. In wet, cold conditions thinly clad runners are prone to developing hypothermia, particularly when they get tired. This is a serious medical condition which occurs when a person's core body temperature drops abnormally low. Look out for stumbles, mumbles and fumbles – key signs of the onset of hypothermia – and make sure these are treated immediately by putting on more clothes and heading for home.

Getting Started

A pair of runners can carry just enough for a relatively comfortable overnight camp

What to carry?

For short routes there is little need to carry anything at all. For longer routes, particularly those in remote areas, food, water and additional clothing are the basic extras. It is most comfortable to carry these in a lightweight rucksack or bumbag designed specifically for runners and sold in specialist running or outdoor shops. It is important to stay well-fed and hydrated. While out on routes lasting several hours runners should aim to eat a small amount regularly. What to eat is a matter of personal preference. Muesli bars, sandwiches, jelly babies, hula hoops and energy gels are just some of the foods popular with experienced runners. Drink when thirsty. The amount of fluid needed varies between individual runners and also depends on the conditions. Water, squash or energy drink can be carried in either a bottle or a bladder and hose. A mobile phone is recommended for safety reasons although coverage is limited in many parts of Scotland. Map, compass and the ability to use both are essential for some of the routes. A basic first aid kit containing at least a crepe bandage, wound dressing and a few sticking plasters is recommended as are a lightweight survival bag and whistle. Head torches prove their worth more often than anticipated.

Use common sense when packing for a run.

Running with a week's supply of muesli bars, three litres of water and five spare tops will not be much fun. On the other hand, omitting waterproofs and a warm layer could lead to a wet, cold and exhausting epic. Fast and light … and well-prepared.

Getting Started

Suggested kit list

	WEAR (CONDITIONS DEPENDENT)	CARRY (CONDITIONS DEPENDENT)
SHORT RUNS	SHOES	(ROUTE DESCRIPTION)
	SOCKS	(MAP AND COMPASS)
	SHORTS OR LEGGINGS	(MOBILE PHONE)
	SUPPORTIVE UNDERWEAR	(MONEY)
	SHORT OR LONG-SLEEVED TOP	(FOOD)
	(CAP)	(WATER)
	(WARM LAYER)	
	(WIND OR WATERPROOF TOP)	
	(HAT AND GLOVES)	
	(SUNSCREEN)	
LONGER RUNS	AS ABOVE	LIGHTWEIGHT RUCKSACK OR BUMBAG
		ROUTE DESCRIPTION
		MAP AND COMPASS
		MOBILE PHONE
		MONEY
		FOOD
		WATER
		WARM LAYER(S)
		WATERPROOF TOP AND BOTTOMS
		HAT AND GLOVES
		FIRST AID KIT
		WHISTLE
		SURVIVAL BAG
		HEAD TORCH
		(SUNSCREEN)
OVERNIGHT CAMPING RUNS	AS ABOVE	LIGHTWEIGHT RUCKSACK (25L IS GOOD)
		ROUTE DESCRIPTION
		MAP AND COMPASS
		MOBILE PHONE
		MONEY
		FOOD
		WATER
		WARM LAYER(S) INCLUDING FULL LENGTH LEGGINGS
		WATERPROOF TOP AND BOTTOMS
		HAT AND GLOVES
		FIRST AID KIT
		WHISTLE
		SURVIVAL BAG
		HEAD TORCH
		(SUNSCREEN)
		TENT OR BIVVY
		STOVE, PAN, FUEL AND LIGHTER/MATCHES
		GROUND INSULATION E.G. CLOSED CELL MAT
		SLEEPING BAG
		(TOTAL WEIGHT 4 – 7KG)

Getting Started

Wee beasties

Scotland's biting insects are legendary. Covering up bare skin with long sleeves and full length leggings is the best way to avoid being bitten. Even with these precautions ticks are liable to sneak a way in regardless. Some ticks in Scotland carry Lyme's Disease. Always do a full body check as soon as possible after running in potentially tick infested areas. In practice this means most of the Scottish countryside and particularly upland areas grazed by deer or sheep. The NHS recommended removal method is to grab the tick as close to the skin as possible using tweezers then extract by pulling straight up gently. See a GP immediately if a target-shaped rash or flu-like symptoms develop.

A map is essential for more remote routes

Skills Development

Trail running technique

There is a real joy and satisfaction to running fast over uneven ground. This is a skill that can be learnt through conscious thought and experience. Running on trails requires concentration and can be mentally tiring. It is important to adapt speed to the terrain and stay within personal limits. Looking ahead and reading the ground to choose the best foot placement is the key to moving swiftly. There may be uneven ground, tree roots, muddy puddles, soft boggy areas, patches of gravel or larger rocks. The skill lies in picking the clear area among the gravel, varying stride length to fit between tree roots, pushing off firm earth instead of soft bog and landing a footstep precisely on top of a rock instead of slipping awkwardly off its side.

Navigation

The routes in this book range from city centre parks to remote wilderness areas in the Scottish Highlands. They cover the whole spectrum from runs where going off route is no problem at all to those where getting lost could be very serious.

Confident navigation is essential for progressing to the more remote routes included in this guide. Each route is rated to indicate the level of navigation required. Confident navigation comes through practice and the rating system is intended to help development of the required skills.

The route descriptions should be read and used in conjunction with maps. Basic map reading starts by relating the hills, valleys and features such as lochs or buildings seen on the ground to the contour lines and features marked on the map. It helps to orientate maps to the direction of travel so that their features line up with those on the ground. While moving, it helps to keep a mental tick list of features shown on the map which must be passed in order to reach the next key point on the route. Get into the habit of memorising the tick list and consulting the map only at key points. It helps enormously to know where one is all the time rather than spend time figuring out the location from scratch at every stop.

The level of navigation required often changes dramatically with weather conditions. A straightforward trot over moorland to a trig point may require counting paces and following a compass bearing when the cloud rolls in.

Navigators must constantly challenge their own assumptions. Look for features that disprove an identified location. It is all too easy to make features fit with the map and inadvertently 'confirm' an incorrect location. Estimate the width and height of a feature as well as the distance to it

Skills Development

before consulting the map. Map measurements should corroborate the estimations. If not, ring the alarm bells.

Developing an awareness of distance and timing is very useful. Try identifying features at varying distances, say 100m, 500m and 1km, and timing how long it takes to run to each of them. Try timing the same distances on rougher terrain.

No times are given for the routes as running time varies so much from person to person. Keep a record of how long each route takes and work out a personalised version of Naismith's Rule. This rule of thumb is used by hillwalkers to calculate the length of time a route will take based on its distance and total ascent. Standard Naismith's Rule allows one hour for every 5km plus one minute for each 10m of height gained. For runners a good starting point is to assume one hour for every 10km plus one minute for each 10m height gain. Rougher terrain will increase the time taken, often very significantly.

Almost all of the routes in this book use paths and tracks that are clear and easy to follow independent of the weather conditions. Some follow fainter paths and need a higher level of navigation. Path recognition is key to finding the way on less distinct routes. Developing an eye for traces of previous footsteps is crucial. Look out for clues such as slightly polished rocks, aligned patches of bare earth, broken, stunted or different types of vegetation. Paths often disappear into boggy or stony areas and reappear on the far side. Humans tend to follow fence lines and head to obvious features. In summertime even usually clear paths may become overgrown, often by bracken, and tricky to identify or run.

Basic navigational techniques such as orientating (also known as setting) the map, pacing, timing, and following a compass bearing can be taught through courses or by studying books. A theoretical knowledge of navigation is not enough. Good navigation only comes through practice. Even excellent navigators need a few hours to get their eye back in after a period of absence from the hills. Orienteering is an excellent way of learning and improving navigation skills.

Measuring distance and height

Grid squares are always 1km

OS Landranger 1:50,000 2cm = 1km, 10m contour interval

OS Explorer 1:25,000 4cm = 1km, 10m contour interval

Harvey Superwalker 1:25,000 4cm = 1km, 15m contour interval

Conversion to imperial units

10km is approximately 6 miles

10m is approximately 33ft

Naismith's rule

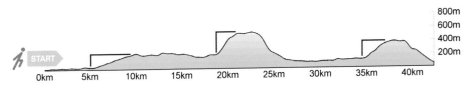

For runners a good starting point is to assume one hour for every 10km plus one minute for each 10m height gain.

EXAMPLE:
approx. 40km run = 4 hours
three climbs total 750m = +75 mins
total estimate = 5 hours 15 mins

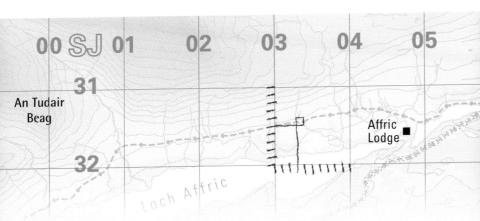

Six figure grid references

On an OS map each 1km square has a four figure reference (look for the blue grid numbers). Divide each square into ten units. Count along then up the square to find your location to within 100m².

EXAMPLE:
the stream crossing is in grid square SJ 03 32;
dividing that square into tenths the crossing is three tenths along and five tenths up
so the grid reference is SJ 033 325

Outdoor Access

The Land Reform (Scotland) Act 2003 gives the general public the right of responsible access to most Scottish land and inland waters including all the trails described in this book. This right only exists if access is undertaken in accordance with the guidelines of the Scottish Outdoor Access Code. The Code is based on three commonsense principles: take responsibility for your own actions; respect the interests of other people; care for the environment. The full Code can be found at *www.outdooraccess-scotland.com*

Stalking and grouse shooting

Some of the routes cross land used for stalking and grouse shooting and specific guidance is given where appropriate. The stag stalking season starts on 1st July and ends on 20th October. September and October are the most active months. As stalking does not normally take place on Sundays this is a good day to head out into the hills during this period. Hind culling continues until 15th February but generally has less affect on access. The grouse shooting season starts on 12th August and ends on 10th December. Runners and other land users must take reasonable steps to find out whether stalking and shooting are taking place and avoid disturbance. The Hillphones answerphone service and the web service Heading for the Scottish Hills provide information for some estates. *www.snh.org.uk/hillphones www.outdooraccess-scotland.com/hftsh* Many estates do not participate in these schemes. In these cases contact the estate office for up-to-date information and obey signs displayed at access points.

Dogs

Keeping dogs under proper control is integral to responsible access. 'Proper control' is defined in the Access Code and Scottish Natural Heritage publishes detailed guidance for dog owners. The basic requirement is to keep dogs on a short lead or under close control when near livestock or crossing ground bird nesting areas during the breeding season (April to July). Many of the trail runs in this book go through unfenced grazing or the breeding areas of ground nesting birds.

Conservation

Adopt a minimum impact approach and leave these trails as it would be good to find them. This may mean carrying out other people's litter. Mesh rucksack side-pockets are particularly handy for this. Running damages soft ground as anyone who has competed in a cross-country, hill race or mountain marathon will be well aware. In recent years a great deal of path construction work has taken place which is helping prevent further erosion by shoes and mountain bike tyres. Without this generous expenditure of many people's time and money many of the trails in this book would be too rough or boggy to run. Support path construction efforts by paying for parking on individual estates and by donating time or money to local footpath trusts or national organisations such as the National Trust for Scotland, the British Trust for Conservation Volunteers and the John Muir Trust *www.nts.org.uk www.btcv.org.uk www.jmt.org*

Leave nothing but footprints

Lammermuirs (Route 13)

Enjoy

Have fun! More than anything else, this book is intended to help runners get out and explore Scotland's amazingly varied trails. There are many hours of trail running contained within these pages. Some routes are easy, others are tough. Sometimes the Scottish weather will co-operate and sometimes it will hurl horizontal hail. Sunny day trail runs make the world feel a better place but a hard run through foul weather is paradoxically even more satisfying. Going running is always the right decision; there is no such thing as a bad run.

Dumfries, Galloway and Ayrshire

Quiet South West Scotland boasts a beautiful coastline, idyllic woodland and rugged hills in the Range of the Awful Hand. To the east lie high moors and rounded summits while venturing north into Ayrshire finds trails through rolling fields, beside rivers and along scenic clifftops.

Castlehill Point (Route 4)

Bluebells, Mabie Forest

Larch Hill

1 Mabie Forest

Distance	9.5km (6 miles)	Ascent	250m (800ft)
Map	OS Landranger 84, OS Explorer 313		
Navigation •••	Yellow, Orange and Brown waymarked trails		
Terrain •••	Smooth gravel tracks and earth paths, short rocky descent on Craigbill Hill		
Wet Feet •••	Occasional puddles		
Start/Finish	Mabie Forest DG2 8HB NX 949 709		

Easy to follow waymarked woodland trails

Mabie Forest is one of the 7stanes: seven mountain biking centres scattered across the south of Scotland. All of the 7stanes are perfect for trail running as well as mountain biking. This route at Mabie wanders through beautiful deciduous woodland with views out over the Nith valley and towards the isolated hill of Criffel. Route finding is simple as this run links three fully waymarked routes through the forest. The run can easily be shortened by completing the Yellow trail instead of continuing on to the Orange Link. At Mabie Forest the waymarked bike and pedestrian routes are cunningly separated except for one or two short sections on forest roads. So there is practically no danger of being run over by the bikers hooning round berms and exploding over jumps elsewhere in the forest.

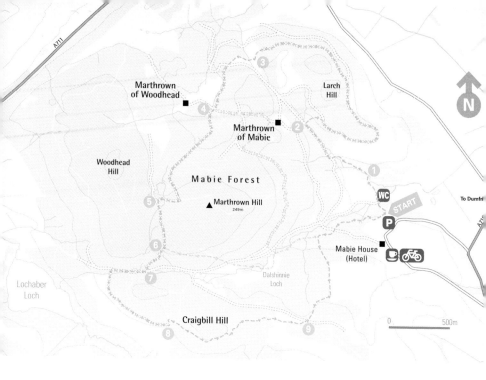

In the lower section of the car park a large board displays a map of the waymarked trails through Mabie Forest. This run starts on the Yellow Trail, joins the Orange Link then finishes on the Brown Trail. 🏃 **START** Head downhill from the information board following the combined trails waymarker on a gravel path that zigzags down to cross a stream. Continue across a grassy area past a shed containing an old sawmill and into woodland to reach a T-junction just after a pond. **1** Turn left and head uphill along the stream for 400m then cross a bridge and go up steps onto a track which continues upstream to another crossing point. **2** Recross the stream, climb uphill and turn right onto a forest road. Follow this around the hill for around 2km to a flight of short steps leading down to a line of tall beech trees. **3** Turn right down the steps and follow the path under the trees to join a forest road. Continue downhill for another 400m to the crossroad. **4** Continue straight ahead onto the Orange Link waymarked trail. After about 600m the forest road ends and the waymarked route forks left onto a grassy path. Follow this path to a T-junction with a forest road. **5** Turn left onto the road and follow it past a pond to a junction of forest roads. **6** Continue downhill, now following Brown Trail waymarkers, to reach a T-junction. **7** Turn right onto a gravel forest road for a couple of hundred metres then left to follow a grassy forest road to its end. **8** Continue onto a path which zigzags up and then contours around Craigbill Hill. On the far side of the hill a rougher path drops down through oak trees and crosses a mountain bike trail to reach a forest road. **9** Cross the forest road and continue on a path

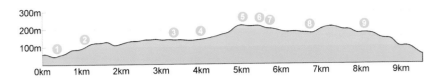

through the woods, along the side of a field, across another mountain bike trail and a forest road. Finally head right, joining the Yellow and Blue Trails for the final 500m to the car park.

Trip Planning

Up-to-date trail information including closures for forestry operations can be found at *www.forestry.gov.uk* 🚌 Mabie Forest, A710 🚗 Follow the A710 Solway Coast road south-west from Dumfries for five miles. Turn right at the Forestry Commission sign for Mabie Forest (not Mabie Farm Park). 🅿 There is a charge for parking. The car park is a loop with walking/running routes leaving from the lower half and biking routes from the upper. 🚾 Toilets are downhill from the car park. 🍴 🚲 The bike hire shop uphill from the car park opposite the Ranger Office doubles as a café and offers tea, cake and excellent bacon butties. 🏠 Mabie House Hotel at the trail head welcomes mountain bikers and other muddy outdoors types. There are wooden camping huts in its grounds and conventional hotel rooms indoors. *www.mabiehousehotel.co.uk* In the middle of the forest is Marthrown of Mabie where the bunkhouse is the least exciting accommodation option. Try the Yurt, Tipi or Iron Age Roundhouse instead. *www.marthrownofmabie.com*

Other Routes

Mabie Forest's waymarked walking trails are up to 7km (4.5 miles). Longer routes can be constructed by linking the trails and following non-waymarked forest roads.

Drumlanrig is a private estate just off the A76 at Thornhill, seventeen miles north of Dumfries. Its woodland paths are perfect for trail running and accessible all year round. An admission charge is levied during the summer (1st April to 31st August) and on winter weekends. Drumlanrig has bike hire, a café, toilets and showers. *www.drumlanrig.com*

7stanes mountain biking

The 7stanes trails attract hundreds of thousands of people each year from all over the world. The 7stanes are also an art project. Look for hidden stone sculptures of a ghost, talking head, well-travelled heart and meteorite inscribed in Klingon. The 7stanes trails run through Glentrool, Kirroughtree, Dalbeattie, Mabie, Ae, Newcastleton, Glentress & Innerleithen Forests.

Mabie Forest

Mabie Forest waymarker

Events

Dumfries Harriers organise a popular 10km trail race through Mabie Forest in June. *www.dumfriesharriers.co.uk*. Running and biking events are held on the Drumlanrig Estate.

Other Activities

Mabie Forest has a range of purpose built mountain bike trails. Bikes and helmets can be hired at the café. *www.7stanesmountainbiking.com*

Culzean Castle

2 Culzean Castle & Country Park

Distance	10km (6 miles)	Ascent	150m (500ft)
Map	OS Landranger 76, OS Explorer 326		
Navigation •••	Link paths and tracks around the park's perimeter		
Terrain •••	Earth and gravel paths, tracks and tarmac road, short section on shingle beach		
Wet Feet •••	Muddy tracks near the Cat Gates and by the caravan site		
Start/Finish	Culzean Country Park Visitor Centre KA19 8JX NS 237 104		

Varied running around a grand country estate

The Kennedy family intended to make an unforgettable impression when they hired architect Robert Adam to design their country home on the Ayrshire coast. They succeeded. The final leg of this run showcases the castle as Adam surely intended it to be seen: a striking array of turrets grandly mounted upon the clifftop. Impressive though it is, the highlight of this run is not the castle. Even the best of architects cannot compete with the view out to Ailsa Craig. This run links scenic coastline with woodland paths, tracks and quiet roads through farmland. Scattered throughout the park are quirky human additions including an otter sculpture and the rather forlorn Cat Gates.

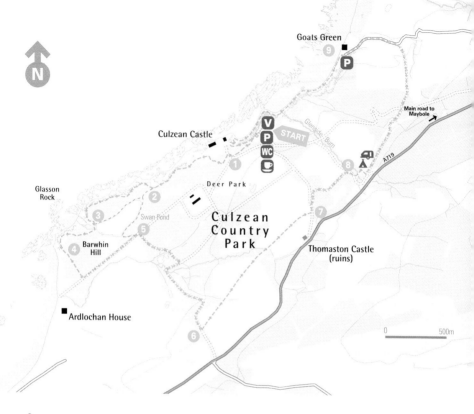

START Leave the Visitor Centre courtyard by the corner opposite the car park. Cross the road and follow a path past buildings and into woodland to reach the castle gates. **1** Turn towards the castle, passing through the gateway, then almost immediately turn left down steps onto a woodland path. Turn off to the right at the first opportunity and head towards the sea through a hole in the wall to the left of the castle. Cross the grass diagonally left to join a woodland path. Join a tarmac road briefly then continue onto a path signed to the Swan Pond for a short distance to the first junction. **2** Turn towards the sea and follow the coastal path until it curves inland to end at the Swan Pond. **3** Turn right across a footbridge then take the first right towards Carrick Beach. Do not go down the steps to the beach but continue along the coastal path to a junction. **4** Leave the coast and follow a wide path downhill through trees, then turn left along a track which returns to the Swan Pond. Continue for 200m past the car park to a path on the right beside a small stream. **5** Follow the stream to a T-junction then turn right and follow the track round to the left and through the Cat Gates. Continue for another 600m until the track crosses a disused railway. **6** Turn left down steps and follow the disused railway through fields.

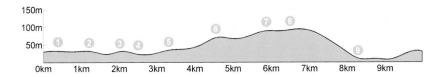

After about 1.5km the railway track goes under a road bridge. ⑦ Turn right up steps, cross the bridge and continue uphill to reach the tarmac entrance road to the country park. Turn right onto this, as if leaving the estate. ⑧ Just after passing the gatehouse turn left onto a path and cross Glenside Burn. Do not enter the caravan site. Instead go right and uphill, then left onto a track just above the site. Continue straight ahead on this track, onto a tarmac road, and head towards the coast to reach Goats Green car park. ⑨ Follow the shore past Segganwell Cottages, then climb uphill past the Gas House and follow the tarmac road back to the Visitor Centre.

Trip Planning

Culzean Castle and Country Park is owned by the National Trust for Scotland. Seasonal entry charges apply. *www.culzeanexperience.org* 🚌 Culzean, Glenside Farm, A719 (near ⑧) 🚗 Culzean Country Park is fourteen miles south of Ayr. Turn off the A77 at either Maybole or Turnberry onto the A719 then follow signs to Culzean Castle and Country Park. Within the Park follow signs to the Visitor Centre. There are other car parks within the park as well as outside at Goats Green ⑨ (242 110). 🚻 💬 Ⓥ Visitor Centre.

Other Routes

A short run of less than 4km starts at the Visitor Centre and follows the described route to the Swan Pond ③. Circle the pond and return to the Visitor Centre. There are many other possible variations. The Cliff Walk is an essential ingredient of any run at Culzean.

The Cliff Walk is part of The Ayrshire Coastal Path, a long distance route developed by the Rotary Club of Ayr. The definitive guide book is the *Ayrshire Coastal Path* by Dr Jimmy Begg. The route links existing paths with beaches and varies from road running to rough, unrunnable ground. *www.ayrshirecoastalpath.org*

Events

The Family Fun Run held at Culzean each April is said to be one of the most scenic 10k races in Scotland.

Culzean Castle & Country Park

Bluebells
Photo: Iain Allison

The letter 'yogh'

Culzean is pronounced 'Kul-ane' rather than 'Kul-zean'. The baffling un-pronounced 'z' is the Old Scots letter 'yogh', a letter which has disappeared from the modern alphabet. It was written like the Arabic numeral 3 and so easily confused with a copperplate tailed z. Use of yogh was already dying out by the time the printing press was invented so early type setters simply replaced it by the similar looking z. Although more than five centuries have passed since the invention of printing this replacement still causes confusion. Current convention pronounces the placename and surname Dalziel as 'dee-ell'. In contrast, MacKenzie, once spoken as 'mackingie' is now universally pronounced with a 'z'. Menzies is arbitrarily pronounced 'ming-is' or 'men-zees'.

River Ayr

3 Auchincruive Estate & the River Ayr Way

Distance	11km (7 miles)	Ascent	150m (500ft)
Map	OS Landranger 70, OS Explorer 326		
Navigation •••	Follow the riverbank and a partially waymarked off-river link		
Terrain •••	Earth and tarmac paths with a short section on pavement and road		
Wet Feet •••	Mostly avoidable puddles and shallow mud		
Start/Finish	Auchincruive Estate Oswald Bridge car park KA6 5AE NS 387 233		

Riverbank and woodland path circuit

Three miles from the sea the River Ayr contorts itself into an impressive meander. This natural loop makes it possible to run almost the whole of this circuit on riverside paths. A short off-river track through the village of Annbank completes the circle. In future, the river will doubtless take the same straight course to create a large oxbow lake. Geography in action. The riverside paths are scenic, straightforward to follow and easy to run. They are shared with anglers whose small shelters are dotted along the riverbank. A highlight is the short section of path just above water level which runs along a level platform cut into the cliff-face.

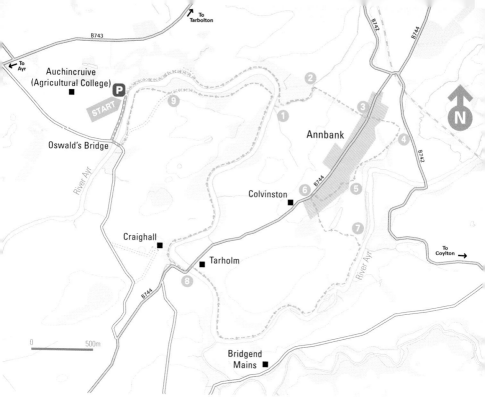

![walker icon] START Follow the blue waymarked riverside path upstream for 1.5km passing through a doorway in a stone wall to nearly reach a small fishing shelter. ① Turn away from the river on the waymarked path, heading uphill beside a stream to reach a T-junction with a track. ② Turn right and head uphill. At the end of the track continue straight on into Annbank. ③ Cross the main road, turn left then immediately right down the gravel of School Brae. At the end of the road continue straight on between fields to a crossroads. ④ Turn right onto a tarmac path and follow it through woodland, keeping left where necessary to avoid entering housing. The path ends at a T-junction where the River Ayr Way (RAW) is signposted to the right. ⑤ Follow the RAW waymarker out of the woodland through a gate, then cross grass by a tarmac path to go between houses onto Whitehall Crescent. Head left along the pavement to reach the main road. ⑥ Turn left onto the main road, then immediately left again, following RAW waymarkers down Mill Road. Follow the road round to the left at the bottom of the hill past a small fishing pond. Continue along the road to reach a small gravel car park on the right just before the road ends at a house. ⑦ Turn right into the car park and follow the path out at the back and onto the river-bank. Head downriver for over 2km to reach Tarholm. ⑧ Cross the river by the road bridge then

Auchincruive Estate & the River Ayr Way

go through a kissing gate to join a path on the opposite bank. The path climbs to a viewpoint then forks right to drop back down to the river. After leaving the river again the path reaches a waymarked fork. ⑨ Take the right branch to stay close to the river, following the waymarked green trail in reverse. After a short rougher section along the river bank climb up steps to Oswald's Bridge, cross the river and turn right to return to the car park.

Trip Planning

A short section of the path between Annbank and Tarholm is just above water level. On the rare occasions when the river is in spate it may be impossible to complete the route. 🚌 Scottish Agricultural College, Auchincruive 🚗 Auchincruive is just over three miles east of Ayr on the B743

Ayr to Mauchline road. Turn off at the sign to the Scottish Agricultural College (SAC) and Woodland Walks. Continue past the main SAC entrance, just before crossing the river turn left through gates and head up the drive to a large car park. These gates are open between 8am and 6pm. Outwith these times the car park can be accessed from the main SAC entrance. At the time of writing the Auchincruive Estate was undergoing redevelopment. Access to the riverside walks was expected to be maintained. 🚻 Ayr (Arthur Street, Blackburn Drive or the Pavilion/Low Green) 🚍 Ayr 🐑 Sheep graze next to the river between Annbank and Tarholm.

Auchincruive Estate & the River Ayr Way

Woodland trail

Other Routes

The source to sea route of the River Ayr is mirrored by a 66km (44 miles) waymarked footpath. One way sections can be tackled from Ayr by taking local buses out to the start point. A map and route guide are advisable as the waymarking is unclear in places. Parts of the River Ayr Way follow roads and tracks away from the river. *www.theriverayrway.org*

Events

The River Ayr Way Challenge is held in September and forms part of the Scottish Ultra Marathon Series. The Challenge is open to both runners and walkers. *www.theriverayrway.org*

Barcloy Hill cliffs

4 Rockcliffe Coastal Path

Distance	16km (10 miles)	Ascent	275m (900ft)
Map	OS Landranger 84, OS Explorer 313		
Navigation •••	Unsigned junctions through Dalbeattie Forest then return by waymarked coastal path		
Terrain •••	Earth and grass paths, forest tracks and short stretches on tarmac road		
Wet Feet •••	Some muddy sections in the forest		
Start/Finish	Sandyhills DG5 4PT NX 890 552		

Woodland trails complete a scenic 'Riviera' circuit

This run is sublime on a sunny spring day with yellow gorse in bloom, lambs gambolling in green fields and deep blue sea sparkling below. The clifftop path between Rockcliffe and Sandyhills is easy running terrain at any time of year thanks to the summer holidaymakers who walk this beautiful stretch of coastline. Outside the main holiday season the area is quiet and it is not unusual to run the whole route with only sheep and seabirds for company. Forest tracks and quiet country lanes connect the two ends of the coastal path. The inland half of the run has its own, more subtle, highlights including Barean Loch and picturesque views across rolling farmland and woods.

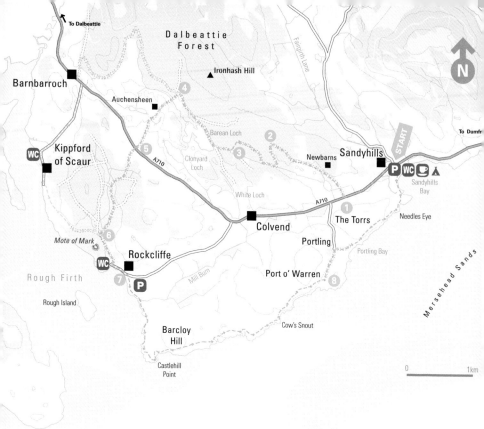

🏃 **START** Cross the river and head uphill for 900m along the A710 towards Colvend to reach the first turn on the right. The road has a grassy verge but no pavement. **1** Turn right through gate posts onto a private road towards Newbarns. Where this turns right towards the house continue straight ahead through a gate into woodland. Follow the sometimes muddy track through trees to a T-junction. **2** Turn left onto a gravel forest road shared with bikes for a few hundred metres to a bridge over a stream. Do not cross the stream. Instead, turn right for around 700m then follow the main path round to the left. This briefly joins the red mountain bike trail (watch and listen for fast approaching bikes) then emerges onto a gravel track. **3** Turn right and follow the track past Barean Loch. Continue for 500m past the loch to a brown-topped way-marker about 20m before the track rises slightly to a junction. **4** Turn left at the waymarker onto a grassy path. Follow this through a kissing gate and along the side of a field towards Auchen-sheen. Avoid the houses by going through a signposted kissing gate about 10m to their right. Cross a small grassy field and go through another kissing gate onto a lane which leads to the

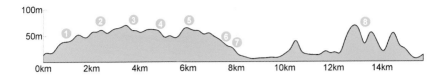

A710. ⑤ Cross the A710, heading slightly left to join a track on the far side. Follow the track into forestry continuing straight ahead at several junctions until the track ends at a gate onto the Rockcliffe-Kippford Jubilee Path. ⑥ Go through the gate and turn left towards Rockcliffe. After passing Baron's Craig Hotel follow the public road down to the sea and along the front until it curves back inland. ⑦ Follow coastal path waymarkers along a lane then onto a shore path. This crosses shingle then climbs up to the clifftops where it becomes a smooth earth path. In a few places the path is narrow and hemmed in by prickly gorse bushes. ⑧ Turn left along the road at Port o' Warren then take the first right, signed to Sandyhills. Instead of descending to the houses go up a set of steps and over a stile to continue on the coastal path. Keep to the right when descending Torrs Hill, cross a footbridge and follow the shore to Sandyhills beach.

Trip Planning

Sandyhills, A710 Sandyhills is nineteen miles south of Dumfries on the A710 Solway Coast road. A charge is made during the summer months (April to October) for the Sandyhills beach car park at the start of the route. There is a free car park at Rockcliffe. Sandyhills' toilets, shop and campsite are open during the summer (April to October). There are also toilets on the sea front at Rockcliffe. Sampling the local Cream o' Galloway ice cream is essential. These ice-cream makers have a visitor centre, kids play area and organise lots of family friendly events at their farm near Gatehouse of Fleet. *www.creamogalloway.co.uk* Sheep and cattle graze along the coastal path and near Auchensheen.

Other Routes

Extend the route to 20km (12.5 miles) by continuing straight ahead at ④ through mature beech woodland then along pavement into Kippford. Climb uphill on the signed Jubilee Path to rejoin the described route at Rockcliffe.

Waymarked walking trails through Dalbeattie Forest start at the Town Wood car park (837 599). The woodland near the car park is attractive with short winding waymarked trails. *www.forestry.gov.uk*

Rough Island can be reached at
low tide by a causeway
Photo: Dougal Ranford

Loch Trool

5 Glen Trool

Distance	26km (16 miles)	Ascent	300m (1000ft)
Map	OS Landranger 77, OS Explorer 319		
Navigation ●●●	First junctions unsigned then follow Southern Upland Way & Loch Trool Trail waymarkers		
Terrain ●●●	Earth and gravel paths, dirt and tarmac roads		
Wet Feet ●●●	Occasional puddles and slippery earth paths		
Start/Finish	Glentrool Visitor Centre DG8 6SZ NX 372 786		

Extended circuit of Galloway's most scenic glen

An inscribed boulder overlooking Loch Trool commemorates an early skirmish between Robert the Bruce and the English. Shortly after returning from exile the Bruce and his supporters were pursued into Glen Trool. As they fled along the steep southern side of the loch their enemies were lured into a trap. Bruce's infantry doubled back above the path and trundled boulders down on top of their pursuers. Today the only creatures scrambling up the hill are Galloway's wild goats. Look out for these multi-coloured beasts as the path crosses steep slopes above the loch. This is the trickiest section of the route where nimble feet are needed to negotiate the uneven path and exposed tree roots. Elsewhere, smooth trails wind through pretty deciduous woodland along the banks of the River Cree, Water of Minnoch and Water of Trool.

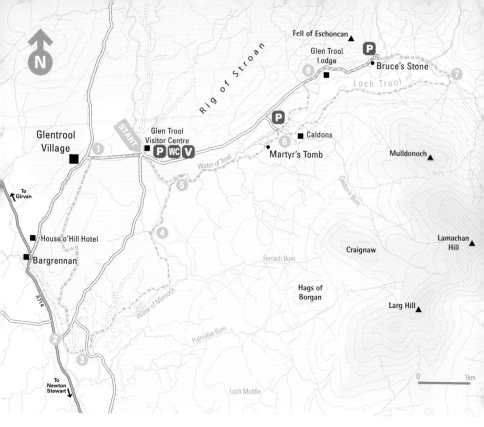

 START Leave the Visitor Centre by crossing the river and taking a path through the trees parallel with the road. The path returns to the road where it crosses a forest track. ① Turn left onto this track and follow it up and around the hill for 2km to a T-junction. Turn right and head downhill for another kilometre to a second T-junction. Turn left for 500m, then right onto the public road to reach a humpback bridge. ② Just before the bridge turn left onto a riverside path. The route now follows the waymarked Southern Upland Way (SUW) to the far end of Loch Trool. After curving away from the stream the path joins a forest road which ends at a T-junction with a public road. ③ Turn left, then immediately right onto a gravel forest road. After 400m turn right onto a footpath which follows the river for 3km to a road bridge. ④ Cross the river then keep left, crossing stiles to return to the river and continue along its bank for just over 1km to a footbridge signed for the Visitor Centre. ⑤ Do not cross, but continue straight ahead on the riverside path. After 1km the path curves away from the river and passes the Martyr's Tomb to reach the road at Caldons. ⑥ Turn right onto the tarmac road then follow SUW and green Loch Trool Trail waymarkers left through the old campsite (closed at time of writing). Shortly after leaving the campsite branch right and climb uphill. The path traverses the steep, wooded hillside

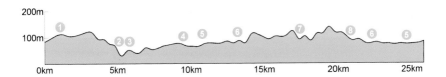

for 3km then drops down to a footbridge over the Glenhead Burn. 7 Leave the Southern Upland Way by crossing the footbridge and following the green waymarker left to join a track. This becomes a dirt road which climbs steeply up to the Bruce Memorial and the end of the public road. Follow the road downhill for 1.5km to reach the gates of Glen Trool Lodge. 8 Continue on the road for another few hundred metres then turn left onto the green waymarked forest trail. This path drops down through the woods and emerges at Caldons car park. Cross the river to 6 then retrace the outward route back to the footbridge at 5. Cross the river then turn left to follow the blue and yellow waymarked trails back to the Visitor Centre.

Trip Planning

Up-to-date trail information including closures for forestry operations can be found at *www.forestry.gov.uk* 🚌 Glentrool Village Road End or Bargrennan, both on the A714. There is no public transport to the Visitor Centre. Join the run by following SUW signs from the A714 bridge over the River Cree (349 764) and returning by the road past Glentrool Village. 🚗 Galloway Forest Park and Glentrool are signposted off the A714 at Bargrennan, eight miles north of Newton Stewart. Turn first right after passing houses following a sign for 🚻 Ⓥ Glentrool Visitor Centre. 🛏 House o' Hill is a small and welcoming hotel, bar and restaurant just off the A714 on the way to Glentrool. *www.houseohill.co.uk*

Other Routes

This route is easily divided into two worthwhile shorter routes. The waymarked 9km (5 miles) green trail around Loch Trool starts at the car park near Caldons (397 791). Start at the Visitor Centre or Bargrennan for a flatter 11km (7 miles) circuit following woodland paths beside the River Cree, Water of Trool and Water of Minnoch.

Events

A popular Galloway hill race is run up the Merrick from the Bruce's Stone car park at the end of Glen Trool. *www.girvanathleticclub.co.uk*

Water of Minnoch

"If the stars should appear one night in a thousand years, how would men believe and adore" – Emerson

Galloway Forest became the UK's first Dark Sky Park in 2009. Light pollution is minimal as the 75,000 hectares of forest far outstrips the land area covered by buildings. Light readings taken in the park average around 22 on a scale of 0 to 25 where 25 is total darkness. In contrast, Glasgow city centre scores a mere 8. About 7000 stars can be seen with the naked eye. Our own Milky Way galaxy appears as a raggedy, star-spangled banner arching overhead. The Earth has made just one rotation around the centre of our galaxy since the dinosaurs became extinct 250 million years ago. *www.forestry.gov.uk/darkskygalloway www.darksky.org*

Scottish Borders

Rolling hills, meandering rivers and miles of well trod yet quiet paths, tracks and forest roads. The Scottish Borders are a fantastic place to run. These routes explore a wide range of Border landscapes from inland hills and waters to coastal cliffs and sandy beaches.

Southern Upland Way

Eildon North Hill

Leaderfoot viaduct

6 The Eildon Hills

Distance	9km (5.5 miles)	**Ascent**	400m (1300ft)
Map	OS Landranger 73, OS Explorer 338		
Navigation ●●●	St Cuthbert's Way signposts followed by obvious paths to the three summits		
Terrain ●●●	Gravel, grass and earth paths and tracks. Steep rough gravel paths on Mid Hill		
Wet Feet ●●●	Earth paths can be slippery in wet weather		
Start/Finish	Pant Well, Bowden TD6 0ST NT 553 305		

A great wee intro to hill running

The triple peaks of the Eildon Hills occupy a commanding position in the middle of the Tweed floodplain. Many myths and legends surround these iconic Borders summits whose tardis-like innards are reputed to conceal a Fairy Kingdom as well as King Arthur's sleeping Knights of the Round Table. The Eildon Hills are also closely associated with the legend of Thomas the Rhymer, a 13th-century prophet. His gift of prophecy was bestowed by the Queen of the Fairies whom he met while out walking on the hills. She fell in love with Thomas and carried him away to Fairy Land. Running the Eildon Hills is a delightful outing even if you fail to be seduced by a Fairy Queen. The North Hill in particular is a fantastic runners' peak with a fine grassy track zigzagging all the way up to the cairn at the top.

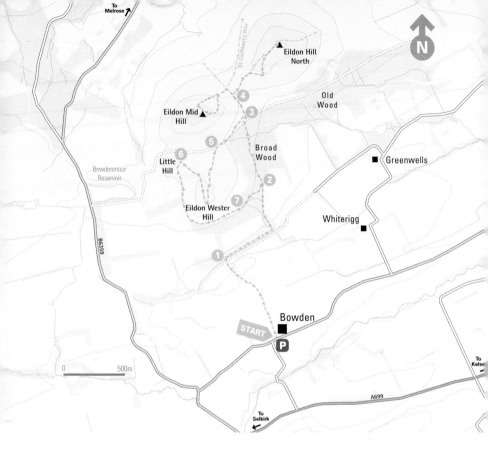

🏃 **START** Follow St Cuthbert's waymarkers up a lane behind the Pant Well and go through a gate into a grassy field with a play area. Continue to follow an obvious wide grassy path which leads into woodland, then across a footbridge and track to reach a second wood. ① Go into the wood and turn right in front of a long flight of steps. The path is level for a few hundred metres then turns sharply uphill. Making this turn requires careful speed control on the return journey. Continue uphill just inside the woodland to reach a track. ② Join the track heading right and uphill. After 500m keep left at a fork to leave the wood by a gate and reach a path junction. ③ Continue straight on and up to the col between North Hill and Mid Hill. ④ Ascend North Hill by a wide zigzag grassy track ignoring more direct walkers' paths. Return to the col and take in Mid Hill following an obvious circuit on steep paths with loose gravel. From the col retrace the outward route to ③ just before re-entering the wood. Turn right and follow the track out of the trees onto a wide flat col between Mid Hill and the lower Wester Hill. ⑤ Turn left onto a wide track heading towards Wester Hill. After a couple of hundred metres turn left again onto a wide

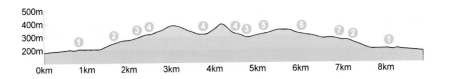

path which leads up to the summit. Return by a narrow path through the heather then rejoin the wide track for a short distance to reach the grassy knoll known as Little Hill. ⑥ Just before the knoll turn left onto a grassy path and traverse the hillside above a stone wall. Continue on this path as it swings left above woodland on a narrow sheep track to reach a gate. ⑦ Go through the gate and descend through the woodland back to ②. Turn right onto St Cuthbert's Way and follow the outward route back to Bowden.

Trip Planning

🚌 Commonside, Bowden 🚗 Bowden is a small village two miles west of Newtown St Boswells on the B6396. Park on the wide main street near the Pant Well, bus shelter and market cross. 🚾 Abbey St, Melrose 9am to 6pm (5pm in winter) ☕ Five miles south of Bowden the colourful Jammy Coo café and gallery in Lilliesleaf has delicious homemade cakes (10:30am to 4pm, closed Mondays) www.jammycoo.co.uk. Alternatively try Newtown St Boswells or Melrose. 🐑 Sheep graze the open hill.

Other Routes

Avoid 70m of height gain by starting at Bowdenmoor Reservoir (539 316), a small fishing loch with roadside parking for a couple of cars. Follow a good track on the south side of the reservoir then head uphill through a kissing gate west of Little Hill to reach ⑥.

Extend the route by following a track through Old Wood then paths around the north side of the hills to meet St Cuthbert's Way above Melrose. The track is excellent but the paths are notoriously muddy.

Events

The Eildon 2 Hills Race is organised by Gala Harriers. It starts in the town of Melrose and goes straight up the untracked north-west side of North Hill, over Mid Hill and back down into Melrose.

www.galaharriers.com

The Eildon Hills

St Cuthbert's Way

St Cuthbert

Cuthbert was inspired to become a monk after seeing strange lights in the night sky while out on the hills guarding sheep as a boy. He grew up to be a man of contrasts. In his younger years Cuthbert was an active missionary who travelled across Scotland spreading the teachings of the Christian gospel. Later, he withdrew completely from society and lived for ten years as a hermit on the remote Island of Inner Farne. He reluctantly left his island to become Bishop of Lindisfarne but returned to his solitary hermitage after only a few years. The 100km St Cuthbert's Way links Lindisfarne with Melrose where Cuthbert began his monastic life.

The Tweed Valley

7 River Tweed Circuit

Distance	12km (7 miles)	Ascent 125m (400ft)
Map	OS Landranger 73, OS Explorer 337	
Navigation •••	Waymarked Tweed Walk then signposted descent	
Terrain •••	Tarmac and earth paths, private and public roads	
Wet Feet •••	Riverside paths can be slippery in wet weather	
Start/Finish	Peebles EH45 9EW NT 251 402	

Quality riverside trail with herons, kingfishers and castles

This pleasant riverside run is finished off by a cracking downhill into Peebles. It is just one of many enjoyable routes that start in or near this Borders town. The trail roughly follows the river and is surprisingly varied. An early section easily traverses a section of steep-sided river bank where Scots pines cling to craggy contours. Further upstream the path leaves the river to follow a disued railway line with views across rolling farmland to the surrounding hills. The Tweed is a haven for wildlife. These quiet paths provide plenty of opportunities for spotting both common species and rarities. A distinctive flash of bright blue betrays a kingfisher streaking past like a feathered bullet. Luckily the rest of the waterfowl are slower moving and more easily observed. This route follows Tweed Walk waymarkers to the viewpoint and car park above Old Manor Brig.

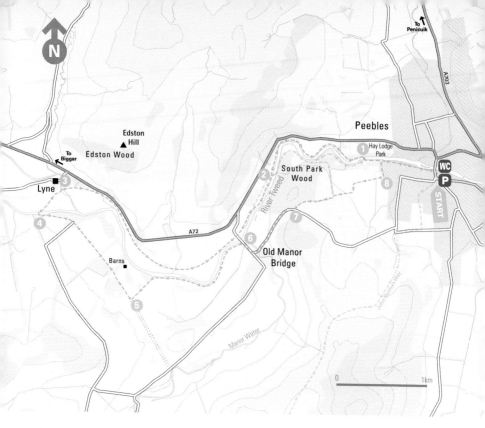

🏃 START Follow the river under the road bridge to join the Riverside Path through Hay Lodge Park and reach the Fotheringham footbridge. ① Cross the river and continue upstream on tarmac and earth paths for 1.5km to an old viaduct. ② Pass underneath the viaduct and follow the path through a field and up onto the disused railway. Continue along the railway for 3km to Lyne crossing Manor Valley road by a gate and steps. ③ At the end of the railway track go down steps and turn right onto a country lane. Continue past houses to the end of the lane then go straight ahead onto a footbridge. ④ After crossing the Tweed follow the path through woodland to a house then continue onto a private road on the Wemyss and March estate. Continue straight ahead past Barns Tower for 350m to reach a signpost and stile on the left. ⑤ Climb over the stile and return to the river. Follow the riverside path for over 1km to the Manor Valley Road bridge and ascend steps to the road. ⑥ Turn right onto the road and after only a short distance turn left past road closed signs to cross Old Manor Brig. Climb the hill by the disused tarmac road looking behind for good views of the valley. Continue for 150m past the car park to reach a signpost at the far corner of the wood. ⑦ Leave the road and take the path along the edge of the woodland

to join a grassy track heading down into Peebles. Continue onto pavement to reach a footpath on the left between the 4th and 5th houses after the industrial estate. ⑧ Return to the river by turning left onto this footpath then follow the river downstream to return to the Kingsmeadows Road car park.

Trip Planning

🚌 Bank of Scotland, High Street, Peebles 🚗 Turn off the A72 in the centre of Peebles onto the B7062 following signs to the car and coach park. Turn left after crossing the river and park immediately in the large Kingsmeadows Road car park. 🚻 Kingsmeadows Road car park 7am to 6pm (5pm in winter) ☕ Peebles High Street. The last section of the run passes an industrial estate housing the Cocoa Black Chocolate and Pastry School. They have a shop and café in the centre of Peebles on the road towards Glasgow. *www.cocoablack.co.uk*

Other Routes

The climb towards the end of this route is easily avoided by recrossing the river by the Manor Valley Road bridge and returning to Peebles by the outward path.

A second alternative finish is to continue on the waymarked Tweed Walk which turns downhill at the viewpoint to follow pleasant trails through South Park Wood.

An excellent trail and hill running extension follows John Buchan Way signposts from Kingsmeadows Road car park through streets to a grassy track up Cademuir Hill. A map is recommended as the waymarked route through the streets is not completely obvious. Continue along the ridge past the remains of several hill forts. Look out for

Follow Tweed Walk waymarkers

River Tweed Circuit

Peebles Old Parish Church and River Tweed

'chevaux de frise' ground defences – a field of pointed stones intended to deter enemy cavalry. Head north-west down the untracked hillside to join the road and turn towards Kirkton Manor. Just after a red telephone box (220 380) turn left through stone gateposts into the Wemyss and March estate to reach ⑤ after about 1km.

Nearby Forestry Commission woodlands have great trail running on and off their waymarked routes. The 9km (5.6 mile) Tower Trail at Glentress is steep with rewarding views.

The Glensax Horseshoe is a good hill run on good, though boggy, tracks and paths. The off-road running starts at the end of Glen Road (259 392) where there is limited parking.

Events

This run shares part of its route with the Beltane 10km Trail Race organised by the Moorfoot Runners. The Gypsy Glen Hill Race is another popular local event. *www.moorfootrunners.co.uk*

Other Activities

There is great mountain biking on purpose-built trails at nearby Glentress and Innerleithen Forests. Glentress is the best place for beginner riders. It has bike hire, a café, toilets and showers. *www.7stanesmountainbiking.com*

Coldingham Bay

8 Berwickshire Coastal Path

Distance	13km (8 miles)	Ascent	250m (800ft)
Map	OS Landranger 67, OS Explorer 346		
Navigation •••	Fully waymarked Coastal Footpath		
Terrain •••	Grass and earth paths, sandy beach, pavement and quiet road		
Wet Feet •••	Earth paths can be slippery in wet weather		
Start	Burnmouth TD14 5RT NT 953 611		
Finish	Coldingham TD14 5NG NT 902 659		

Sea views and grassy clifftop paths

Think of the Scottish Borders and landscapes of rolling hills and green pastures come to mind. So it is something of a departure to head over to the east coast where high rocky cliffs present a completely different kind of scenery and running experience. To increase wildlife spotting opportunities extend the run out to St Abb's Head. St Abb's is a National Nature Reserve and home to many thousands of seabirds. Almost the whole of this route hugs the clifftops with great views out to sea and firm short turf underfoot. There is no shelter so it is worth considering the wind direction prior to the run. Strong North Easterlies will turn this gentle seaside jog into an exhilarating battle with the elements.

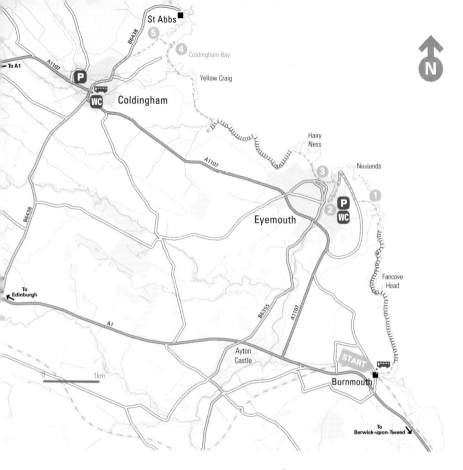

This route entirely follows Coastal Path waymarkers. From the bus stop in Burnmouth follow the Coastal Path sign up a tarmac lane and left onto a grass path to avoid a house. Continue around the edge of a field to reach the coast. Turn left onto the signed footpath and follow it for nearly 4km along the clifftop to reach a golf course on the outskirts of Eyemouth. ① Part way along the golf course turn left onto a gravel footpath and cross the fairway. Turn right onto a wide road and follow the pavement round to the left to reach the harbour. Cross the road and a footbridge onto a pier heading towards the back of the harbour. ② Cross the river and turn back towards the sea then along the promenade and beach. ③ Climb steps at the far end of Eyemouth beach then follow the path straight ahead around the edge of the caravan park. Continue along the coast to Coldingham Bay with its row of brightly painted beach huts. ④ Climb steep steps beyond the huts then turn left onto a tarmac path signposted to Coldingham

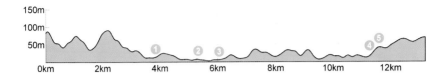

by the Creel Path. After a few hundred metres take the right hand fork at St Abbs Haven (a private home) and continue for a short distance to a T-junction. **⑤** Turn left onto the Creel Path. Follow this path, pavement then quiet road into the centre of Coldingham.

Trip Planning

🚌 Village Hall, Burnmouth and Bus Shelter, Coldingham An hourly bus service links the two stops. The Coldingham bus stop is at the crossroads in the centre of the village. Get off the bus just as it reaches houses at Burnmouth. The Coastal Path is signed from the bus stop. 🚗 Follow the A1107 to Coldingham and park in the signposted Priors Walk car park (901 660) next to a playing field. 🚻 Coldingham village centre near the bus stop, Coldingham Sands on the beach front, Eyemouth Harbour Road 7am to 6pm (5pm in winter) 🍽 A couple of pubs in Coldingham serve food and have small beer gardens. The seaside staples of fish and chips and ice cream dominate in Eyemouth. Alternatively, eat al fresco in the Springbank Cottage Tea Garden at St Abbs Harbour. It has no indoor seating but umbrellas, awnings or a tea-tray to take to the car can all be provided if the rain sets in. 🏠 Scoutscroft Caravan Park, several hotels and plenty of B&Bs.

Other Routes

The 24km (15 miles) Coastal Path runs from Berwick-upon-Tweed to Coldingham.

Other Activities

Diving is popular on this part of the east coast. Several dive boats and schools operate out of St Abbs and Eyemouth. *www.stabbs.org*

The string of sandy beaches between Edinburgh and Coldingham have bags of surfing potential. Surfboards, sit-on-top kayaks and wetsuits can be hired at St Veda's in Coldingham Sands.

www.stvedas.co.uk

Berwickshire Coastal Path

Heading north on
the Coastal Path

Beneath the Waves

Scuba diving gives a completely different perspective on this section of coastline. A Voluntary Marine Reserve, the first of its kind in the UK, was established here in 1984. Unusually clear water and spectacular underwater scenery make this a popular spot for divers. The shore diving is some of the best in the UK and many more dive sites can be reached by boat. Top of the marine wildlife tick list for all divers visiting the Reserve is the wolf-fish, a formidable looking creature that grows to be over a metre long and is usually found in Arctic waters.

The Minchmoor Road

9 The Three Brethren & the Minchmoor Road

Distance	15km (9 miles)	Ascent	500m (1700ft)
Map	OS Landranger 73, OS Explorer 337		
Navigation •••	Waymarkers, signposts or obvious features		
Terrain •••	Earth, grass and stony paths and tracks		
Wet Feet •••	Short muddy field above the Youth Hostel		
Start/Finish	Yarrowford TD7 5NA NT 408 299		

Ridge-top running with views over the Borders

The Three Brethren can be seen from miles around and are a distinctive Borders landmark. These nine foot high cairns mark the intersection of three estate boundaries. Every summer a cavalcade of riders and foot followers climb the hill from Selkirk to the Three Brethren. This tradition harks back to the days when Border territories were bitterly disputed. Back then Selkirk townsfolk regularly patrolled the 'marches' or boundaries of their land. So if in Selkirk on the Friday of the second week in June go to the Common Riding. On any other day head over to the Yarrow Valley for this great hill run on excellent tracks. The climb up from Yarrowford is steep and sustained

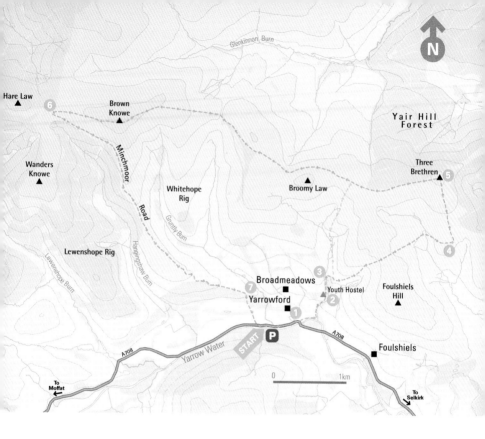

but once the ridge is gained the track becomes undulating and the views superb. The Minchmoor Road descent is the highlight of the run. This old droving route quickly becomes a path of sheep cropped turf perfect for gravity-assisted running.

START Head east along the A708 for 500m to a road on the left just before the A708 crosses Yarrow Water. There is a grassy verge but no pavement. ❶ Head uphill, then after just 100m turn right onto a fenced footpath signposted to the Youth Hostel. Once in woodland follow the path steeply uphill to the Youth Hostel. ❷ Cross the lawn to the right hand side of the hostel and continue uphill onto a track. This becomes a path which goes through woodland to a gate onto the open hill. ❸ Go through the gate and turn right then continue through another walkers' gate to cross the muddy field by a boardwalk. Turn right at the end of the boards where the Southern Upland Way (SUW) marker points left. At the corner of the woodland turn left onto a good track which climbs steeply uphill. Follow this track over the brow of the hill, drop down to cross the head of the Long Philip burn and climb back up, passing through a wooden field gate.

The Three Brethren & the Minchmoor Road

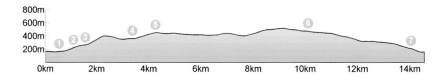

④ Turn left onto an obvious grassy track leading up to the Three Brethren. ⑤ Continue along the SUW towards Traquair for nearly 6km to a signposted junction near stands of forestry. ⑥ (379 327) Turn sharp left onto the Minchmoor Road and descend the ridge for 3km to woodland. Follow field edges just above the trees until the way is blocked by a stone wall. ⑦ Turn right through a gate onto a stony track. Where this track goes right into houses go left down steps onto a lower track. Run past the startlingly red Village Hall to return to the A708.

Trip Planning

🚐 Yarrowford, Broadmeadows Farm Road End 🚗 Yarrowford is five miles west of Selkirk on the A708. Park opposite houses in a lay-by with a red telephone box. 🚾 Selkirk Market Square (9am to 6pm, 5pm in winter) or Dovecot (8am to 7pm) 🍴 Between Yarrowford and Selkirk are the Bowhill Estate Tearoom (summer only) and the Waterwheel Restaurant on the Philiphaugh Estate. Both are signposted off the A708. *www.bowhill.org www.salmonviewingcentre.com* 🏠 Broadmeadows Youth Hostel is open June, July and August. It can also be booked through the RentaHostel scheme. *www.syha.org.uk* 0845 293 7373 🐑 Sheep graze the open hill and in fields towards the end of the route.

Other Routes

Shorten the route by paths which meet the Southern Upland Way on either side of Broomy Law at (420 318) and (402 327).

A 14.5km (9 miles) waymarked Forestry Commission trail climbs up to the Three Brethren Cairn from Yair Forest (439 349). It gives good fast running on wide forest roads. *www.forestry.gov.uk*

Drove road sign

The Three Brethren & the Minchmoor Road

The Three Brethren

The 11km (7 miles) Duchess's Drive is a circular track through woodland and over open moor on the Bowhill Estate. The Drive was designed as a scenic route for horse-drawn carriages. The route can be accessed all year round although the house, gardens and tearoom are only open during summer when a parking charge applies. Bowhill Estate (428 279) is on the A708 three miles West of Selkirk. *www.bowhill.org*

Cowgill Upper Reservoir

10 Lamington Hills

Distance	19km (12 miles)	Ascent	625m (2100ft)
Map	OS Landranger 72, OS Explorer 336		
Navigation •••	Straightforward to Hardrig Head. Short stretch of indistinct path then track and road		
Terrain •••	Grassy tracks, paths, tarmac, faintly tracked heather moorland		
Wet Feet •••	Some soft ground and occasional puddles		
Start/Finish	Lamington ML12 6HW NS 978 309		

Grassy tracks over and through rolling Border hills

Grassy tracks as good as these are hard to find. Save them for a dry day when their fragile surface is at its most robust. Clear weather is also best for the views: range after range of pudding bowl hills stretch far off into the distance. Steep-sided Key Cleuch is the gateway to this never-ending landscape which feels a world away from the busy A702. Technically this route lies within South Lanarkshire but its gills and rigs place it linguistically in the Borders. The names of the hills and valleys around Lamington trip off the tongue from the weird Snickert Knees to the evocative Deil's Barn Door.

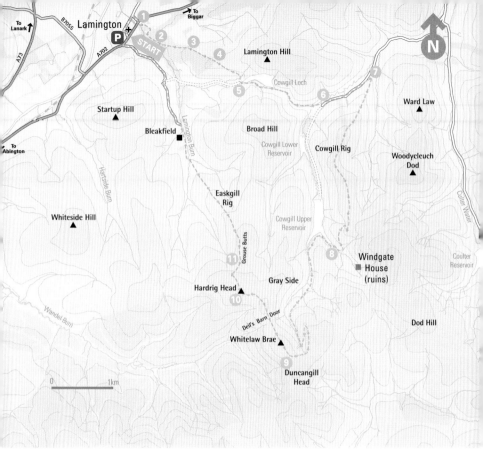

START Follow the minor road past the church and through the village. Soon after crossing a stream take the first right towards the A702. ① Cross the A702 and continue down a lane. Turn left between the last two houses and follow a track round the back of the last house to reach a T-junction after another 100m. Turn right then left at the next junction to reach a fork. These turnings are all signed for walkers by the Baitlaws Estate. ② Take the left-hand track at the fork to climb uphill through woodland for about 750m to a stile at the edge of the wood. This is an old route called Nips Road. ③ Climb over the stile and continue uphill along the side of the field to reach a gate and stile over a stone wall. ④ Climb over the stile and follow a grassy path diagonally across the field to drop downhill and meet a wide grassy track at a stand of isolated Scots pine trees. ⑤ Turn left onto the track and follow it past Cowgill Loch and through the steep sided glen beyond. Cross a footbridge and continue uphill on the farm drive to meet a tarmac

road. Turn left and follow the road for nearly 1km until a gate can be seen on the skyline to the right. Take a short cut across the field to the gate or continue for another couple of hundred metres then turn sharp right onto a track. After about 1km the track levels out and continues for a further 1.5km before dropping down zigzags to Cowgill Upper Reservoir. Follow the track along the left hand side of the reservoir then continue above Duncan Gill. The path becomes narrower as it is partially overgrown by heather. In a couple of places streams have washed away short sections which are easily negotiated. The track eventually climbs up onto the hilltops and reaches a fence. Turn right along the fenceline past the trig point on Whitelaw Brae, through the Deil's Barn Door (a col) over a smaller summit and up to the cairn on Hardrig Head. The initial rough track becomes a narrow path through the heather which disappears completely just before Hardrig Head. Go through the gap in the fence next to the cairn and pick up a faint track which bisects the two fences. Follow this north-north-west and downhill for 400m then turn sharp right onto another faint track which leads downhill to grouse shooting butts. Continue north on a faint track just left of the shooting butts and contour around the hill to reach a good grassy track. Follow this downhill and along Lamington Burn to Bleakfield. Continue on the tarmac road through Baitlaws and down to the A702.

Trip Planning

Access may be restricted during the grouse shooting season, starting August 12th, particularly near Hardrig Head. Observe all signs and flags. Emahroo, Lamington Lamington is on the A702 five miles north-east of Junction 13 of the M74. The car park is at the south-west end of the village, next to the A702. Abington Services at Junction 13 of the M74 is the closest pit stop for toilets and refreshments. Biggar is on the A702 six miles north-east of Lamington. It has several cafés and a fish and chip shop. A sign near the start of the trail requests that dogs are kept on a secure lead. The route crosses grouse moors and unfenced grazing.

Lamington Hills

Sheep roam freely over these hills and trails

Long Distance Waymarked Paths

There are several waymarked routes in the Scottish Borders which are mainly but not entirely off-road. Some are based upon geography while others are inspired by historical events and figures.

Southern Upland Way – Britain's first coast-to-coast footpath runs for 340km (212 miles) from Portpatrick in the west to Cockburnspath in the east (Route 9).

Berwickshire Coastal Path – 24km (15 miles) along the east coast from Berwick-upon-Tweed to Coldingham (Route 8).

Borders Abbeys Way – A 105km (65 miles) circular route linking the four great ruined abbeys in Kelso, Jedburgh, Melrose and Dryburgh.

John Buchan Way – 22km (13 miles) from Peebles to Broughton through countryside immortalised in Buchan's series of Richard Hannay novels (Route 7).

St Cuthbert's Way – 100km (60 miles) linking Melrose Abbey with the Holy Island of Lindisfarne (Route 6).

Edinburgh, Falkirk & the Lothians

In running terms, Edinburgh is a microcosm of the whole of Scotland. Within the city limits lie top quality fell runs, woodland trails and seaside paths. Further afield are hill tracks over the Lammermuirs and Pentland Hills, east coast beach runs and West Lothian waterway trails.

Arthur's Seat, Edinburgh

Arthur's Seat from Blackford Hill

City Centre Running

Edinburgh offers loads of opportunities for urban off-road running starting with the popular Meadows and Bruntsfield Links just south of the city centre. Arthur's Seat dominates the skyline and runners can be found here at any time of day and sometimes night. Some climb to the summit or over the top of Salisbury Crags while others enjoy the views from the road circling the hill. In the north-east of the city a network of disused railway paths connect with Inverleith Park and the Water of Leith Walkway. For a long run follow this walkway out of town and up Poets Glen into the Pentland Hills. An alternative, trickier to navigate, route out to the Pentlands follows the Braid Burn past Dreghorn Barracks then ducks under the city bypass at Bonaly Burn. Heading west, the Union Canal crosses the Water of Leith near Slateford or can be followed to Falkirk where it joins the Forth and Clyde Canal.

Hermitage, Braids and Pentlands

11 Braid Hills

Distance	4.5km (3 miles)	Ascent	100m (350ft)
Map	OS Landranger 66, OS Explorer 350, Harvey Edinburgh Seven Hills		
Navigation ●●●	Easy to follow bridleway around the golf course		
Terrain ●●●	Gravel track and earth paths		
Wet Feet ●●●	Short, muddy section behind houses at 3, otherwise dry		
Start/Finish	Braid Hills Drive car park EH10 6GZ NT 253 700		

360° views from the southernmost of Edinburgh's seven hills

Even though these hills are within the city bypass, running over the Braids feels like an escape to the country. The broad hilltop is covered in golf fairways. This short, circular run follows a bridleway around the perimeter of the course. A gradual climb leads to a trig point with a superb panoramic view over the city and surrounding countryside. Close at hand the Pentland Hills loom almost overhead while the coastline leads the eye to Bass Rock and North Berwick Law. On the return leg Edinburgh Castle assumes a commanding position with the silvery Forth and patch-worked Fife countryside beyond. This route is perfect for gaining great views with minimal effort. On a warm summer day blue skies set off the brilliant yellow gorse blooms to perfection while the heady scent of coconuts fills the air.

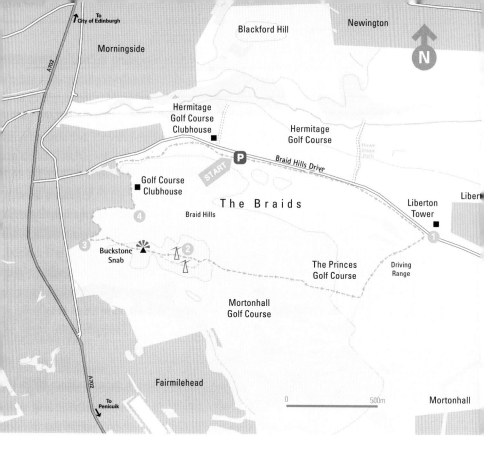

The Braids

START Head east towards Liberton for 1km on a path through low shrubs which ends at a red dirt road. ① Turn right and follow the dirt road for over 1.5km around the golf course perimeter to a left hand bend just before the masts. ② Continue straight ahead taking an obvious grassy path to the right of the masts. Rejoin the bridleway briefly then continue straight uphill to the trig point where the bridleway contours left. Drop steeply down the far side of the hill on a narrow path through gorse to a junction. ③ Turn sharp right onto a path behind a row of houses. This short section is usually muddy. ④ After the last house turn left between fences. Go through the car park. At the far end of the car park turn right through gates then immediately left onto the signposted bridleway. Follow this narrow path around the side of the hill to return to the start of the route.

Trip Planning

🚌 Braid Hills Hotel, Comiston Road A702 (1.2km from start) or Liberton Drive, Liberton Brae A701 (2.3km from start) 🚗 Braid Hills Drive links the A701 and A702 four miles south of the centre of Edinburgh. A signposted off-road car park is on the south side of the road a few hundred metres east of the entrance to the Hermitage Golf Course. 🚾 Cameron Toll Shopping Centre A701/A7 ☕ Opposite the car park at the Queen Cake Café in the Hermitage Golf Course club house. *www.queencakecafé.co.uk*

Other Routes

Add this loop onto a run through Hermitage of Braid and over Blackford Hill. The small parking area at Blackford Pond (255 709) is a good place to start. A few hundred metres west of the end of Blackford Glen Road cross a footbridge over the Braid Burn and climb up to Braid Hills

Follow the bridleway around the golf course

Braid Hills

Drive on the Howe Dean Path. Return to Hermitage of Braid by the Lang Linn Path which crosses Hermitage Golf Course to the east of the club house.

Events

The Edinburgh University Hare and Hounds Club organise a race around the Braids every November. Any left-over energy can be used up on the dance floor as the post-run ceilidh is just as much part of the event as the race itself.

The Hunters Bog Trot is a 6.5km trail/hill race held in Holyrood Park in April and organised by the Hunters Bog Trotters. *www.huntersbogtrotters.com*

Edinburgh's Seven Hills

Each June a motley crew of runners line up on Calton Hill to compete in the Edinburgh Seven Hills Race. With no marked course the event is a mix of road running, cross country, hill running and urban orienteering. The sole rule is that competitors must pass through each summit checkpoint in the correct order: Edinburgh Castle, Corstorphine, Craiglockhart, the Braids, Blackford, Arthur's Seat and back to Calton Hill. Optimal route choice is the essence of the challenge and veterans know all the cunning shortcuts. Running the Seven Hills is a great way of seeing the city and should be on the tick list of all Edinburgh runners. Enjoy the event's friendly atmosphere by trying the 14 miles, 2200ft Race or shorter Challenge. Alternatively, trot round on any sunny Sunday morning for a leisurely tour of Edinburgh. *www.seven-hills.org.uk*

Dechmont Law Park

12 Dechmont Law

Distance	6km (3.5 miles)	Ascent 100m (300ft)
Map	OS Landranger 65, OS Explorer 350	
Navigation ●●●	Over the M8 and along the far side, returning via an underpass and trig point	
Terrain ●●●	Gravel, earth and grass paths	
Wet Feet ●●●	A few soft, muddy sections	
Start/Finish	Eastwood Park cul-de-sac next to Deans Community High School	
	EH54 8P NT 032 694	

Short woodland trail criss-crossing the M8 motorway

Slap bang next to Scotland's busiest motorway is an unlikely place to find a good run but this short circuit belies its location. Firm trails through pretty deciduous woodland are a surprise discovery in the heart of industrial 'Silicon Glen'. In just a few kilometres this route ticks off open grassland, leafy woodland, dense conifer plantation and a rocky hilltop. It is always satisfying to reach a trig point and the one on top of this modest volcanic pimple has views to rival many of its loftier cousins.

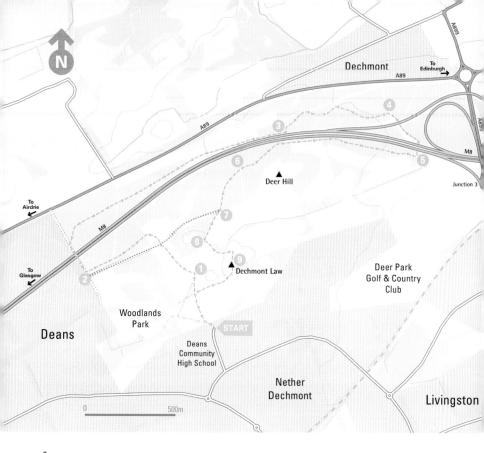

Dechmont

To Edinburgh →

A89

A899

A899

M8

Junction 3

A89

A89

Deer Hill

To Airdrie ←

M8

To Glasgow ←

Deer Park
Golf & Country
Club

Woodlands
Park

Deans

Dechmont Law

START

Deans
Community
High School

Nether
Dechmont

Livingston

0   500m

🏃 START   Follow the path from the end of the cul-de-sac leftwards into the park. Within the first 100m keep right at a fork and climb uphill to the third path on the left marked by two benches. ① Turn onto the path to pass by the benches. Continue straight across a gravel path then curve left through a field and into woodland to reach a T-junction. ② Turn right and cross a footbridge over the motorway then take the first right onto a path through the North Wood. This may become a bit muddy as it crosses a grassy field to reach coniferous woodland. ③ Ignore the first path into the wood and continue beside the motorway for another hundred metres before turning left onto a less muddy path marked by a short wooden post. Keep to the strongest path through the trees while heading right to reach a tarmac road. ④ Turn right to cross a footbridge and then go under the motorway. ⑤ After emerging from the underpass take the first path on the right, just in front of a fence. This runs through trees close to the motorway then moves away from the road to reach a fork. ⑥ Take the right-hand branch which leads uphill to a second fork at a seat. This time take the left-hand branch and head uphill to the edge of the

250m							
200m							
150m							
0km	1km	2km	3km	4km	5km		

trees. ⑦ Turn right then immediately left at a stone to follow the edge of the woodland along a twisty path between the trees. ⑧ Leave the woodland and cross boggy ground to head directly up Dechmont Law. ⑨ Continue straight past the trig point to drop down an obvious grassy path and meet the outward gravel path. Turn left to return to the start of the route.

Trip Planning

🚌 Harburn Avenue, Deans North Road outside Deans Community High School. 🚂 Livingston North (1km from start) 🚗 Dechmont Law is on the north side of Livingston. Leave the M8 at Junction 3 and follow signs to Livingston and Deans. Turn right just before the High School then first left onto Eastwood Park cul-de-sac where there is a small car park 🚾 Carmondean Shopping Centre.

Dechmont Law

Dechmont Law

Walker on Dechmont Law

Other Routes

South and west of Livingston there are paths through Oakbank Park, Calder Wood and along the River Almond that can be linked to form longer off-road runs.

Events

Lothian Running Club organise a 10km Trail Race and shorter fun run at Dechmont Law each June. *www.lothianrunningclub.co.uk*

Ascent from Hopes Reservoir

13 Lammer Law

Distance	11km (7 miles)	Ascent	350m (1200ft)
Map	OS Landranger 66, OS Explorer 345		
Navigation •••	Onto the tops by an obvious track, return by the ridge north of the reservoir		
Terrain •••	Gravel and grassy tracks, narrow and uneven paths through heather		
Wet Feet •••	Jump the stream at the end of the route		
Start/Finish	West Hopes EH41 4PL NT 556 633		

Wide hill tracks gain high moorland and sea views

On a hot summer day splashing through the ford at the end of this run is the perfect way to revive tired, dusty feet. The first half of this route follows wide gravel roads and tracks up to the summit of Lammer Law. The second half returns by way of narrow heathery paths along a broad ridge followed by a fast, grassy descent. The large cairn on top of Lammer Law provides an opportunity to rest and admire the view. Greens, yellows and browns of farmland give way to deep blue sea stretching to the horizon. Traprain Law and pointy North Berwick Law are easily picked out while just offshore the Bass Rock sparkles in its coat of white guano.

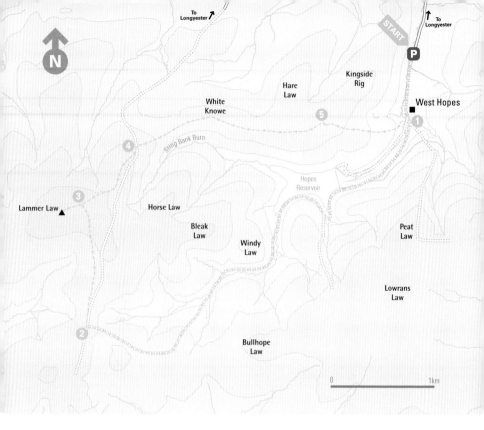

Follow the gravel road towards Hopes Reservoir to the houses at West Hopes. ❶ Go through a gate and continue along the lower road on a gradually rising traverse. This contours above the reservoir then turns into a stream valley after nearly 3km. Continue following this track up onto the top of the moors to a gate and T-junction with another track. ❷ Turn right then after 200m continue straight on where a rougher Scotways signposted track goes off to the right. Continue climbing for another 1km to the brow of the hill. ❸ Take a short detour left to the summit cairn then return to and cross the track. Go through a gate and head downhill on a narrow path through the heather. Follow this down and left for around 800m to meet a grassy track at a fence corner. ❹ Cross the track and continue downhill on a narrow path through heather to the left hand side of the fence. Continue following this fence along the ridge for about 2km. After the second small summit (spot height 398m) look for a gate in the fence on the right. ❺ Go through the gate and a few metres on the far side of the fence turn left onto a grassy track. (This track runs parallel to the fence from the first summit.) Follow the grassy track downhill, jump or wade the river then follow the reservoir road back to the start.

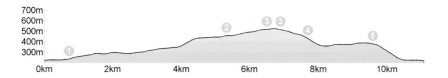

Trip Planning

In wet weather the stream crossing at the end of the run (556 627) should be inspected before starting out. Under normal conditions the stream is easily jumped or waded. Access may be restricted during the grouse season starting on August 12th. Observe all signs and flags. There is no public transport to the start. 🚙 Hopes Reservoir is twenty five miles east of Edinburgh by road. Turn off the B6355 south-west of Gifford onto a minor road signed to Longyester. Follow the road round left at Longyester then turn right after the houses towards Hopes Reservoir. There is a large car park on the left just past cottages at the end of the public road. 🚻 Gifford 🍺 Log fire and real ales at the Goblin Ha' pub in Gifford. *www.goblinha.com* 🐕 Keep dogs on a short lead or under close control during the ground bird nesting season (April to July). Sheep graze the hills and fields around the reservoir.

Other Routes

Extend the run by linking the hill tracks past Hopes Reservoir and over Lammer Law with the two dead-end roads heading south from Longyester. The best parking is at West Hopes. Roadside parking for one or two cars is possible at Longyester but care must be taken not to block entrances. There is rough off-road parking for several cars at Blinkbonny Wood. Scotways, the Scottish Rights of Way and Access Society, have waymarked 127km (80 miles) of historic hill tracks which are described in a free leaflet *Walking in the Lammermuir Hills*. *www.scotways.com*

Ridge north of Hopes Reservoir

79

Lammer Law

Running off Lammer Law

Medieval cadgers

On the descent off Lammer Law the path swings left to follow the line of an old track parallel with the modern track marked on maps. A closer look reveals multiple parallel tracks. Most are very faint, marked only by intermittent lines of grass or blaeberries through the heather. These faint traces are all that remain of an old trading route that once linked Lauder with Haddington. Unlike earlier Roman roads, medieval trading routes were simply trodden out by the feet of men and beasts. Wherever terrain permitted the route would spread out into multiple parallel paths like those on the shoulder of Lammer Law. Cadgers, the Scots term for carriers or packmen, travelled north with wool from the Borders and returned south with Lothian grain. Paths further east were used by fish cadgers. In the mid 1600s up to 20,000 people gathered in Dunbar at Lammas to buy their winter supply of salt fish.

Union Canal

14 Union Canal & River Almond

Distance	13km (8 miles)	Ascent	100m (300ft)
Map	OS Landranger 65, OS Explorer 350		
Navigation ●●●	Signed track to canal, signs to Country Park, signed road junctions return to canal		
Terrain ●●●	Canal towpath, earth paths, quiet public road, steps and stiles		
Wet Feet ●●●	Occasional puddles and shallow mud		
Start/Finish	Canal bridge, Ratho EH28 8RU NT 139 709		

Level running along the canal and river valley

The Union Canal towpath is an unlikely place for a life changing experience. Yet this is precisely what happened to a young engineer in 1834. After John Scott Russell observed a soliton wave on the canal he devoted the rest of his life to explaining the phenomenon. Do today's academics from nearby Heriot Watt University experience similar flashes of insight during their lunchtime towpath runs? Along the way there is plenty to inspire even the least academically minded runner. This route follows a long canal feeder which runs high above the scenic River Almond. Across the valley is Illieston Castle. Look behind to see an impressive aqueduct which is crossed later in the route. While running back along the canal look out for Santa's island. A December run by head torch provides the full colourful Christmassy experience.

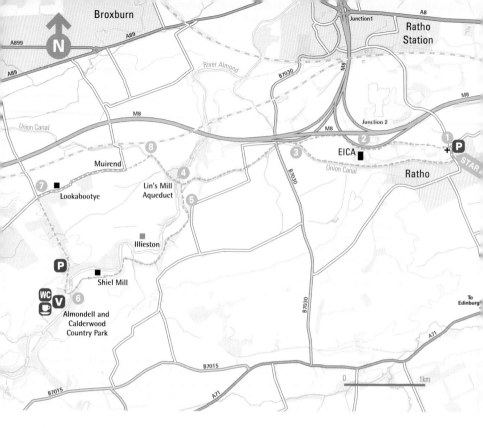

🏃 **START**   Follow the road uphill past the war memorial to a road junction. ❶ Turn left onto a track signposted to Wilkie Basin via Platt Hill. Continue along the right-hand side of a small wooded hill to reach the Edinburgh International Climbing Arena (EICA) just over 1km into the run. ❷ Continue straight ahead through boulders where the road turns left, then follow around two sides of the field to reach the canal. ❸ Turn right onto the towpath and follow it for over 1.5km to reach signposted steps just before the aqueduct. ❹ Head down the steps signed to the Country Park and turn left under the aqueduct. Follow the road along the side of the field for a few hundred metres to a sign for the Country Park. ❺ Follow the sign to turn right down steps to reach the canal feeder. Continue for just over 2km crossing stiles and a house drive to reach a small suspension bridge. ❻ Cross the river and continue straight ahead to climb up to a tarmac road. At this point the Visitor Centre with toilets and a café is a short detour left. Turn right and follow the road out of the country park to a crossroads. ❼ Turn right towards Muirend and the Union Canal. At the farm continue straight ahead onto a track which crosses the canal. ❽ From the bridge, the towpath on the right, south-east, leads all the way back to Ratho.

Trip Planning

🚌 Ratho Canal Centre 🚗 Ratho is eight miles west of the centre of Edinburgh. Follow the Glasgow Road (A8) turning south onto Gogarstone Road then Freelands Road just east of Ratho Station. Park in the public car park just north of the canal. 🚾 Almondell and Calderwood Country Park Visitor Centre 🍴 The Bridge Inn serves pub meals and afternoon tea and cake. *www.bridgeinn.com* The Country Park Visitor Centre and the EICA also have cafés.

Other Routes

The Union Canal links Fountainbridge near the centre of Edinburgh with the Forth and Clyde Canal at Falkirk. Unusually the canal was designed with no locks other than a flight at Falkirk. Cuttings, embankments and aqueducts maintain the level of the canal as it follows the 240ft contour. Bus and train connections help create a range of one way runs.

Events

The 56 miles Glasgow-Edinburgh Ultramarathon follows the Forth and Clyde, then Union Canal towpaths from Ruchill on the outskirts of Glasgow to Edinburgh Quay near Haymarket Railway Station. *www.resoluteevents.co.uk*

Other Activities

The Edinburgh International Climbing Arena is a huge climbing wall built in an old quarry. Technically it is indoors (it has a roof) but take a down jacket in winter. The EICA is also the home of the JudoScotland National Training Centre. *www.eica-ratho.com*

Union Canal & River Almond

Ratho

The Soliton Wave

John Scott Russell was a talented engineer who spent an early part of his career designing barges for the Union Canal Company. While watching trials of a new design he saw that the bow wave continued on down the canal after the barge itself stopped. Russell followed the wave on horseback for over a mile as it continued at constant speed and with no change in height. This behaviour contradicted all theories of the time. Russell was convinced that this phenomenon must be hugely important and spent the next three years studying the 'Wave of Translation' in a water tank he built in the garden of his New Town flat. Sadly for Russell his fellow scientists were uninterested in his discovery. It was long after his death that soliton waves were understood theoretically and identified in fields as diverse as oceanography, plasma physics, superconductors and fibre optic communications.

Aberlady Nature Reserve

15 Aberlady Bay & Gullane Sands

Distance	14 km (8 miles)	Ascent	50m (150ft)
Map	OS Landranger 66, OS Explorer 351		
Navigation •••	General direction is straightforward although multiple paths can be confusing		
Terrain •••	Grass paths and tracks, sandy beach, optional rocky scrambles		
Wet Feet •••	Dry and sandy		
Start/Finish	Aberlady Bay EH32 0QB NT 471 805		

Gorgeous sandy beaches and grassy tracks through the dunes

Wandering off-route is practically obligatory on this scenic coastal circuit. The aim is to get from Aberlady Bay to the far side of Gullane and back. The outward journey follows grassy tracks and the return is mainly along the beach. Simple. In a few places there are lots of path options on the ground but it doesn't matter which one is taken providing the overall direction is maintained. Avoiding the golf course is advisable and if in doubt head towards the sea as the beach running is fantastic in either direction. Woodland at the far end of the run provides contrast and a welcome shelter in windy weather. The highlight is dropping down from Gullane Point onto the beach to see a vast expanse of runnable sand stretching away into the distance. While Gullane Bents are often busy Aberlady Bay is quiet and shared with the occasional sea bird rather than humans. A great place to run.

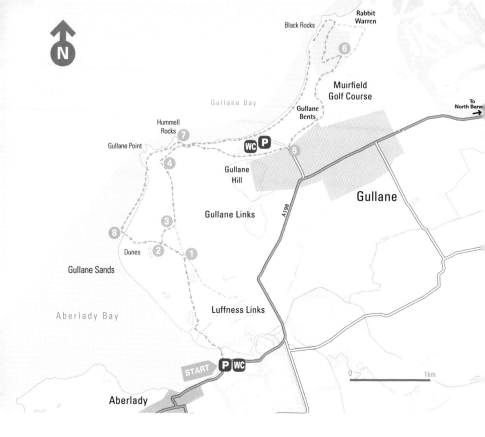

🏃 **START** Cross the footbridge into the nature reserve then continue through a tunnel of shrubbery and past the tiny Marl Loch to reach a T-junction with a grassy track. ❶ Turn left onto the track for 300m to reach the end of the golf course. ❷ Turn right following footpath signs around the edge of the course to reach a track junction. ❸ Turn left onto a long straight track for 800m. This climbs gradually uphill past tank defences then curves left and downhill to a fork. ❹ Keep right at the fork then follow paths over the top of the cliffs through tank defences. Keep right, following the edge of the golf course, then continue just below the row of houses on Gullane Hill. ❺ Cross the road and go around an emergency access barrier onto a track. Follow this past pine trees and into shrubs. Keep right at three forked junctions to follow a fence and finally reach a building. ❻ Turn left onto a little used but obvious path into woodland. After about 200m the path drops down into a clearing. A narrow path continues on but instead turn right to cross the clearing and join a wide path through the trees. After emerging from the woods turn left to follow grassy shore paths back to Gullane Bay. Scramble over rocks below the head-

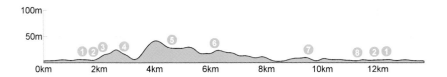

land or rejoin the outward path over the top of the cliffs then continue along the shore to the Aberlady Bay Nature Reserve sign. ⑦ Follow a grassy path along the edge of the dunes then drop down onto the beach. ⑧ A footpath sign indicates the way back through the dunes. Shortly after reaching the golf course turn right onto the outward grassy track to return to the car park.

Trip Planning

🚌 Aberlady, Community Hall (800m from start) 🚗 Aberlady Bay is about eighteen miles east of Edinburgh. If travelling from Edinburgh turn off the A1 onto the A198. The car park is on the left about half a mile after passing through Aberlady village. 🅦🅒 Aberlady Bay car park 9am to 9pm (6pm in winter) 🍴 Falko Konditorei, a German bakery on Stanley Road, Gullane. Incredible cakes and probably the best pretzels in Scotland. 🐕 Dogs are not permitted on the Nature Reserve between April and July (inclusive) and must be kept on a lead or under close control during the rest of the year. There are no restrictions outside the Nature Reserve.

Other Routes

The route is easily shortened by running from Aberlady to Gullane Bents and back. Or by starting at Gullane Bents and running either the east or west halves of the circuit.

A good one-way route follows the coast from Aberlady Bay to North Berwick which has bus and train connections. The beach is sometimes rocky and dune paths can be faint or overgrown. Turn this longer route into a circuit by

Tyninghame, East Lothian

Aberlady Bay & Gullane Sands

Gullane Bay

returning to Aberlady from Yellowcraigs along the waymarked John Muir Way.

The John Muir Way is a 73km waymarked route from Fisherrow to Dunglass, just south of Dunbar. It combines pavement with off-road paths and tracks. The John Muir Way forms the East Lothian section of the North Sea Trail (NAVE Nortrail) which runs through Scotland, England, the Netherlands, Germany, Denmark, Sweden and Norway.

Birdwatching

Aberlady Bay is one of the best places to birdwatch in East Lothian. It was designated Britain's first Local Nature Reserve in 1952. In winter look out for ducks, geese and waders. Come here at dusk to see up to 15,000 pink-footed geese fly in from surrounding fields to roost on the salt marsh. Common species on the shore include lapwings, golden plovers and widgeons. In summer skylarks sing above the grass tracks through the dunes while reed buntings and warblers flit between the thin branches of shrubs near the Marl Loch.

West Kip

16 The Western Pentlands

Distance	16km (10 miles)	Ascent	675m (2200ft)
Map	OS Landranger 66, OS Explorer 350, Harvey Pentland Hills		
Navigation •••	Intermittently signed, footpaths faint in places		
Terrain •••	Grassy and stony paths and tracks		
Wet Feet •••	Some boggy ground and stream crossings		
Start/Finish	Nine Mile Burn EH26 9LZ NT 177 577		

Mixed trail and hill running at the quiet end of these popular hills

The Pentlands are a great place for running off excess energy with their grassy slopes, well-worn paths and steep but short ups and downs. As a general rule, the further one ventures from Edinburgh the quieter the Pentlands become. This route in the far western end of the range follows old rights of way. These include a path trod by monks travelling between Queensferry Abbey and their hospice and travellers rest near Nine Mile Burn. The "font stone" by the side of the path over Monks Rig is in fact the socket stone of a wooden cross which used to stand on the hillside. Open landscapes, a wide variety of views and mixed, though always runnable, terrain characterise this run. The long grassy descent off Monks Rig provides a fitting finale.

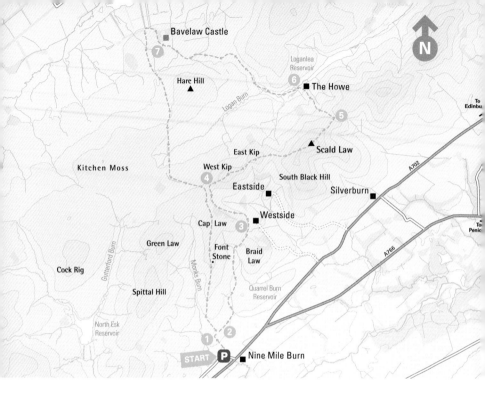

🏃 **START** Go through the kissing gate signposted to Balerno and follow footpath signposts around the edge of the field and uphill to a stile. ① Cross the stile and turn right along the stone wall then continue over the next stile towards Braid Law. ② As the field begins to descend towards a stream head left and uphill to the top corner of the field. Follow an obvious path which traverses rough hillside, crossing a stone wall after 300m then jumping a small stream after a further 600m. Continue over the brow of the hill to a track junction above Westside Farm. ③ Take the uphill, left-hand track and contour around the valley to the col just west of West Kip. ④ Cross a stile and quad tracks to reach the path up West Kip. Go over West Kip, East Kip and Scald Law. ⑤ Turn left off the ridge onto an obvious path down to The Howe. ⑥ Turn left along the burn and follow the path through Green Cleuch towards Bavelaw Castle. ⑦ Cross the stile onto the castle drive and keep turning left to join the signposted track back to Nine Mile Burn. This track has a boggy stream crossing but otherwise is very runnable and easily followed back to the col at West Kip near ④. Go right over a stile signposted to Nine Mile Burn by Monks Rig and climb gradually uphill on a grassy track. Take the right hand branch where the track forks just before the brow of Cap Law. Continue on the obvious grassy path to cross signposted stiles and return to ①. Retrace the outward route back to Nine Mile Burn.

Trip Planning

Trail shoes with excellent grip or fell shoes are recommended. 🚌 Nine Mile Burn 🚗 Nine Mile Burn is thirteen miles south-west of Edinburgh city centre on the A702. Turn north off the road at Nine Mile Burn and park opposite a row of cottages. 🚾 Flotterstone Ranger Base, just off the A702, five miles closer to Edinburgh. 🍴 The Flotterstone Inn is a popular haunt after running, walking, biking or skiing in the Pentlands. *www.flotterstoneinn.com* If heading south on the A702 try the Allan Ramsay at Carlops. *www.allanramsayhotel.com* 🐕 Sheep graze the fields and open hillside.

Other Routes

There are plenty of other routes through the Pentland Hills. Information is available from the Ranger Base at Flotterstone or *www.pentlandhills.org*

Heading uphill from Nine Mile Burn

The Western Pentlands

The Font Stone on Monks Rig

The shortest variant of this route is to omit the loop over the Kips and return directly to Nine Mile Burn by Monks Rig. Alternative short cuts omit Scald Law or follow a path south of Hare Hill. For a longer run simply continue over the hills.

The Red Moss Nature Reserve car park above Balerno (166 639) is an alternative starting point. The steep climb up the tarmac drive to Bavelaw Castle is soon forgotten and makes a fast descent on the return. The roads up from the bus terminus at Balerno (Mansfield Road/Cockburn Crescent) (165 656) are quiet and often run, walked and cycled.

Events

The Pentland Skyline is a classic fell race held in October. Competitors tick all the main Pentland summits in one 16 mile, 6200ft round. This race as well as shorter Pentland races are organised by the Carnethy Hill Running Club. *www.carnethy.com*

Drum Wood

17 Falkirk Community Woodlands

Distance	17km (10 miles)	Ascent	200m (700ft)
Map	OS Landranger 65, OS Explorer 349		
Navigation •••	Many junctions are signposted although the route is not waymarked		
Terrain •••	Canal towpath, gravel paths, farm track, forest road, pavement		
Wet Feet •••	Shallow mud on farm track and forest road		
Start/Finish	Falkirk Wheel (South) FK1 4RR NS 853 799		

Good trails link woods, farms, a Roman fort and a canal

This longer run explores farmland and woods to the south of Falkirk. Most of the very run-nable trails are purpose built walking paths through community woodlands. There is also a long section on an old farm track. Although straight as a die this track is never dull as it undulates along slightly higher ground with views towards the Ochils. Running through the trees lining the Antonine Wall at Rough Castle is a highlight, as is turning a corner to see the impressive Falkirk Wheel. The long list of directions makes this route appear complicated. Once on the ground the navigation feels much more straightforward. Many different permutations are possible and worth exploring.

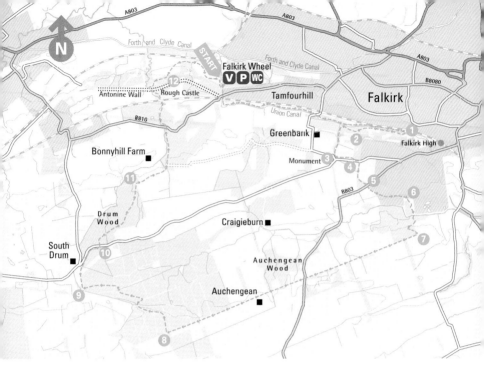

🏃 **START**   Follow the towpath south from the wheel, through the tunnel and along the north side of the canal for about 2.5km until opposite the Seagull Trust Boathouse. **1** Cross the canal then go through the car park of the Boathouse to join a path which returns along the south side of the canal. After 500m the path climbs uphill away from the canal to a junction just before a bridge. **2** Turn right onto a path signed to Greenbank Road then after 200m turn left at the next junction to follow a small stream uphill towards the Falkirk Monument. **3** Turn left at the monument and follow the field edge or road to the entrance of South Bantaskine Estate. **4** Cross the road and go through a gate onto a path signposted to Lionthorn. Follow this for 500m as it turns away from the road down a strip of woodland then across a field to Slamannan Road. **5** Cross the road and follow the pavement down Lionthorn Road, signposted Edinburgh (M9), for about 750m to reach the next woodland. **6** Follow the path to the left of the woods, cross a footbridge and continue uphill towards Kilbean Strip, turning left at a T-junction to reach the track running along the ridgeline. **7** Turn right onto the track and follow it for nearly 4km. The track crosses Slamannan Road and passes Auchengean Farm to reach a cross roads with Scots pine trees on both sides of the track. **8** Turn right onto a dirt forestry road and follow this main track through the trees to a T-junction with a dirt road at the edge of the plantation. **9** Turn right onto the road and right again just before a barrier onto a walkers' path. This path runs

parallel to the public road and ends after 500m. ⑩ Cross the road onto a gravel path. Soon after, turn right at a T-junction and continue for 1km to a T-junction with the Drove Loan. ⑪ Turn right and follow signs to Rough Castle. The route turns off the Drove Loan through a gate and straight on to cross a road and go under the railway then left to reach the site of the Roman fort. ⑫ Leave the fort by a path at its north-west corner which leads back to the Falkirk Wheel.

Trip Planning

🚌 Lime Road Turning Circle 🚂 Falkirk High (600m east of ①) 🚗 Follow signs to the Falkirk Wheel to park either north of the wheel (A883 Park & Ride free) or to its west (Lime Road pay & display). 🚻 🍴 Falkirk Wheel Visitor Centre *www.thefalkirkwheel.co.uk*

The final section of the route passes through the Roman fort of Rough Castle

Falkirk Community Woodlands

The Falkirk Wheel
Photo: Chris Upson

Other Routes

Shorten the route to 10km by turning right at the Battle of Falkirk Monument ❸ and following the Old Drove Loan to the Rough Castle turn-off. Part of this shortcut follows a quiet public road with no pavement.

Other Activities

The Callendar Estate has developed a network of mountain-biking trails accessed from Greenrig car park (858 765). *www.callendarestate.co.uk*

The Falkirk Wheel

This monstrous structure towers over the canal, dwarfing people, barges and even the substantial Visitor Centre. The 24 metre height difference between the two canals was originally resolved by a flight of eleven locks. The Wheel is a much more dramatic solution to the problem. The 35m diameter wheel carries two diametrically opposed caissons. One caisson contains 360,000 litres of water and can carry up to eight boats. As the two caissons are perfectly balanced it takes relatively little energy to power the wheel. A 180 degree rotation uses about the same energy as boiling 10 kettles of water.

Glasgow and the Clyde

Although rumours of near-constant rainfall are exaggerated it is a fact that the West of Scotland is luxuriantly green and leafy. Some of the best woodland trail running in the whole country is found here. Rising above the Clyde Valley are low hills with fabulous views towards Arran, Argyll and Loch Lomond.

Kelvingrove Park

City Centre Running

Every sunny summer day sees office workers swarming out of air conditioned offices and onto the River Clyde walkway. This walkway allows sensible lunchtime-sized circuits both east and west of the city centre. To the east is Glasgow Green which can be circled on level tarmac paths. Kelvingrove Park in the West End offers a longer and more hilly alternative. Kelvingrove also gives access to a wooded path along the River Kelvin which feels a world away from the hustle and bustle of the city. Wildlife likes it here too: secretive otters and kingfishers have both been spotted in recent years. Combining the River Kelvin walkway with the Speirs Wharf branch of the Forth and Clyde Canal creates a 13km circuit from the city centre. The M8 motorway is easily crossed by footbridges at Charing Cross and east of Port Dundas. Within the city limits is Pollok Park whose stately trees and tarmac paths are an oasis for Southside runners. Several off-tarmac paths through the North Wood and an old farm track to the south of White Cart Water are well worth exploring.

North of the Pad

18 Neilston Pad

Distance	3.5km (2 miles)	Ascent	50m (200ft)
Map	OS Landranger 64, OS Explorer 342		
Navigation •••	Obvious track around the foot of the hill		
Terrain •••	Wide stony track		
Wet Feet •••	Good grip even in wet weather		
Start/Finish	Car park south of Neilston Pad G78 3DA NS 472 544		

Easy to follow track circuit through fields and forestry

This is the easiest route in the book: a short straightforward trail looping around a flat-topped hill south-west of Barrhead. The wide track gives easy running through pleasantly varied scenery: forests, reservoirs, picturesque farmland and a fine view of the Campsie Fells. A trip to the top of the Pad doubles the ascent to gain an even better view over Neilston and its surrounds. Neilston's large parish church is a reminder that in its heyday this sleepy village was a bustling mill town. Despite its size, the church was still too small for its congregation and a seat rent was applied during the 1820s. The minister, Dr Alexander Fleming, objected to this levy and preached from a tent in the graveyard for eight years. As he put it, "the people of the Parish are entitled to hear the Gospel". Any minister prepared to deliver an outdoor sermon in Scotland surely made it to the top of his local hill, although probably at a dignified walk rather than a run.

🏃 START Go through a kissing gate onto a wide gravel track and follow it around the hill. After about 1km the track descends into a stream valley then climbs above a small fishing loch through a couple of gates. ❶ Continue on the track up to the brow of the hill where there is a good view of the Campsie Fells. Descend a short distance to a track junction in front of a wood. ❷ Turn left and follow the track along the edge of woodland and through a couple of kissing gates. Continue on the track past a reservoir and through forestry then along a line of tall beech trees. ❸ Just after the track curves left to cross the line of trees turn right onto a narrow, sometimes muddy, path which heads directly back to the car park. Or continue slightly further along the track to a T-junction then turn right onto the outward route.

Trip Planning

If using public transport, join the route at ② by following a farm track from Neilston. 🚂 Neilston (1.7km from ②) 🚌 Loanfoot Avenue on Kingston Road (1.2km from ②) 🚗 Neilston is just off the A736 a couple of miles south-west of Barrhead. Turn off Neilston's Main Street opposite the Parish Church onto High Street which becomes Kingston Road. Continue out of town for two miles. Turn left and park in a car park at a bend in the road just after gas works. 🚾 Neilston Railway Station. 🚻 Neilston.

Other Routes

For longer runs head up onto Fereneze Braes just north of Neilston. The signposted routes vary from good tracks and paths to rough ground. From Brownside car park (489 607) a runnable track leads up onto the hills. This track can also be linked through Glen Park to the path network on Gleniffer Braes. Brownside and Fereneze Braes tend to be quiet while the area near the Robertson Car Park (459 602) on Gleniffer Braes is usually busy with dog walkers. This low range of hills has a superb view north across the Clyde towards the Arrochar Alps and Campsie Fells.

Further west are trails through Clyde Muirshiel Country Park starting from the Castle Semple Visitor Centre. There are circular trail routes near Lochwinnoch. Most tracks heading into the moors are out and back or connected by rough footpaths and untracked ground.

www.clydemuirshiel.co.uk

Events

A trail race around Neilston Pad forms part of the annual village show in May.

www.neilstonshow.co.uk/padrace

The Kilbarchan Klassic is a 5.5 miles out and back trail race organised by Kilbarchan AAC.

www.kilbarchanaac.org.uk

Neilston Pad

Descent to Snypes Dam

Long Lost Languages

The word Glasgow is derived from "glas chu" which means "green hollow" in the Cumbric tongue. This translation has evolved to the affectionate modern moniker "dear green place". Cumbric is closely related to Welsh. It is a P-Celtic language which was spoken in southern Scotland and northern England between the 6th and 11th centuries AD. East of Glasgow Cumbric was superseded by Old Northumbrian while Scots Gaelic, a Q-Celtic language derived from Irish, spread south from the Western Isles and Argyll. Modern Welsh speakers will recognise Cumbric-derived Scottish placenames such as Lanark – 'llannerch' is Welsh for glade.

Mugdock Wood

19 Mugdock Country Park

Distance	4km (2.5 miles)	Ascent	50m (150ft)
Map	OS Landranger 64, OS Explorer 348		
Navigation •••	Straightforward circuit around the park and loch with some signage		
Terrain •••	Gravel and grass paths and tracks		
Wet Feet •••	Occasional muddy puddles		
Start/Finish	Mugdock Country Park Visitor Centre G62 8EL NS 546 779		

Woodland trails beneath the Campsie Fells

Mugdock Country Park lies just beyond Glasgow's suburban sprawl and offers a wide range of easily accessible running trails. The easiest circuit at Mugdock simply goes round the loch. The route described here explores different areas of the park and is a good introduction to trail running on a variety of surfaces. It is also a good introduction to Glasgow's varied history. The route passes Mugdock Castle which was ransacked twice in the 17th century. 20th-century conflict is recorded in the gun battery built to protect the Clyde shipyards. Less obvious are the cages cut into the bedrock of Gallow Hill near the start of the route. These were occupied in the early 1950s by the animals, reptiles and birds of Craigend Zoo. The zoo's most popular resident was Charlie the elephant who made quite an impression on Milngavie. On one memorable occasion he demolished the doorway of a local pub by attempting to follow his keeper into the bar.

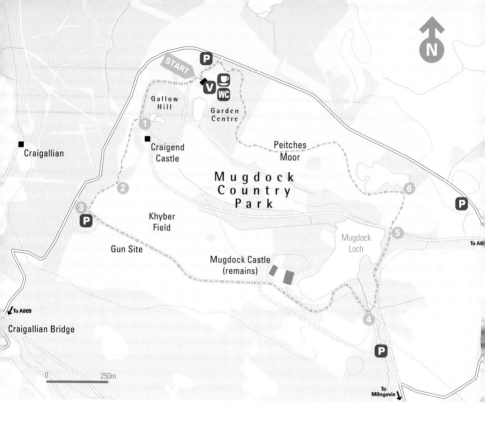

🏃 START From the archway on the park side of the Visitor Centre head to the right past the play park. Follow the track round the foot of Gallow Hill for 250m to a footbridge. ① Cross the bridge then follow a grassy path left for 300m to a T-junction. ② Turn right and head uphill to a kissing gate. ③ After going through the gate turn left onto a long straight track. This goes past WWII gun emplacements and has good views of the Campsies and of the Clyde Valley. Continue through a gate, past Mugdock Castle and stay on the main track as it curves left down to the loch. A few hundred metres after heading away from the loch the track reaches a junction. ④ Turn left across a bridge and follow this track for about 400m to a T-junction of tracks at the north-east corner of the loch. ⑤ Continue straight ahead on a rough path, cross a stile and follow grassy paths straight ahead to reach a fence. ⑥ Turn left at the edge of the old quarry and follow a grassy path across Peitches Moor to woodland. Head through the trees, keeping right at each junction, to return to the main car park and the Visitor Centre.

Mugdock Country Park

Trip Planning

Mugdock Country Park visitor information can be found online at *www.mugdock-country-park.org.uk*
🚌 No timetabled service to Visitor Centre. Strathclyde Partnership for Transport operate a ring 'n' ride service. *www.spt.co.uk* Free buses run from Milngavie railway station during the school holidays. 🚗 Follow the A81 out of Milngavie towards Strathblane. After leaving the 30mph limit turn left signposted to the Country Park. At the next junction head diagonally right and continue for another kilometre to the Visitor Centre. **WC** **V** 🅿 The Visitor Centre has a café as does the nearby Plantaria.

Other Routes

There are many possible variations as Mugdock Country Park has an extensive path network and several different access points. The West Highland Way provides a waymarked off-road path from Milngavie town centre into the park.

A perfectly level trail goes round the two Mugdock Reservoirs and has a good view over the Clyde Valley. Park at the Drumclog car park (NS 554 759) on Mugdock Road.

Mugdock Loch and Castle

Mugdock Country Park

Khyber Field

Hunting Lodge
and Grand Avenue

20 Chatelherault Country Park

Distance	8km (5 miles)	Ascent	100m (350ft)
Map	OS Landranger 64, OS Explorer 343		
Navigation •••	Signposted paths lead out to Green Bridge and return by the far side of the river		
Terrain •••	Wide woodland paths		
Wet Feet •••	Good grip even in wet weather		
Start/Finish	Chatelherault Visitor Centre ML3 7UE NS 737 539		

Soft pine needle strewn trails through an old hunting estate

This route is the epitome of woodland trail running. Chatelherault is particularly lovely in spring when bluebells carpet the ground and oak leaves are just unfurling. Winding between the trees are wide gravel paths littered with pine needles which give a soft yet firm running surface. The trails follow the woodland's edge with views out over the surrounding farmland. Both trees and farmland were once part of a vast hunting estate owned by the Dukes of Hamilton. Their hunting lodge is now a Visitor Centre; its original architect referred to it as the "dogg kennel". The building's proportions scream out its primary purpose: to impress visitors to the ducal palace at the far end of the Grand Avenue. Emerging out of shady woodland into the bright open space of this grassy avenue is a great way to end the run.

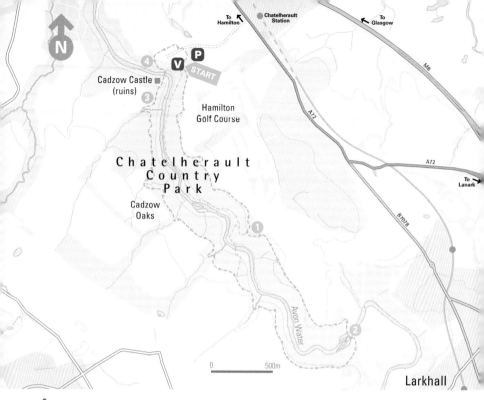

START Head towards the river from the information board outside the visitor centre entrance and almost immediately take a left turn signposted to Green Bridge. This path follows the north-west edge of the woods for nearly 2km to a fork. ① Keep left, continuing to follow signs to Green Bridge. 1.5km further on the path drops down steps to the river. ② Cross the Green Bridge and climb up the far bank following the path round to the right. Follow this path along the top of the riverbank for 3.5km to reach the Cadzow Oaks. ③ After the oak trees keep right at an unmarked fork to take a shortcut to Duke's Bridge. The left fork takes a slightly longer route past the ruin of Cadzow Castle. ④ Recross the river to reach a T-junction where the Visitor Centre is signposted to the right. Turn left here then bear slightly right to emerge from woodland onto the Grand Avenue. Turn right up steps to return to the Visitor Centre or continue straight on to reach the car park.

Trip Planning

🚂 Chatelherault 🚌 Allanton, Chatelherault Country Park entrance on A72 🚗 Chatelherault Country Park is signposted from Junction 6 of the M74 and off the A72 just south of Hamilton. It is about sixteen miles south of Glasgow city centre. 🚻 ♿ Visitor Centre

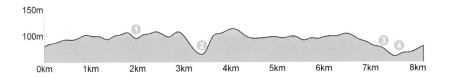

Other Routes

Nearby Strathclyde Country Park was also part of the Hamilton hunting estate. Good running is found around the loch and through the Dalzell Estate as well as along the Clyde Walkway which passes through the park.

Further south a similar but even more scenic 10km (6.3 miles) trail goes through the Falls of Clyde Nature Reserve. Start at New Lanark Heritage Village and follow superb woodland trails past Corra Linn waterfall to the weir above Bonnington Linn. Paths and tracks along the far bank lead to the old road bridge at Kirkfieldbank then follow Clyde Walkway signs back to New Lanark. Run this route after heavy rain or snow-melt to see the waterfalls at their most awe-inspiring.

Events

Free weekly 5km runs in Strathclyde Park are organised by Parkrun volunteers. Prior registration is required. *www.parkrun.org.uk*

Avon Water

Chatelherault Country Park

Cadzow Oaks

Calderglen Harriers organise 5km and 10km races on excellent woodland trails at Calderglen Country Park. *www.calderglenharriers.org.uk*

The Clyde Stride Race along the Clyde Walkway forms part of the Scottish Ultra Marathon Series. The 40 mile race starts at Partick Railway Station in Glasgow and finishes at New Lanark.

www.clydestride.webnode.com

The Cadzow Oaks

These gnarled trees have been dated back to the 1400s although folklore claims they were planted in the 12th century by King David I. Many are stag-headed, so called because of the antler-like spread of dead branches growing out of their crown. The trees at Cadzow are sessile oaks, *Quercus petraea*, a native British species common in the north and west of the country. The acorn of the sessile oak sits directly on its twig. This differentiates the tree from Britain's other native oak species. The acorns of the pedunculate oak, *Quercus robur*, are attached to stalks or 'peduncles' from which the tree derives its name.

Summit view: Loch Lomond
and the Highlands

21 Doughnot Hill

Distance	10km (6 miles)	Ascent	325m (1000ft)
Map	OS Landranger 64, OS Explorer 347		
Navigation •••	Waymarked Crags Circular Path		
Terrain •••	Quiet public road, farm road, forestry track, grass paths and a short section of hillside		
Wet feet •••	Boggy just before the summit		
Start/Finish	Overtoun House, G82 2SH NS 424 761		

Hill circuit with a fast grassy descent

This route up Doughnot Hill is gradual and easily runnable. A downhill start loosens up muscles before the steady climb on good tracks up to Black Linn Reservoir. The short summit section is off the beaten track and gaining the panoramic view of Loch Lomond from the trig point is well worth a little bit of bog. The grassy descent down the Overtoun Burn is one of the best around and has a fantastic view towards Dumbarton Rock and the Firth of Clyde. During the Middle Ages Dumbarton Rock became a vital frontier fortress as the Norwegian border was a mere ten miles downriver. Today it is rock climbers rather than Vikings who mount assaults on the Rock's near-impregnable defences. Dave MacLeod's Rhapsody was the world's first E11 and remains one of the hardest traditional rock routes ever climbed.

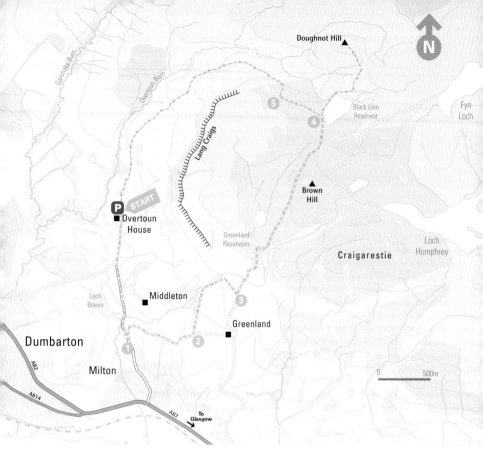

START Head down the Overtoun House drive and down Milton Brae for just over 1km to the second road on the left. On the far side of the junction a signpost indicates the continuation of the Crags Circular Path down into Dumbarton. **1** Turn sharp left and follow the private dirt road uphill towards Greenland Farm for about 1km. **2** Turn left at the signpost to go through a kissing gate onto a narrow earth path between a wall and a fence. Follow this path for 800m past an oak wood, uphill along a stream and right between fields to reach a farm track. **3** Turn left onto the track, cross a stream and continue through a gate into forestry. Continue uphill for nearly 2km to reach Black Linn Reservoir. Towards the top of the hill keep left to stay on the Crags Circular Path where a track goes right to Loch Humphrey. **4** Detour to the summit of Doughnot Hill by crossing the dam and following an indistinct path across the bog. Heading right and then cutting back left to the trig point avoids the worst of the bog. After returning to **4** continue on the signed stony track for less than 500m until a sign indicates an unlikely looking path through

thick plantation. ⑤ The route between the lines of trees is easier than it appears and quickly emerges onto a grassy path. Go through a gate and follow the grassy path downhill for 2km. Continue through a gate onto a track through woodland surrounding Overtoun House.

Trip Planning

🚉 The Crags Circular Path continues downhill on roads and pavements to Crosslet Road just north of Dumbarton East railway station (3km from ①). 🚌 Milton, Whyte Corner at the Arnold Clark garage (600m from ①). 🚗 Turn off the A82 opposite the Arnold Clark garage. Follow Milton Brae uphill for just under one mile then continue straight on through a stone gateway into the grounds of Overtoun House, a Christian centre. There is a large car park on the left before the house. Access times 9am to 6pm (October to March) and 8am to 9pm (April to September). Dumbarton is about thirteen miles from Glasgow city centre. 🚾 ☕ A simple tea room at Over-

Doughnot Hill

Doughnot Hill

Dumbarton Rock and
the Firth of Clyde

toun House is open 10am to 4pm on Fridays and Saturdays. The BP garage on the A82 is a quick
and convenient post-run pit stop.

Other Routes
There is fine running over the Kilpatrick Hills on good though often boggy paths and untracked
ground. Park on the pavement at the gas works just off the A82 (470 732) to climb on a good
track up to Loch Humphrey then follow a clear path to Duncolm. Cochno is an alternative start
point (496 736). Westerlands Cross Country club often train here. *www.westerlandsccc.co.uk*

Clyde Valley from Bar Hill

22 The Antonine Wall & the Forth & Clyde Canal

Distance	10km (6 miles)	Ascent	200m (700ft)
Map	OS Landranger 64, OS Explorer 349		
Navigation ●●●	Along the canal, over small hills then return by a signposted path or the canal		
Terrain ●●●	Canal towpath, pavement, farm track, grass and gravel paths		
Wet Feet ●●●	Hill paths soggy in places after rain		
Start/Finish	Auchinstarry Quarry G65 9SG NS 719 770		

Scenic running along canal towpath and over small hills

The east and west coasts of Scotland are linked by two great feats of engineering. In the 1st century AD Roman soldiers built the Antonine Wall to protect the northern edge of their empire. Sixteen hundred years later the Forth and Clyde Canal was constructed across the same narrowing of the land. This route links both epic constructions in a varied and scenic circuit. The canal towpath is a good warm up with views of the Campsie Fells. Croy and Bar Hill summits are gained by gentle climbs although the two have quite distinct characters. Croy Hill is open while Bar Hill is wooded with bluebells and a Roman fort on its broad summit area. Two long, grassy descents along the Antonine Wall are highlights of the run.

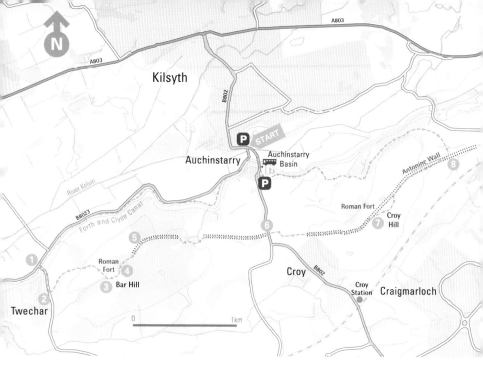

🏃 START Cross the B802 and briefly follow the minor road towards Twechar to join the canal towpath. Head west for about 2.5km to the road bridge at Twechar. ① Cross the canal and head up past houses to the brow of the hill. ② Turn left onto a farm track signposted to The Bar Hill Fort and Antonine Wall. Follow this track past a house with noisy (locked in) dogs and up to the top of the hill. ③ Turn left through a gate onto a grassy track between two fields then go through a gate onto the site of the Roman fort. ④ Head over the grass towards the north-east corner of the site and pick up a path leading to a short, steep climb up to the trig point. ⑤ Continue straight on down a grassy avenue following the line of the Antonine Wall. At the end of the avenue go right then immediately left onto a farm track which leads to the road. ⑥ Cross the road and go through a gate to reach an electricity substation. Turn right, then left before houses onto a grassy track past a boulder carved with the words Antonine Wall. The path follows the crest of the ridge then splits just before the summit. ⑦ Take any path and return to the crest of the ridge after the summit. Continue in the same direction as before, heading downhill along the line of the Antonine Wall towards pylons to meet a gravel path. ⑧ Turn left onto this path, the Antonine Walkway. Follow it around the hill above the canal. Stay on good gravel paths or dirt tracks turning downhill after about 1km to return to the canal and Auchinstarry Basin. Head just left of the Boathouse restaurant and up a path to cross the canal by the road bridge and return to the quarry car park.

The Antonine Wall & the Forth & Clyde Canal

Trip Planning

🚂 Croy (1.3km on pavement from ⑥) 🚐 Auchinstarry Farm 🚗 Auchinstarry is on the B802 between Kilsyth and Croy. It is about fourteen miles from the centre of Glasgow. Park in the large quarry (disused) car park just north of the canal. There is also a Scottish Waterways car park at Auchinstarry Basin on the south side of the canal. 🚻 Kilsyth has Comfort Scheme toilets at Burngreen Community Hall, Kilsyth First Stop Shop or Kilsyth Library during opening times. Also Croy Railway Station. 🍽 🏠 Auchinstarry Basin is home to a bar-restaurant and small hotel called the Boathouse. If planning a post run meal or pint take a change of clothes as this place is fairly upmarket. Or head to one of several Kilsyth chippies. Try Marini's on Main St, just off the A803 east of the B802 junction.

Other Routes

Shorten the route to 6.5km (4 miles) by running the first half along the canal and over Bar Hill. Just before ⑥ turn left off the farm track onto a footpath signposted to Auchinstarry Basin.
An alternative ending follows the towpath back to Auchinstarry by dropping down to the road 200m after ⑧ and crossing the canal by the road bridge.
The Forth and Clyde Canal towpath can often be linked to railway stations by short stints of road running.

Events

Adventure Zone Scotland organise a half marathon on off-road trails near the route of the Antonine Wall. *www.adventurezonescotland.com*

Other Activities

Auchinstarry Quarry is a popular evening hang out for rock climbers, fishermen and local kids. The rock routes range from Diff to E6. The wall next to the car park has the easiest routes and is therefore clean and popular. Battling with the brambles on the far side of the flooded quarry unearths routes graded VS and above.

The Antonine Wall & the Forth & Clyde Canal

Forth and Clyde
Canal near Twechar

Bar Hill Roman Fort

Pausing to explore the remains of the Roman fort and bath house on top of Bar Hill is optional but recommended. Information boards describe the original purpose of each ruin and depict what they may have looked like while in use. The line of the Antonine Wall runs west through Bearsden to meet the Firth of Clyde at Old Kilpatrick and east through Falkirk to Bo'ness on the Forth. Other well preserved Roman sites to explore include a bath house near Bearsden Cross and Rough Castle fort near Falkirk (Route 17).

The Cut and Argyll hills

23 Greenock Cut

Distance	12km (7 miles)	Ascent	100m (350ft)
Map	OS Landranger 63, OS Explorer 341		
Navigation ●●●	Over the hill then left along the Cut		
Terrain ●●●	Tarmac and dirt road, gravel path		
Wet Feet ●●●	Good grip even in wet weather		
Start/Finish	Greenock Cut Visitor Centre PA16 9LX NS 247 721		

A straightforward trail with spectacular views

High above the roofs of Greenock a small canal traverses the steep hillside. The Greenock Cut was the brainchild of hydraulics engineer Robert Thom. Crucially, he decided to build a much larger system than 1827 Greenock needed for its drinking water supply. The excess water powered the textile mills of Greenock's Industrial Revolution. During its heyday workmen walked the Cut in all weathers removing rubble or breaking ice to keep the water flowing and the mill wheels turning. Their path has been renovated and is now an easy, level trail. A hill track links the two ends of the Cut. This steady climb is well rewarded by views across the Firth of Clyde towards Helensburgh. The views get better and better as the route continues west along the Cut.

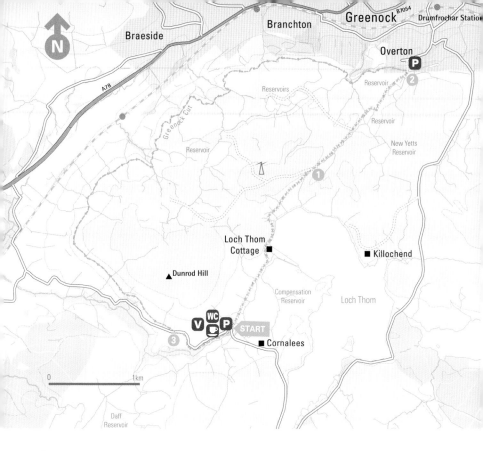

START Head north-east from the Visitor Centre on the tarmac road past Ardgowan Fishery. After about 1km the tarmac ends at Loch Thom Cottage and a dirt road continues rising gradually to a col. ① There is a good view from here over to Helensburgh on the far side of the Firth of Clyde. Head downhill on the track to reach houses at Overton. ② Turn left onto the Greenock Cut path. After about 5km the Cut turns inland and reaches the road at Shielhill Farm. ③ Cross the road and continue along the Cut for a further 1km to return to the Visitor Centre.

Trip Planning

There is no public transport to the Visitor Centre. 🚆 Drumfrochar (1km to ③) 🚌 Overton, Glen Douglas Road (250m from ③) 🚗 Turn off the A78 between Inverkip and Greenock near the old IBM factory following signs to the Greenock Cut Visitor Centre (formerly known as the Cornalees Visitor Centre). It is about thirty miles from central Glasgow. WC 🚻 Visitor Centre or café across the road at Ardgowan Fishery.

Greenock Cut

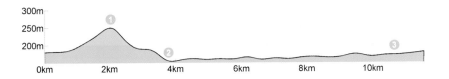

Other Routes

The Kelly Cut was built in 1845 when the Greenock Cut alone proved insufficient to meet Greenock's thirst for water and power. The 6.5km Kelly Cut starts at Kelly Reservoir and runs into the Compensation Reservoir at the Visitor Centre. The path along Kelly Cut is easily runnable though not as well made as the Greenock Cut path. Linking the two Cuts gives a one way run of about 18km (11 miles) from Drumfrochar Station to Wemyss Bay Station. Only the first 1km is on road.

Events

Local club Greenock Glenpark Harriers hold an internal club handicap along the Greenock Cut path. *www.glenparkharriers.webs.com*

Centenary fountain at Overton

Greenock Cut

Bute and Arran

Robert Thom's greatest contribution to the world was not the hydraulics that powered Greenock's Industrial Revolution. It was in fact the slow sand filter. This simple device uses naturally occurring bacteria to filter out water impurities. By improving its design Thom revolutionised public health. In 1804 Paisley town council asked Thom to install the world's first municipal water treatment plant. This immediately halted outbreaks of typhoid and cholera which at the time were rife in Britain's squalid, overcrowded cities. After the success in Paisley, Parliament passed an Act requiring slow sand filtration of London's entire water supply. While most 19th-century technologies have been superseded slow sand filtration has stood the test of time. Even today most British drinking water passes through sand filters before reaching our taps.

Dumgoyach

24 West Highland Way & the Waterworks Road

Distance	25km (16 miles)	Ascent	400m (1400ft)
Map	OS Landranger 64, OS Explorer 348, Harvey West Highland Way		
Navigation •••	WH Way then unsigned waterworks road and tracks back to Mugdock Country Park		
Terrain •••	Gravel and earth paths and tracks		
Wet feet •••	Muddy before Dumgoyach Farm and in woods between Strathblane and Mugdock CP		
Start/Finish	West Highland Way Obelisk, Milngavie G62 6PB NS 553 745		

Woodland and open country beneath the Campsie Fells

It is inevitable that some sections of a long distance route will be better than others. Many West Highland Way walkers can't wait to leave the lowlands behind for spectacular scenery further north. This run proves that dismissing the lowlands is a mistake. Mugdock Country Park is a great place for trail running and the stretch of woodland just before Craigallian is arguably the loveliest in the whole of the park. The highlight of the route is the descent into the Blane valley with its view of the Campsie Fells and Dumgoyne. As the West Highland Way settles into mile after mile of railway path this route heads back to Milngavie along a track beneath the fells.

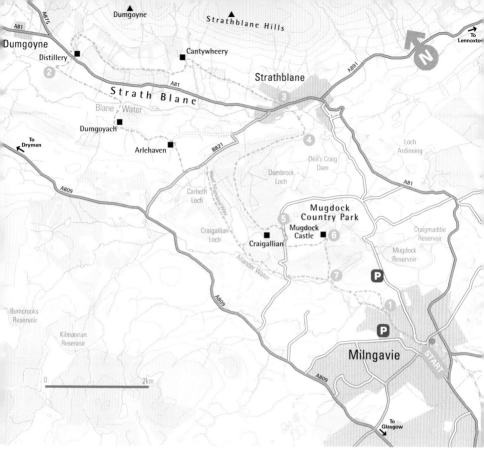

The section of this route which follows the West Highland Way is well waymarked. The route description concentrates on the unmarked paths. 🏃 START From the West Highland Way obelisk in Milngavie pedestrian precinct follow waymarkers down the ramp, across the car park and onto a tarmac path which quickly diverges from the road. Follow the West Highland Way until it is signed uphill away from the river. ① Avoid a steep hill by continuing along the river for another 500m to a playing field. Turn right after the field, head gently uphill for 250m then turn left onto the West Highland Way. Continue following West Highland Way markers through Mugdock Wood, Craigallian and Carbeth to reach Dumgoyach Farm. Continue past the farm and left onto a disused railway line. Follow this for nearly 1.5km to a gate soon after drawing level with Dumgoyne Distillery. ② Turn right and follow a rough track along the side of a field to the distillery. Cross the A81 and go up a minor road past houses approximately 100m left of the

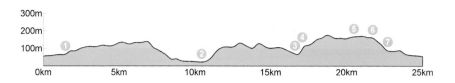

distillery. After crossing a bridge and climbing uphill on hairpins go through a gate onto a level track across a field. Continue on this track for 4.5km to Strathblane. ❸ Recross the A81 and go down a tarmac path opposite the war memorial. Continue up the far side of the valley on a faint path up the right hand side of a horses' field. From the top of the field follow a path right over a stile then up to a track. ❹ Turn right and follow the track for 3km to the Khyber Pass road. As the track emerges from forestry towards the end of the 3km keep left and follow a clear path along the edge of the plantation to reach the road. ❺ Turn right onto the road for 350m then left past the Khyber Pass car park onto a track past WWII gun emplacements. Go through a gate to a path junction just before Mugdock Castle. ❻ Turn right towards Mugdock Wood. Keep right to follow a narrow path down into the woods and across boardwalks to reach a fork. ❼ Keep left and descend to rejoin the West Highland Way. Follow waymarkers back to Milngavie, taking care to turn right before the track across Drumclog Moor goes into housing. Descend the hill avoided on the outward journey and return along Allander Water.

Trip Planning

🚉 Milngavie (250m from start) 🚌 Main Street, Milngavie (200m from start) 🚗 Milngavie is seven miles north of Glasgow on the A81. Park at Milngavie Library (552 748) or on Clober Road (550 751) a short distance into the route. 🚻 Milngavie Railway Station or the Library. 🍴 By the pedestrian underpass to Gavin's Mill and Tesco is Colpi which sells the best Italian-style ice cream around. For tea and cake try the café at Milngavie Bookshop on Douglas Street.

Other Routes

A shorter 12km (7.5 miles) circuit can be run from Strathblane along the West Highland Way and waterworks road. Follow Stockiemuir Road (B821) to its first switchback then turn off onto a track to join the West Highland Way before Dumgoyach Farm. Follow the route description from just before ❸ to ❺. Cars may be parked in the church car park near the war memorial. Please do not use this car park on Sundays.

Mugdock Wood
Photo: Dougal Ranford

The West Highland Way

This waymarked 153km (95 miles) route starts in the Lowlands and ends in the Highlands at the foot of Ben Nevis. It is the oldest and most famous of all Scotland's long distance waymarked paths. The route is almost entirely off-road following old droving roads, farm tracks and disused railway lines. In 1985 Bobby Shields of Clydesdale Harriers and Duncan Watson of Lochaber set out from Milngavie and ran to Fort William in a time of 17 hours, 48 minutes and 30 seconds. Their adventure was the beginning of an annual race. The current course record of 15:39:15 was set in 2012 by Terry Conway. Lucy Colquhoun's 2007 women's record is 17:16:20. The Highland Fling and Devil O' The Highlands are shorter ultramarathons run along the first and second halves of the West Highland Way respectively.

www.westhighlandwayrace.org www.highlandflingrace.org www.devilothehighlandsfootrace.co.uk

Lochaber and Argyll

The rocky peaks and narrow glens of the West Highlands are a dramatic landscape to run through. From north to south, high Lochaber peaks give way to forested Argyll peninsulas stretching out into the sea. These routes are rare gems as runnable circuits are hard to find outwith plantation forestry. Knoydart's sea and mountain views stand head and shoulders above the rest.

Loch Linnhe and Ardgour from Sgorr nam Fiannaidh

Ben Nevis and Cow Hill
(right) from Corpach

25 Cow Hill

Distance	7.5km (4.5 miles)	Ascent	250m (800ft)
Map	OS Landranger 41, OS Explorer 392, Harvey Ben Nevis & Glen Coe		
Navigation •••	Fully signed along the Peat Track and a Multi-use Trail		
Terrain •••	Gravel paths and track		
Wet Feet •••	Good grip even in wet weather		
Start/Finish	Lochaber Leisure Centre PH33 6BX NN 110 741		

Ben Nevis views from a straightforward circular trail

Fort William is the UK's self-proclaimed outdoor capital. The town has a magnetic attraction for outdoor enthusiasts thanks to its prime location at the foot of Britain's highest mountain. But there is far more to being an outdoor capital than just one summit. World class rock or ice climbing, river or sea kayaking, mountain biking, skiing? Try them all here. For an endorphin rather than adrenalin inducing adventure try this straightforward trail run instead. Panoramas down the length of Loch Linnhe are followed by remote moorland then by views down into Glen Nevis with steep mountains rearing up on either side. This route has a sting at the start. After the initial steep zigzags the trail becomes a mix of gradual climbs and smooth descents.

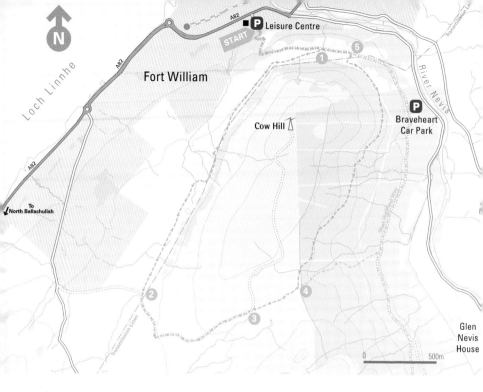

🏃 **START** There is an information board behind the leisure centre. Climb up the zigzags behind the board keeping to the strongest path which goes left to a junction just before the Sugarloaf viewpoint. ① Turn right onto the signposted Peat Track for a gently rising traverse then descent to a gate onto a landrover track. ② Turn left and climb uphill on the track for 1km to a signed junction. ③ Turn right to follow the Peat Track downhill towards Glen Nevis, reaching a gate after less than 500m. (The landrover track continues out and back to the mast at the top of Cow Hill.) ④ Go through the gate then turn left onto a signed multi-use path. This descends gradually for 2km across a steep, forested hillside to a T-junction at a corrugated iron shack. Between the trees are stunning views down Glen Nevis. ⑤ Turn left and climb a short distance up to the Sugarloaf viewpoint. Continue straight ahead to rejoin the outward path and zigzag down to the leisure centre.

Trip Planning

🚂 Fort William (400m from start) 🚌 Leisure Centre, Belford Road 🚗 Parking at the Leisure Centre is for customers only. Alternative route access is from the Braveheart Car Park in Glen Nevis. 🚻 Leisure Centre showers can be used for a small fee. Public toilets are at the Bank

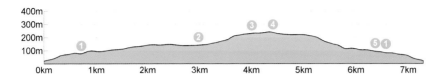

Street car park. Morrisons supermarket has customer toilets. 🖥 Nevisport Café during daytime for tea, cake and bacon butties. The bar below Nevisport is popular in the evenings with local and visiting outdoor enthusiasts. ⌂ Alan and Sue Kimber of West Coast Mountain Guides run Calluna, a self-catering hostel and private bunkhouse on the slopes of Cow Hill. It has an indoor bouldering wall and guides can be booked for winter and summer mountaineering adventures. *www.fortwilliamholiday.co.uk* Glen Nevis has an SYHA hostel and a Caravan and Camping Park. *www.syha.org.uk www.glen-nevis.co.uk*

Other Routes

The Peat Track can also be accessed from Henderson Row (107 736) or the cattle-grid at the top of Lundavra Road (097 724). The described route cuts off the Glen Nevis section of the Peat Track because the Multi-use Trail shortcut is less steep and has good views. The full Peat Track starts at the Braveheart Car Park in Glen Nevis (122 736).

The Braveheart Car Park is also an excellent starting point for level trail runs through Glen Nevis.

The forest road extends all the way to the Lower Falls at Achriabhach. A path, rough and boggy in places, leads back along the north-east bank of the River Nevis from the cottages at Polldubh.

There are plenty of longer routes in the area. Two of the best and most runnable are the final section of the West Highland Way and a circuit which climbs halfway up Ben Nevis. The 23km (14 miles) from Kinlochleven to Fort William goes through a broad glen then has stunning views

Peat Track waymarker

Cow Hill

Peat Track above Loch Linnhe

of Ben Nevis on the descent into Glen Nevis. The off-road part of the Half Ben route starts at the Glen Nevis Visitor Centre or Achintee and climbs up to the Halfway Lochan. Descend to the CIC Hut then down the Allt a' Mhuilinn path to join the landrover track. Turn off the track onto a woodland path and head down the side of distillery buildings to the A82.

Events
Nearby Leanachan Forest is the setting for a half marathon trail race and fun run.
www.nofussevents.co.uk
The 14km (8.7 miles) Ben Nevis Hill Race climbs from near sea level to the 1344m summit. The current records were set in 1984 by Kenny and Pauline Stuart of Keswick AC in times of 1:25:34 and 1:43:25 respectively. *www.bennevisrace.co.uk*

Other Activities
Head to Nevis Range for winter skiing and summer mountain biking on the Witch's Trails through Leanachan Forest. Nevis Range is home to the UK's only World Cup downhill mountain biking course. *www.nevisrange.co.uk*
The west coast is perfect for sea kayaking, particularly the rocky islands and sandy beaches near Arisaig. Rockhopper offer guided trips from Fort William. *www.rockhopperscotland.co.uk*

Loch Fyne

26 Ardcastle

Distance	8km (5 miles)	Ascent	200m (700ft)
Map	OS Landranger 55, OS Explorer 358		
Navigation •••	Follow the yellow waymarked trail		
Terrain •••	Grassy forest paths and gravel forest roads		
Wet Feet •••	Grass paths are squidgy in wet weather		
Start/Finish	Ardcastle Forestry Commission car park NR 942 920		

Secluded trails through woodland and by the loch shore

Ardcastle Forest guards its secrets well. The gravel drive which turns off the A83 betrays no sign of the quality trail running concealed within. The first hint comes on stepping off the wide gravel road of today onto its predecessor from yesteryear – now soft, grassy and shaded by tall trees. This trail winds through the forest to Loch Fyne then turns to follow the rocky, tree-lined lochshore stretching tantalisingly off into the distance. There are all manner of fleeting delights along the way: glimpses deep into dark, primordial woodland; sunlight dappling the grassy path underfoot; craggy outcrops wreathed in ferns and creepers; the well-kempt oasis of St Bride's churchyard above Loch Gair. Light-footed and lucky runners may even spot one of Argyll's elusive otters playing offshore.

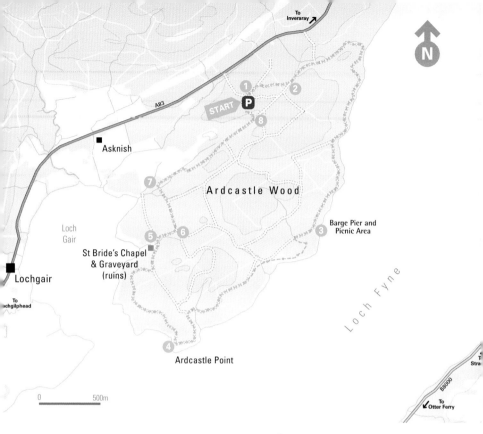

This route is fully waymarked by yellow waymarkers. 🏃 START▶ Head out of the car park entrance and take the forest road on the right, past a 'no vehicles' sign. ① After about 20m turn left onto a grassy old track, keep right at the fork and continue between the trees for nearly 400m to reach a wide gravel forest road. ② Turn left onto the road for 200m then take the right hand fork onto a grassy ride. This becomes a narrow path leading down to the shore. Follow the shore path to a clearing then continue on forest road for another 1.5km to reach a small quay and picnic area. ③ Keep on the forest road for 200m then turn left onto a grassy path following the near bank of a stream. This path crosses the stream, runs along the shore then climbs up to a viewpoint high above Loch Fyne. Drop down steeply through the trees, to join a track and weave around craggy outcrops to the end of a wide forest road. ④ Follow this road around the bay and past St Bride's Chapel. ⑤ Head round to the right on the main forest road for 200m to another right hand bend. ⑥ Turn off left onto a path which leads through the trees to the edge of the forest. ⑦ Turn right along a track along the edge of the trees. A short, steep uphill leads to a couple of gates and a long straight forest road. ⑧ Turn left and climb a short, steep path to return to the car park.

Ardcastle

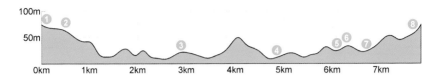

Trip Planning

Up-to-date trail information including closures for forestry operations can be found at *www.forestry.gov.uk* 🚌 There are no official bus stops on the A83 near Ardcastle. 🚗 Ardcastle is signed off a long straight stretch of the A83 between Minard and Lochgair, fifteen miles south-west of Inveraray. 🍴 Lochgair Hotel is two miles towards Lochgilphead while the Quarry View café is towards to Inveraray. The head of Loch Fyne is a magnet for foodies with its Oyster Bar/Shop and Fyne Ales Brewery. 🏠 Claonairaigh House B&B is owned by the Corner family who are all keen runners. *www.inveraraybandb.co.uk*

Fyne Fruits of the Sea

This route's first glimpse of Loch Fyne is a perfectly framed view of a fish farm. Fishing has made an important contribution to Argyll's economy and dinner tables from the time of its first settlers. This area's brief dalliance with heavy industry ended abruptly with the 1833 explosion of the gunpowder works in Furnace. Fishing continued and oysters, mussels and langoustines from Loch Fyne are now exported all over the UK to the loch's eponymous restaurant chain.

St Bride's Chapel

Ardcastle

Loch Fyne

Lairig Eilde

27 The Two Lairigs

Distance	14km (9 miles)	Ascent	500m (1700ft)
Map	OS Landranger 41, OS Explorer 384, Harvey Ben Nevis & Glen Coe		
Navigation ●●●	Over the Lairig Eilde and back by Lairig Gartain		
Terrain ●●●	Gravel path and old track		
Wet Feet ●●●	Patches of shallow bog on the old Glencoe road		
Start/Finish	Glencoe (opposite large cairn) NN 187 562		

Good paths and dramatic mountain scenery

Glencoe's Little Shepherd hides shyly behind his big brother letting his brasher neighbours grab the limelight. Buachaille Etive Beag doesn't have a fabulous Curved Ridge or exposed Rannoch Wall like Buachaille Etive Mor. He doesn't have a Lost Valley or high snowy corries like the Three Sisters to the west. But circling this otherwise unremarkable hill is the best trail run for miles around. The views are better in a clockwise direction but running anti-clockwise keeps feet dry until practically the finish. The Lairig Eilde is a beautiful glen with a dramatic ridge at its head. On another day this ridge makes a good technical scramble. Resting on the climb up the Lairig Gartain is compulsory in order to properly admire the view behind of Glen Etive. The old Glencoe Road provides a suitably fast downhill finish.

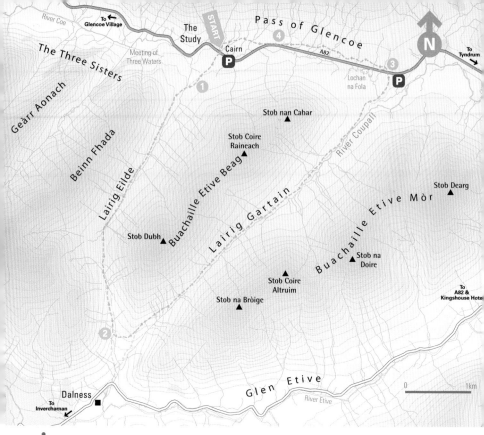

🏃 `START` Take a path uphill from the south-west corner of the car park for a few hundred metres to a fork. ① Bear right to cross the stream and continue on a clear path up the glen and down towards Glen Etive. ② Turn left to cross the stream and climb up into Lairig Gartain. The most obvious route is to cross just above a deer fence. Higher up the hill is a faint alternative traverse path. The path up Lairig Gartain is initially a narrow trench which improves towards the top of the pass. The 4.5km down to the A82 used to be a bog but is now a good gravel path. ③ Cross the road onto a path heading left over the top of a small quarry then join a wet and overgrown but easily runnable section of the old road. ④ After nearly 2km the old road crosses to the far side of the A82. As it recrosses after just 200m it is easiest just to run along the side of the modern road. Continue on the old road which becomes a drier grassy track. Leave it after about 500m and cross the river by stepping stones to reach the large cairn and the car park.

Trip Planning

🚗 The Lairig Eilde car park is on the south side of the A82 through Glencoe opposite a large round cairn. It is 500m east of the waterfall at The Study. WC 🗪 National Trust Visitor Centre on

the west side of the A82 one mile south of Glencoe village. The Clachaig Inn is on the Old Glencoe Road. If heading south through Tyndrum, the Real Food Café is highly recommended for its good food and cheerful service. The Kings House Hotel on Rannoch Moor is a traditional Scottish hotel with a small usually quiet bar. *www.kingy.com* On the Old Glencoe Road are a SYHA, an independent hostel and the Red Squirrel campsite. *www.redsquirrelcampsite.co.uk www.syha.org.uk www.glencoehostel.co.uk* The Inchree Centre at Onich has a good bar-restaurant, hostel and private bunkhouse accommodation. *www.inchreecentre.co.uk*

Other Routes

A good one way trail goes round the south side of the Ballachulish Horseshoe from Ballachulish Primary School to Glen Duror. On the north side of the hills are forestry tracks through Gleann a' Chaolais, some of which are waymarked by the Forestry Commission.

Across the Ballachulish Bridge are short trails through the Forestry Commission's Glen Righ Forest at Onich. These are steep in places but very enjoyable to run with good views of waterfalls and Loch Linnhe.

Cairn opposite the car park

The Two Lairigs

Glen Etive

The King's House

King's Houses are dotted throughout Scotland and indicate the location of camps housing the workmen who built the 18th-century network of military roads. General Wade and his successor Major William Caulfeild supervised the construction of 1600 kilometres of road. The roads were built with care and some are still good tracks in use today. They inspired the ditty "Had you seen these roads before they were made, you would lift up your hands and bless General Wade." Many have been reclaimed by nature and further investigation is recommended before setting out to run a route marked on maps as 'military road'. The West Highland Way partly follows Wade's military road over Rannoch Moor to The Kings House Hotel.

Loch Ossian from
Sgor Choinnich

28 Loch Ossian

Distance	14km (9 miles)	Ascent	50m (200ft)
Map	OS Landranger 41 and 42, OS Explorer 385		
Navigation •••	One left fork then right turns to circle the loch		
Terrain •••	Gravel and stony track		
Wet Feet •••	Some puddles on the final stretch of loch side		
Start/Finish	Corrour Station NN 355 664		

An easy trail round a beautiful loch reached only by train

The train journey alone is worth the trip whether travelling north across the subtle-hued barrens of Rannoch Moor or south above Loch Treig. Although it is possible to run this route and return home in the same day this is not the way to make the most of a trip to Corrour. Loch Ossian is breathtaking at dawn when its still waters reflect the pastel sky. Low sun rays bring out the pink-orange of Scots pine bark on the small wooded islands near the youth hostel. The surrounding peaks will keep hill runners happily occupied for days. For trail runners the hostel itself is the objective as 11+ mile tracks approach Loch Ossian from all points of the compass. When tackling these longer routes be aware that the circuit of Loch Ossian is the only trail in the area without a section of shoe-sucking bog.

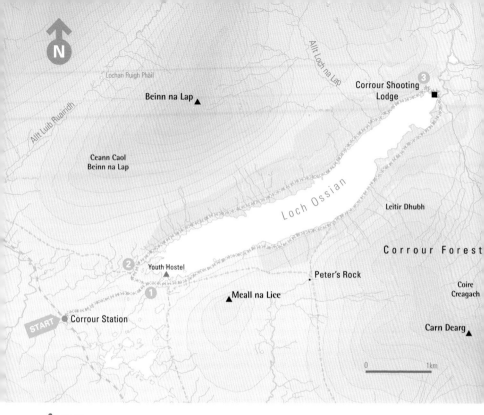

🏃 **START** Head east, signposted Tulloch, on a good dirt road to reach a fork after nearly 1.5km.
1 Take the left hand track for a short distance, following a Scottish Rights of Way signpost.
2 At the next junction head right towards the loch then follow the north shore for 5.5km to a T-junction. Three cattle grids along the track are momentary impediments. **3** Turn right towards Corrour Shooting Lodge then follow the track left behind the lodge buildings. On the far side of the lodge continue across a river and keep right at the next few junctions to stay by the shore of the loch. The 5km of track along the south shore is slightly rougher and has a few muddy puddles towards the end. Near the west end of the loch a rough track goes right to the youth hostel but continue straight ahead to return to **1**. Turn left to return to Corrour Station.

Trip Planning

🚂 Corrour 🏠 The SYHA Loch Ossian Hostel has one of the most scenic locations in Scotland. It is on the shore of the loch less than 2km from the railway station. 🍴 Corrour Station House offersteas and beers as well as a full restaurant menu.

www.corrour-station-house-restaurant.co.uk

Loch Ossian

Other Routes

Both the youth hostel and the Station House are good bases for train and trail runs. Sensible folk run towards their accommodation rather than risk missing the last train. These are some of the low level options listed clockwise from the north. All have rough and boggy sections.

Tulloch Station (**355 802**) (25km, 15 miles) Roads to Fersit then rough path east through the forest (very boggy). Dry path south across moorland to Strathossian then estate road to Corrour.

Dalwhinnie Station (**634 849**) (37km, 23 miles) Good estate road to Ben Alder Lodge then track to Culra (bothy). Path over Bealach Dubh fades into rough, boggy ground then reappears by Uisge Labhair. Track from Corrour Shooting Lodge.

Rannoch Station (**423 579**) (18km, 11 miles) 2.5km east on tarmac road then take track north-east. Take path north-east past Corrour Old Lodge, North to Peter's Rock, then west to Corrour.

Fort William Station (**105 742**) (33km, 20 miles) Footpath from behind Leisure Centre (**110 741**)

Corrour Station

to Glen Nevis then forest track up the glen to Achriabhach. Tarmac road then path past Steall Falls to Tom an Eite (boggy). Path along north side of Abhainn Rath (boggy) to Loch Treig. Good track to hostel then station. Avoid the boggy path next to the railway track.

Spean Bridge Station (**222 244**) (25km, 15 miles). Minor road to Corriechoille then south through the Lairig to Loch Treig then by good tracks to Corrour.

Ardgoil from Portincaple

29 Ardgoil Peninsula

Distance	22km (14 miles)	Ascent	750m (2500ft)
Map	OS Landranger 56 OS Explorer 363 and 364		
Navigation •••	Faint path and widely spaced marker posts over the bealach to Lochgoilhead		
Terrain •••	Forest tracks and paths, boggy and tussocky ground		
Wet Feet •••	Boggy bealach and muddy descent		
Start/Finish	Coilessan Events car park, Ardgarten Forest G83 7AR NN 258 011		

A wild bealach and scenic forest trails lead to a remote lochan

Long sea lochs split Argyll into fingers stretching out into the Firth of Clyde and Irish Sea. These rugged fingers are clad in conifers networked by miles of forest tracks. When these tracks have a view the running is superb. This route is a mixture of everything Argyll has to offer. Narrow sea lochs, rugged mountains, plantation forestry, pretty mixed woodland, smooth tracks, winding woodland paths... and rough, boggy hillside. The north and south sides of the peninsula are linked by crossing a boggy bealach and descending a muddy, tussocky path. This is a relatively short section of the route. On a clear day the view from the top is worth the wet feet and un-runnability. In low cloud a compass bearing comes in handy. The majority of the route follows easy to run forest paths and tracks. The path above Loch Goil is particularly enjoyable with pretty mixed woodland, waterfalls and views down the loch.

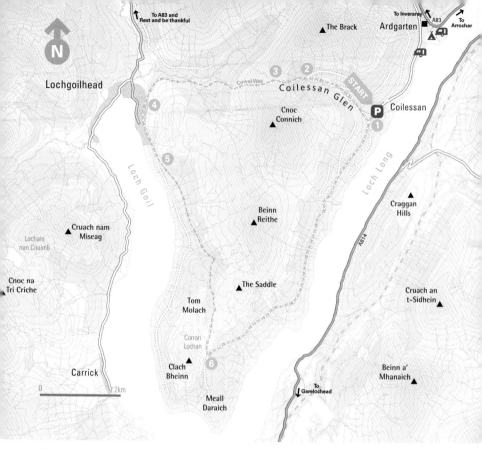

START Go round the barrier and head uphill on the forest road for about 250m to the first junction on the right. ① Turn right onto Coilessan Glen Road and continue uphill. After 600m continue straight on across a stream and climb uphill for another 1km to a track junction. ② Take the path on the left signed for the Cowal Way. After crossing a footbridge this climbs steeply to the edge of the forest. Cross the stile and follow the faint path across boggy ground to a cairn on top of a knoll to the right of the stream line. ③ Continue following white-topped posts which go along the slightly raised hillside on the left (south) side of the pass. Descend a rough and muddy path to join a good path once well into the trees. Follow signs to Lochgoilhead, crossing a river and continuing out of the forest to reach a T-junction just above the village. ④ Turn left onto the dirt road signed for The Duke's Pass. Follow this for 1.5km to junction with a path signed for Duke's Pass and the Corran Lochan. ⑤ Turn left onto the path and head steeply uphill. Continue on this path for 6km to reach the lochan. ⑥ Turn left onto a forest road and follow it back to the car park, ignoring all turns to left and right. This road has gradual climbs and descents, testing stamina to the very end.

Trip Planning

Up-to-date trail information including closures for forestry operations can be found at *www. forestry.gov.uk* 🚗 Turn off the A83 three miles north of Arrochar into the Forestry Commission's Ardgarten Forest. Drive past the car park and buildings to a T-junction, turn left and follow the single track road for two miles to a barrier. The Coilessan Events car park is a large gravel, unsigned, parking area on the right before a barrier. 🚻 Ardgarten Forest car park ☕ Café at the nearby campsite or Arrochar which has a chip shop and several hotels. ⛺ Ardgarten Caravan and Camping Site and Argyll Cabins are both on the shore of Loch Long. Instructor-led canoeing, rock climbing and gorge walking activities are available and bikes can be hired. *www.forestholidays.co.uk* There are hotels and B&Bs in Arrochar. 🐎 Unfenced grazing over the bealach.

Other Routes

Forestry Commission waymarked walking and biking routes start at the main Ardgarten car park. The 32km (20 miles) Ardgarten Peninsula bike route avoids the boggy bealach by travelling further on forest and public roads.

If a boggy bealach doesn't appeal then try the 17km (11 miles) Glen Loin Loop from the car park at the head of Loch Long (295 049). Start up The Cobbler hill path then follow a level forest road to Coire Grogain, along the waterworks road, then right across the river to join the signed Glen Loin path. This path is fun to run despite the unattractive overhead pylons. Another great run continues up the surprisingly runnable zigzag Cobbler path then descends an untracked steep tussocky slope from the bealach between Beinn Ime and Beinn Narnain to join the Glen Loin Loop in Coire Grogain.

Other Activities

Explore the Glen Loin caves. These have a long history as a climbers' doss. Finding them is not totally straightforward.

Loch Long is popular with scuba divers. Three underwater reefs near Argarten are home to plenty of conger eels.

Above Loch Goil

Glasgow Hard Men

In the early days of Scottish climbing The Cobbler was one of the most accessible mountain crags. By today's standards the journey from Glasgow by train and boat was epic. Many tardy climbing parties ended up running off the hill, through Arrochar, to catch the last Loch Lomond steamer. Early pioneers included Willie Naismith and Gilbert Thomson from Glasgow. The Cobbler's merits even persuaded Edinburgh climbers, including Raeburn and the Inglis Clark brothers, to make the long trek west. Between the wars Glen Loin's caves were well occupied. Jock Nimlin put up many routes and wrote the first guidebook. 1945 saw the start of the Creag Dhu Club assault with John Cunningham and Bill Smith leading the way. Line after line fell to these notoriously tough Clydeside shipbuilders.

Barisdale Bay

30 Knoydart

Distance	60km (38 miles)	Ascent	2400m (7800ft)
Map	OS Landranger 33, Harvey Knoydart		
Navigation •••	Tricky route finding near Lochan nan Breac		
Terrain •••	Well made but overgrown stony tracks, some faint and pathless sections		
Mud •••	Stretches of wet path, particularly Mam Unndalain descent and around Carnoch		
Start/Finish	Kinloch Hourn PH35 4HD NG 949 066		

An epic adventure in the Rough Bounds

The Knoydart peninsula is hard to reach even in today's connected world. Travelling there requires either a boat trip or an interminable car journey along winding single track road. No-one who has been to Knoydart questions whether or not the journey is worthwhile. This northern part of the Rough Bounds is a wild land of high peaks, narrow glens and fjord-like sea lochs. Traces of an attempt to tame the wilderness are clear in the old though well-made paths connecting the glens. These routes were constructed by engineer James Watt and two labourers early in the 20th century. Despite their age this legacy path network provides exceptional running through tough terrain. Spectacular views and descents, of which there are many, are well-earned. Knoydart is an inspiring place. Leaving is only made possible by vowing to return.

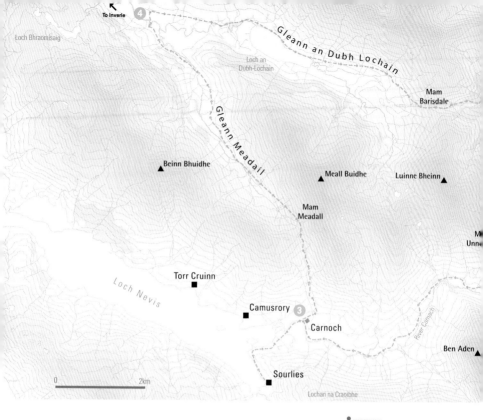

The route is described as a two day adventure with a camp at Sourlies. **START** Day 1 Follow
the coastal path from the end of the road to Barisdale Bay. This scenic path is anything but flat
with three significant climbs and descents. Continue past Barisdale Lodge and the bothy to cross
the river. ① 300m after the river crossing take the second turn on the left and follow the track
up Gleann Unndalain. Care is needed to stay on the faint zigzag path as it heads left over the pass
at the top of the glen. The descent from Mam Unndalain is wet but the path is obvious. Continue
until Lochan nan Breac appears on the right. ② (909 998) This path junction is not obvious. An
indistinct path doubles back along the near side of a narrow boggy valley. Overshooting the
junction is indicated by dropping into and skirting round the edge of a flat grassy valley with a
meandering stream. The path crosses the river on boulders then climbs up the far bank. It levels
out to pass between the ring contour and the main slope then descends to recross the river in
the shallows. (Alternatively, avoid the two river crossings by carefully descending steep slopes on
the north side of the river before the gorge.) Follow the river on variable paths to Carnoch.
③ (865 965) Cross the river by wading or by a rickety bridge (marked as dangerous so use at
your own risk) and go round the headland to Sourlies bothy (867 951). (If safety is in doubt
due to high water levels omit the out and back to Sourlies and camp at the Carnoch ruin.) At low

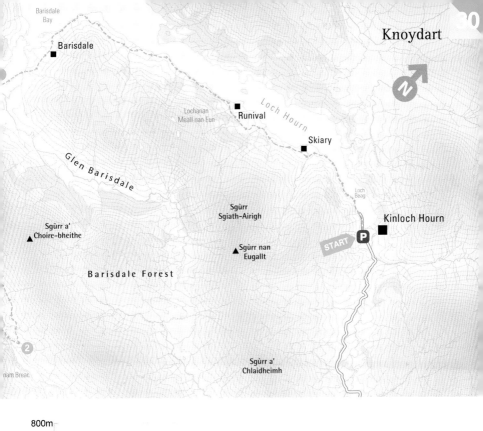

tide the easiest route to Sourlies is along the shore. At high tide follow deer tracks across boggy scrubland and a rough path over the tip of the headland.

Day 2 Return to Carnoch ③. A good path climbs up from behind the ruins to the pass between Meall Bhasiter and Sgurr Sgeithe. Descend on an excellent though rocky track down Gleann Meadail to the Inverie-Barisdale track. ④ Turn right and follow the track then path over Mam Barisdale and back to Barisdale Bay. Retrace the outward route to Kinloch Hourn.

Trip Planning

This is a serious run in a remote area with limited escape routes. Most runners will want to tackle it over two days. Knoydart is not a place to be rushed and wild camping at Sourlies definitely adds to the experience. 🚗 Turn off the A87 about 5 miles west of Invergarry onto a single track

Knoydart

Descent to Lochan nan Breac

road signed for Kinloch Hourn. It is just over twenty miles to the end of the road where a small charge is made for parking. **WC** 🥤 A toilet is available at the farmhouse at Kinloch Hourn which also offers hot drinks and a limited selection of snacks. ⌂ The short turf outside Sourlies is perfect for wild camping. Sourlies is a small and popular bothy maintained by the Mountain Bothies Association. *www.mountainbothies.org.uk* Other accommodation is at Kinlochhourn, Barisdale or Inverie. *www.kinlochhourn.com www.barisdale.com www.knoydart-foundation.com www.theoldforge.co.uk* Invergarry Lodge Hostel is a good base for the wider North West Highlands. Its owners, Jenny and Matt Jenneson, are outdoor enthusiasts and hill runners. *www.invergarrylodge.co.uk*

Other Routes

The 34km (21 miles) 1600m (5200ft) circuit at the heart of this route can be linked to any of the Knoydart access points. The best of the alternatives starts at Inverie (765 002) adding 8km (5 miles) 200m (600ft) to the basic circuit. Run the route in either a long day or with a camp at Barisdale or Sourlies. There is no good camping ground near Lochan nan Breac. The Strathan (Loch Arkaig) start adds 33km (11 miles) 1000m (3200ft). The usual walking path into Sourlies bothy is fairly obvious on the ground although it is muddy and difficult to run in places. Poor to non-existent paths and a notoriously difficult crossing of the Abhainn Chosaidh make starting at Loch Quoich (988 036) the least appealing access point.

The West Highland Line enables multi-day one way trail and hill runs. Catch the train to Mallaig then the boat to Inverie. Make a way through the Rough Bounds to Glenfinnan or one of the other West Highland Line stations. As a general rule, the paths marked on the map exist on the ground and are reasonably runnable.

Stirling and Perth

The Highland Boundary Fault separates the flood plains of the Forth and Clyde from the Southern Highlands. Stirlingshire bridges the fault with woodland trails and hill runs on Lowland volcanic outcrops as well as around Highland hills. Perthshire's rugged Central Highlands have more than their fair share of leafy woodland paths through the straths as well as hill tracks perfect for longer trail runs.

Stirling Castle and the
Wallace Monument

North Third Reservoir

31 North Third & Sauchie Crags

Distance	5.5km (3.5 miles)	Ascent	125m (400ft)
Map	OS Landranger 57, OS Explorer 366		
Navigation •••	Along the clifftop and back round the reservoir		
Terrain •••	Grass and dirt paths; a short, steep and rocky downhill		
Wet Feet •••	Paths can be muddy between hill and reservoir		
Start/Finish	Lay-by west of Bannockburn FK7 9QS NS 757 878		

Unexpectedly accessible clifftop running

This route is a real hidden gem. Tucked away to the west of the M9 it is passed every day by hundreds of unheeding drivers. From the motorway there is little to see: just a patch of woodland merging into low-lying tussocky hills. But the east and west sides of the hill are as chalk and cheese. Crossing over to the west side enters into a new world of steep rocky cliffs and bird's eye views over a pretty lochan. A superb grassy path runs all the way along the clifftop and back beside the reservoir.

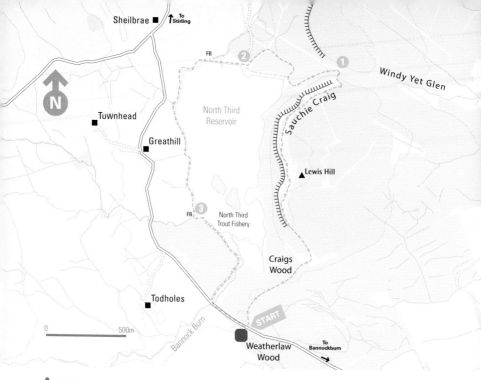

To Stirling

START Head uphill away from the lay-by on a strong path between mature mixed woodland and forestry plantation. A short, steep climb gains the level grassy path along the top of the escarpment and the trig point. At one point the path forks but the two branches rejoin after only a couple of metres. At the end of the crags drop down rocky zigzags into Windy Yet Glen. ❶ Turn left onto a path below the plantation to meet the reservoir fence. The waymarked route follows the fenceline downhill and climbs back up to a metal gate at the far side of the first dam. A well used path also cuts straight across the dam to the gate. ❷ Cross the second dam onto a grass path which follows the shore of the reservoir for nearly 1.5km to the trout fishery. ❸ After crossing the bridge turn left onto a gravel path. Continue on this path as it leaves the reservoir and follows the Bannock Burn to meet the road a few hundred metres from the start of the route.

Trip Planning

🚗 Turn off the A872 at the Bannockburn Heritage Centre and immediately left onto New Line Road. Continue over the M9 following signs for North Third Fishery and keeping right where the road forks. After the second fork continue for three quarters of a mile and park in a lay-by on the left opposite the start of the route. 🚌 Cambusbarron or Bannockburn.

156

Other Routes

Explore the network of paths and forest roads between Windy Yet Glen and Cambusbarron. Many are not shown on maps and require a sense of adventure or a local guide.

The Darn Road and Old Glen Road between Bridge of Allan and Dunblane can be linked to form scenic riverside and woodland circuits of varying lengths.

Dumyat is a good peak to tackle for first hill runs. The easiest start is from roadside parking on the Sherriffmuir Road. The Dumyat Hill Race follows a more challenging route straight up from the Stirling University campus.

Events

The Ochils' undulating grassy tops are perfect for hill running and are a popular racing venue. The Run of the Mill Hill Race route is a great circuit in its own right. Start at Ochil Hills Woodland Park, Alva (898 975) and follow good paths up the east side of Mill Glen onto Andrew Gannel Hill, over Ben Cleuch, down Ben Ever to a zigzag track and back through Wood Hill Wood to Alva. This race raises funds for Chris Upson's Scottish Hill Racing website. *www.scottishhillracing.co.uk*

Tartan tales

Ancient clan dress or Victorian invention? The 1746 'Dress Act' attempted to quash rebellious Highlanders by prohibiting the wearing of tartan. The repeal of this act in 1782 caused an explosion in popularity of traditional Highland dress and customs. This great interest was fuelled by the romanticised portrayal of Highlanders by Victorian novelist Sir Walter Scott. Everyone, even those with the flimsiest Scottish connection, wanted their own personal tartan. Bannockburn weaver William Wilson travelled extensively over Scotland collecting all the tartan patterns he could find. By the time he undertook his journeys it is likely that many of the patterns had already lost their link with place and clan. Undeterred, Wilson matched these ancient orphan patterns to the required names in order to satisfy his nostalgic clientele.

Sauchie Crags

River Earn

32 Laggan Hill & Lady Mary's Walk

Distance	9km (5.5 miles)	Ascent	150m (500ft)
Map	OS Landranger 52 or 58, OS Explorer 368		
Navigation •••	Signposted junctions out over Laggan Hill and back by Lady Mary's walk.		
Terrain •••	Tarmac road and pavement, earth and gravel paths and tracks		
Wet Feet •••	Seasonally muddy farm track and paths		
Start/Finish	Taylor Park PH7 4JJ NN 857 221		

Woodland trails, views of the strath and tranquil riverside running

Once a year Strathearn Harriers issue an open invitation to visit Crieff and run the terrain the locals take advantage of all year round. Leading out from this small Perthshire town are off-road paths and quiet farm lanes perfect for running. Although this route is based on the race it is worth taking longer than the course record of 33 minutes 22 seconds in order to fully appreciate the scenery. A particularly fine view looks up Strathearn towards Comrie's gleaming White Church set against a backdrop of rugged hills. Closer to Crieff are picture perfect views of the River Earn from Lady Mary's Walk. This mile-long stretch of riverbank was the favourite walk of the daughter of the Laird of Ochtertyre. In the early 1800s he named the walk after her and opened it up for the townspeople of Crieff to enjoy. It remains a beautiful, tranquil place and a fitting end to this woodland trail.

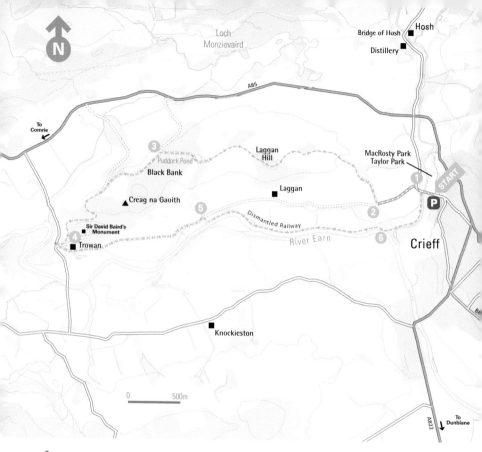

🏃 **START** Cross the river and head uphill for a few hundred metres. ① After passing a red post box on a lamp post turn left onto Laggan Road and follow this to the end of the public road, continuing onto a narrow lane to reach the gates of Laggan Estate. ② Turn right and head uphill continuing onto a grassy track leading leftwards through woodland above fields. Continue straight ahead on this track past Puddock Pond to a T-junction at the edge of the woods. ③ Turn left towards Trowan and follow the path round an old stream bed and left onto an old track to reach another T-junction. ④ Turn right (signed Trowan) to reach the road. Go left for a short distance along the road then turn left onto a farm track signposted to Crieff. At the end of the track continue onto an obvious path between the fields which re-enters woodland. ⑤ A few hundred metres after reaching the trees go right under an old railway bridge and down to the river. Follow Lady Mary's Walk for almost 2km until the path forks. ⑥ Follow the sign to Turret Bridge across a small sandy beach then onto a narrow path. This turns away from the Earn along the River Turret. Stay close to the river to return to the road at Turret Bridge.

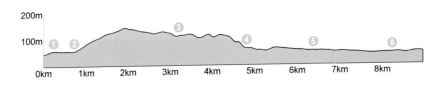

Trip Planning

🚃 Taylor Park 🚌 Turn off the A85 in the centre of Crieff onto Milnab Street and continue onto Turretbank Road. There is an off-road car park at Taylor Park. (Signs at the car park read MacRosty Park.) 🚻 James Square, Crieff town centre. A small charge is made. 🅿 The oldest craft bakery in Scotland is Campbell's on King Street, a few blocks downhill from James Square in the centre of Crieff. Nine miles west, the Dalchonzie Fruit Farm Shop just beyond Comrie is worth a detour, particularly in strawberry and ice cream season. *www.dalchonzie.co.uk* 🏠 Comrie Croft is less than five miles west of Crieff on the A85. This self-catering hostel and campsite also hires out mountain bikes. *www.comriecroft.com*

Laggan Hill & Lady Mary's Walk

Shady riverside trails are a Perthshire speciality

Other Routes

Shorten the run by turning downhill at a gate just before Puddock Pond. This path meets the continuation of the Laggan Estate drive just before the river. A quick right then left goes under the railway bridge and down to Lady Mary's Walk.

Nearby Knock Hill has good trails and fantastic views over Strathearn. Or head up to Turret Reservoir for longer track runs through the hills.

Events

Strathearn Harriers organise the Crieff 10k Trail Race and the Comrie Hills Relay.

www.strathearnharriers.org.uk

Fast running on the long, gradual descent to the river

33 Glen Tilt

Distance	9km (5.5 miles)	**Ascent**	250m (800ft)
Map	OS Landranger 43, OS Explorer 386		
Navigation ●●●	Follow Atholl Estate's Yellow Trail waymarkers		
Terrain ●●●	Earth paths, gravel and grassy tracks		
Wet Feet ●●●	Occasional muddy puddles		
Start/Finish	Glen Tilt car park, Old Bridge of Tilt PH18 5TP NN 874 663		

Waymarked circuit at the mouth of a grand Highland glen

This is a straightforward and scenic circuit on old and new tracks through the lower reaches of Glen Tilt. A narrow humpback bridge leads over the road and on to a steady run on estate roads and tracks. The route climbs up to the shooting range to gain a view down into the heart of the long glen. Glen Tilt is one of Scotland's classic through routes. From Blair Atholl a right of way runs over twenty miles to Linn of Dee near Braemar. The circuit described here turns back at Gilbert's Bridge to return to Bridge of Tilt by a high grassy track with good views over wide Glen Garry. A fast descent on a quiet tarmac road completes the circuit.

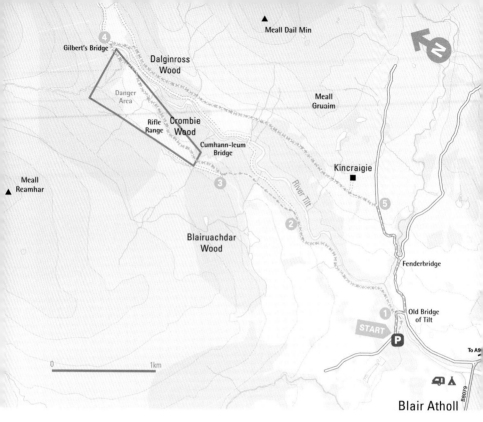

This route follows the waymarked Yellow Trail. Check the information board at the car park for firing times at the rifle range. If the range is in use follow the riverside track from ② to Gilbert's Bridge. 🏃 START▶ Head right through trees behind the information board and go over the old humpback bridge. Turn right and follow the path for about 150m to reach the estate road. ① Turn right and follow this dirt road along the edge of woodland for nearly 1.5km. (Along the way the Yellow Trail takes a couple of short optional detours off to the right.) A few hundred metres after the road turns into the trees a grassy track heads off to the left. ② Head uphill on this track which undulates through trees then climbs around a forestry plantation to meet a wide dirt road. ③ Turn right and follow the dirt road through the rifle range. (Access is restricted at firing times.) Once past the range the track heads down into the glen. Keep right at two forks to reach Gilbert's Bridge. ④ Cross the river and turn right across a cattle grid onto a wide forest road. After 600m turn left up steps through trees then right at the top onto a grassy track above the forest. Follow this track for 2.5km keeping left at a fork after 1.5km to eventually join a farm road. ⑤ At the end of the farm road follow the tarmac public road downhill. At the bottom of the hill turn right towards Old Blair and follow the road under the humpback bridge to return to the car park.

Trip Planning

The trail is managed by the Atholl Estates Ranger Service. *www.athollestatesrangerservice.co.uk* Tilt Hotel, Blair Atholl (1.4km from start) Turn off the A9 onto the B8079 towards Blair Atholl. In the village turn off towards the signed Glen Tilt car park, Old Bridge of Tilt and Old Blair. After less than one mile turn left to cross the river and take the next left into the car park. **WC** Blair Atholl, near the Post Office, and Village Hall The Bothy Bar at the Atholl Arms Hotel serves local ales from the Moulin microbrewery in Pitlochry. *www.athollarmshotel.co.uk www.moulininn.co.uk* On the far side of the railway track the bread, scones and cakes at the Blair Atholl Watermill Tearoom are made using home-ground flour and oatmeal. *www.blairathollwatermill.co.uk*

Access for all

In the mid-1800s a group of Edinburgh citizens banded together to fight attempts by landowners to block public access to the nearby countryside. The 'Association for the Protection of Public Rights of Roadway in and around Edinburgh' was quick to expand its horizons. In 1847 an Edinburgh University Professor, John Balfour, took a group of botany students on a field trip to the Grampians. They were confronted in Glen Tilt by the Duke of Atholl who tried to force the group to retrace their steps. Led by Balfour, the students leapt a wall to evade the Duke's ghillies and ran off down the glen to continue on their chosen route. Balfour, supported by the fledgling Association, won the ensuing court case and the public right of way through Glen Tilt was established once and for all. The Association, now renamed the Scottish Rights of Way and Access Society, is as active as ever and their book Scottish Hill Tracks is the definitive catalogue of routes through the Scottish hills. *www.scotways.com*

Other Routes

Several waymarked routes start from the Glen Tilt car park. A longer route goes up pretty Glen Banvie and returns on pleasant forest roads. A short and worthwhile detour off this route leads to the picturesque Falls of Bruar.

Glen Tilt

Gilbert's Bridge

An excellent track and then path runs through Glen Tilt to White Bridge (32km starting at Blair Atholl Railway Station). Either head out to Linn of Dee and Braemar or continue through the Lairig Ghru to Aviemore (30km to Aviemore Railway Station).

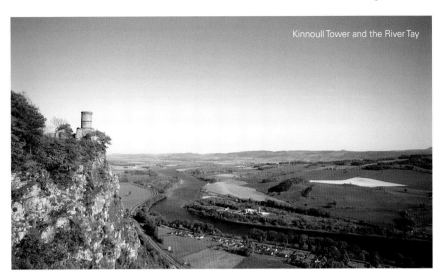

Kinnoull Tower and the River Tay

34 Kinnoull Hill & Deuchny Wood

Distance	9.5km (6 miles)	Ascent	300m (1000ft)
Map	OS Landranger 58, OS Explorer 369		
Navigation •••	Signed paths round the two woods		
Terrain •••	Forest road, earth and gravel paths		
Wet Feet •••	Good grip even in wet weather		
Start/Finish	Jubilee Road PH2 7LN NO 144 235		

A figure of eight on woodland paths and tracks

The Coronation Road links an old ferry crossing on the Tay with Scone Palace. Many centuries ago the Thanes of Fife rode this way to crown Scotland's monarchs at Scone. In later years Stuart Kings and Queens used the route to travel between their palaces at Scone and Falkland. Running in their footsteps gives great views over the surrounding countryside. The tracks around Deuchny Wood are quieter than the more popular paths across the road on Kinnoull Hill. Kinnoull's clifftop path has a spectacular view over the meandering River Tay as well its own crumbling folly.

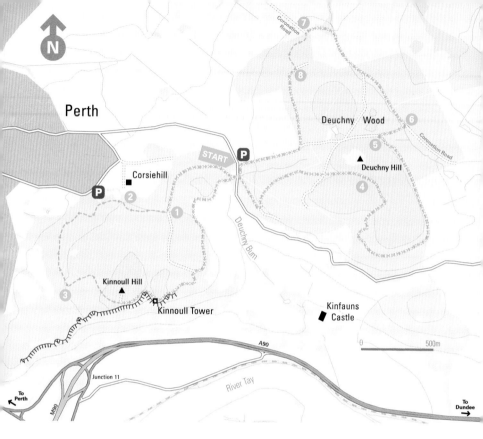

The first half of this route follows the Blue Trail round Kinnoull Hill. On the opposite side of the road to the car park an information point dispenses maps of the waymarked trails.

START Take the right-hand forest track away from the information point to head into the woods past a building. Keep left at an unsigned fork, then continue for 100m past the first waymarked junction to a second signpost where a path goes off on the right towards Corsiehill. ① Take the Corsiehill path. (At the time of writing the Blue Trail was incorrectly signed straight ahead at this junction.) The path runs through beech trees then crosses a footbridge. ② Turn downhill then almost immediately left above a small quarry. Contour around the side of the hill for another 800m to a junction signed to the summit. ③ Climb very steeply uphill. After visiting the trig point return to the gravel path along the top of the escarpment and follow this past the ruined tower. Continue along the clifftops then keep right around the edge of the trees and back to the car park.

The second half of the route follows unsigned forest paths and tracks through Deuchny Wood as well as the waymarked Coronation Road. **START** Climb gradually uphill from the car park round a long hairpin bend on the forest road and straight over a junction to the brow of the hill.

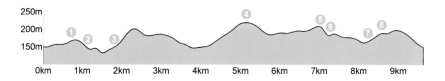

④ Follow the road right then down and around the east side of the hill. The track re-enters forestry and climbs uphill for nearly 500m to a path junction. ⑤ Turn sharp right to head steeply downhill to a T-junction with the Coronation Road track. ⑥ Turn left and follow the Coronation Road for 1km as it goes through a gate, crosses a stream and cuts across a field of crops to the edge of the forest. ⑦ Leave the Coronation Road by going through a gate into the forest to reach a T-junction with a track. ⑧ Turn right to follow this track downhill to Jubilee Road.

Trip Planning

Find out more about Kinnoull Hill Woodland Park at *www.kinnoull.org.uk* 🚌 Branklyn Gardens, Barnhill (Climb uphill from the A85 on paths through Barnhill Wood to join the route at ②) 🚗 Turn off the A85/A93 onto Muirhall Road, signed Woodland Walks, and drive uphill past the hospital. The Jubilee Road car park is on the col between Kinnoull Hill and Deuchny Wood. Several other roads are also signed Woodland Walks from the A85/A93. Following any of these will eventually lead to the top of the hill.

The Royal Stewards

The surname Stewart was adopted by Walter, the 3rd High Steward of Scotland in the early 13th century. High Steward was a hereditary political position given to the family by David I of Scotland. The 6th High Steward married Marjorie, the daughter of Robert the Bruce. Their son, another Robert, became King and the Royal House of Stewart was born. Robert's several times great grand-daughter was Mary, Queen of Scots. She was crowned at nine months old, betrothed to the French Dauphin at the age of five and swiftly packed off to France, safely out of reach of the English King. Mary's French hosts struggled to pronounce "Stewart" correctly so Mary authorised removal of the confusing "w" to give the new spelling "Stuart".

Other Routes

This figure of eight can easily be split into two shorter circuits. The Deuchny Wood circuit is 5.5km (3.5 miles) while the Blue Trail round Kinnoull Hill is slightly shorter at 4km (2.5 miles). To avoid

Kinnoull Hill & Deuchny Wood

Deuchny Wood

the descent and steep re-ascent of Kinnoull Hill simply continue straight on at ❶ instead of turning right towards Corsiehill.

Kinnoull Hill is the most westerly of the Sidlaw Hills which offer good hill running on paths, tracks and rough ground.

Events

The Kinnoull Hill Race is one of the shortest and fastest of the hill running season. It is all on good trails with a steep start and finish. *www.strathtayharriers.co.uk*

Ben Ledi

35 Bochastle & Falls of Leny

Distance	10km (6 miles)	Ascent	175m (600ft)
Map	OS Landranger 57, OS Explorer 365		
Navigation •••	Forest road then return along the loch and river		
Terrain •••	Dirt and tarmac roads, gravel and earth paths		
Wet Feet •••	Woodland paths can be slippery		
Start/Finish	Bochastle car park, Kilmahog FK17 8HD NN 607 080		

Classic Trossachs views and woodland running

Water tumbles dramatically through a narrow rocky gorge at the Falls of Leny. This waterfall and several sets of rapids further downstream are popular challenges for river kayakers. The golden nugget for runners lies in pretty deciduous woodland downstream of the paddlers' playground. The path that weaves through the trees is much more entertaining than the parallel gravel cycle path. These sun-dappled oak woods contrast with the first section of the run on forestry tracks. The easily runnable trail climbs up through plantation forestry to quickly gain a good view of Ben Ledi as well as a vantage point looking down the length of Loch Lubnaig. All in all, this route is a great tour through classic Trossachs scenery.

🏃 **START** Follow either path from the car park to join the forest road above. This climbs gradually up and around Bochastle Hill and traverses the hillside to reach the Ben Ledi walkers' path coming up from the river. ① Continue straight on past a track coming in from the left to head downhill on the forest road. A series of zigzags descend to the valley floor. ② Turn right onto a track briefly then follow a signpost left through a hedge onto a tarmac road. This respects the privacy of cottages further along the track. Follow the road past the bridge and through the parking area to the end of the dirt road. ③ Continue through a gate onto a cycle path and follow this for nearly 1km through the trees to a large concrete block in the centre of the path. ④ The cycle path continues along the old railway line which used to cross the river at this point. Instead, head left into woodland and follow narrow paths down to a viewpoint above the waterfall. After visiting the falls return to a strong path along the top of an embankment. At an obvious fork keep right to stay on top of the embankment. ⑤ Where the path ends at a stream go up onto the railway cycle path and follow this back to the road. Turn right onto a gravel track which leads back to the car park.

Trip Planning

The forest is part of the Queen Elizabeth Forest Park *www.forestry.gov.uk* 🚐 Dreadnought Hotel, Callander (2.5km along an off-road cycle path from start) 🚗 Forestry Commission Bochastle car park on the west side of the A821, south of the A821/A84 junction at Kilmahog. The National Park's Kilmahog car park is on the cycle path 200m closer to the river. 🚻 Callander, behind the Dreadnought Hotel. A small charge is levied. 🍴 The Lade Inn serves real ale and local food. Drivers can take home a doggy bag of bottled beers from the shop next door. *www.theladeinn.com*

Other Routes

A level 4km (2.5 miles) run follows the cycle path from the A821 to ⑤ then returns along the last section of the described route. The steep Ben Ledi walkers path at ① is an alternative means of shortening the route.

Lengthen the route by turning left a few hundred metres after ① and following a well-made path round Stank Glen. Rejoin the route near ② by a waymarked woodland path past a waterfall.

Bochastle is a good place to start a hill run up Ben Ledi. This approach avoids the normal route's

Oaks and birches beside the Leny.

Narrow paths above the Falls of Leny
Photo: Dougal Ranford

steep ascent from the Stank car park (586 092). The descent from Bealach nan Corp into Stank Glen is not obvious. Overshooting is indicated by rising ground and a small lochan.

A few miles along the A821 towards Brig of Turk is a 27km (17 miles) route circling Meall Cala. Start at the Woodland Trust Glen Finglas car park (546 065) east of Brig o' Turk and follow a woodland path to the reservoir road. The track round Meall Cala is runnable throughout.

Events

The Trossachs 10k Trail Race follows forest roads and paths through Loch Ard Forest just south of Aberfoyle. The race is run at the end of May and raises money for the Anthony Nolan Trust.

Loch Ordie

36 Loch Ordie

Distance	19km (12 miles)	Ascent	350m (1100ft)
Map	OS Landranger 52 or 53, OS Explorer 379		
Navigation •••	Signed tracks to Loch Ordie then unsigned path and track descent		
Terrain •••	Stony tracks and earth path		
Wet Feet •••	Occasional puddles		
Start/Finish	Cally car park PH8 0EP NO 024 437		

A high loch is the goal for this longer circuit

Loch Ordie and its more remote sister lochans Oisinneach Mor and Beag lie cupped in the hills above Dunkeld. The whole area is criss-crossed with paths and tracks which enable many hours of happy off-road running. The landscape is typical Perthshire with knobbly heathery hills and pockets of woodland. The route up to Loch Ordie is all on good landrover track and the return follows a mix of runnable path, track and a short stretch on tarmac road. As a general rule, running is prone to cause injury rather than cure it. This route offers the prospect of both. Folklore tells of lame men walking and sick children healed by drinking from the Santa Crux Well near Grewhill. The well can still be seen today although its efficacy is doubtful.

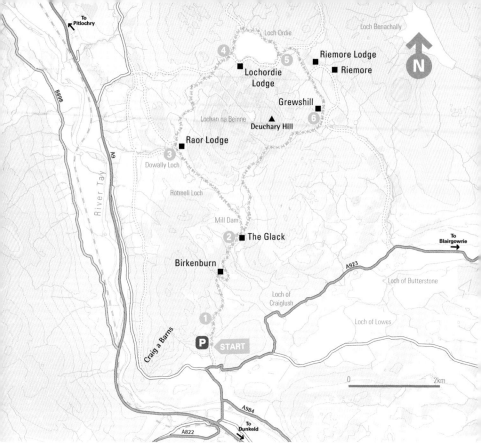

🏃 START Follow the dirt road uphill from the entrance to Cally car park. ① After 400m keep right at a fork to continue uphill on the road for a further 2.5km to a gate and path junction just before a house at The Glack. ② Turn left through the gate and continue straight ahead following the sign to Loch Ordie. The track passes a couple of fishing lochans and reaches Raor Lodge after about 2.5km. Hens and guinea fowl roam freely so take care to close gates after passing through. ③ Turn right just after the house and continue uphill on the main track to reach Loch Ordie. ④ Continue on the track to the left of the loch then turn onto a rougher lochside path around the north side of the loch. ⑤ Turn away from the loch onto a track for 400m then go right onto a waymarked track heading south. This joins the tarmac road from Riemore Lodge. Continue past Grewshill for 300m to a signed junction. ⑥ Turn right onto a grassy track signposted to Mill Dam. This becomes a narrow path crossing the southern slopes of Deuchary Hill. At the end of the path head downhill on a rough track which leads past Mill Dam to the path junction near The Glack. ② Retrace the outward route back to Cally car park.

Trip Planning

🚆 Dunkeld (3km from start) 🚌 North Car Park, Dunkeld (1km from start) 🚗 Head north out of Dunkeld then turn right onto the A923 towards Blairgowrie. Turn left soon after passing the industrial estate. The turn has an array of signs pointing to Cally car park, The Glack and other B&Bs but the signs are invisible until the last minute. 🚻 Dunkeld North Car Park (for a small fee) 🍴 Folk music lovers should head straight for the Taybank near to the river. It has outside seating for sunny days. Next door is the Atholl Arms. The main street has several cafés including Howies bar-café which stays open later than the rest. 🏠 Runner Adrian Davis owns a guest house in nearby Birnam. He also organises guided wildlife and running holidays. *www.birnamguesthouse.co.uk www.wildoutdoors.info* 🐕 Free range poultry at Raor Lodge and unfenced grazing elsewhere on the route.

Other Routes

Runnable paths continue past Loch Ordie to Lochan Oisinneach Mor, Lochan Oisinneach and beyond. These paths are rougher and muddier than the tracks leading up to Loch Ordie.

Waymarked routes around Dunkeld and Birnam make good trail runs. Try the 6.4km (4 miles) Braan Path. Start at the Inver car park (016 419), a few hundred metres past the caravan site near the A9/A822 junction. Lovely woodland paths lead upriver, cross over into the Hermitage and continue upstream to Rumbling Bridge. The return is on farm tracks, paths and forest roads. A 22km (14 miles) route on tracks and woodland paths links two branches of the Rob Roy Way above Aberfeldy. From the car park (NN 855 486), follow the road to Urlar, then a track across the moors to a minor road (800 431) with a great view of the Ben Lawers range. The return track (789 446) overlooks the valley, crosses the outward road and finishes on woodland trails through the famous Birks of Aberfeldy.

Events

The Highland Boundary Races at Birnam provide entertainment for everyone. The weekend of races includes a flattish 5 mile trail run, a short run up Birnam Hill and a longer run up Deuchary Hill.

Loch Ordie

Track to Raor Lodge

The Cateran Trail is a 103km (64 miles) waymarked circular route through Perthshire run as part of the Scottish Ultra Marathon Series. The 32km (20 miles) Mini Trail includes the best section of the route – a grassy descent to Spittal of Glenshee. The Mini Trail is runnable except for the link between Lair and Kirkmichael which is partly rough, faintly tracked moorland. *www.caterantrail.org*

Ben Vorlich and Stuc a' Chroin
Photo: Dougal Ranford

37 Glen Kendrum & Glen Ogle

Distance	25km (15 miles)	Ascent	600m (2000ft)
Map	OS Landranger 51, OS Explorer 365		
Navigation ●●●	Signed track over pass then return by cycle path		
Terrain ●●●	Stony track and gravel cycle path		
Wet Feet ●●●	Occasional puddles		
Start/Finish	Lochearnhead FK19 8PS NN 592 238		

Highland views from hill tracks and the old railway line

A very fine track winds up Glen Kendrum and over a low pass into Glen Dubh. Although the hills on either side are low their craggy sides are interesting with cracking views down both glens. It is essential to pause and turn around on the way up Glen Kendrum to admire Ben Vorlich and Stuc a' Chroin. Once over the pass another fine view awaits. Technically, this route takes in five glens as it starts up the Glen of Strathyre before turning into Glen Kendrum. After descending through Glen Dubh to Glen Dochart the route returns through a fifth glen: Glen Ogle. The old railway track from Killin Junction to Lochearnhead gives an easy running surface with gentle inclines. The only disadvantage to running along this path is that it becomes impossible to appreciate the graceful viaduct built to carry the railway along the side of the glen.

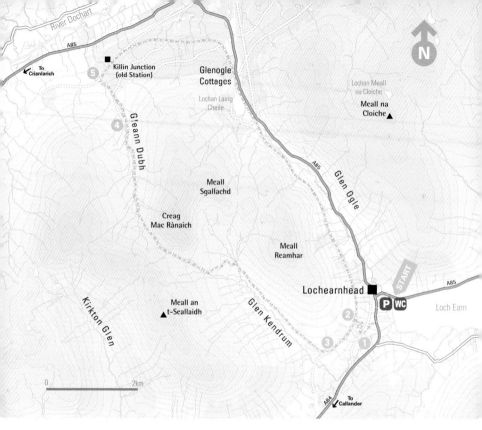

🏃 **START** Cross the river and turn left onto the A84. After 500m turn right at the church and follow a minor road uphill to a bridge. ❶ Just before crossing the bridge follow Sustrans signs left down a ramp and turn right underneath the bridge. Climb uphill on the zigzag cycle path to reach the disused railway path. ❷ Turn left and follow the track for nearly 1km passing through a couple of gates to reach a bridge over the track. ❸ Just before the bridge turn left through a gate, then cross the bridge following a signpost to Glen Kendrum. Follow this rocky track for 5km up Glen Kendrum to the col. Continue down into Gleann Dubh for another 3km until the main track curves left to ford the river. ❹ Leave the main track for a rough, wet track down the right hand side of the river. Continue into forest and take the left hand path next to the river to reach the disused railway line. ❺ Turn right along the track going past the platform of Killin Junction station then taking the right hand branch to head uphill. The track climbs gradually to Lochan Lairig Cheile and Glenoglehead Station which is now a private house. Continue downhill for 5km to return to ❷. Turn left down the zigzags and retrace the outward route back to Lochearnhead.

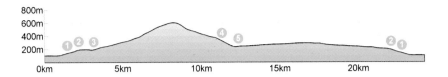

Trip Planning

🚐 Cameron Court, Lochearnhead 🚗 🚾 Lochearnhead's public car park and toilets are on the A85 Perth Road opposite the Watersports Centre. They are signed off the A84. 🥧 Hot pies, tea and coffee are available from the village shop. For a sit down snack try the Lochside Café at the Watersports Centre. ⌂ There are a couple of hotels next to Loch Earn which also serve food and drink to non-residents. *www.clachancottagehotel.co.uk www.lochearnhead-hotel.com*

Other Routes

An alternative ending follows the old military road through Glen Ogle. This grassy path crosses the A85 lower down the glen and can be boggy in places. Linking this alternative route with the described ending creates a shorter 12km (7 miles) circuit known as the Glenogle Trail.

The forest roads south of Loch Tay offer level running as well as a few steep climbs. They have fantastic views across Loch Tay to the Lawers range. Start from Killin near Falls of Dochart or from a car park next to the RAF memorial near the top of Glen Ogle. These forest roads link with hill tracks and paths which can be followed to Glen Lednock and Comrie.

Railway Mania

In the late 18th century James Watts' patent kept a lid on steam engine development. With its expiry in 1800 came an explosion of new inventions. Cornish engineer Richard Trevithick's miniaturised high pressure steam engine powered the first car and then the first locomotive. Train lines spread from town to town as Railway Mania gripped the nation. At its peak in 1846 272 new railway companies were authorised by Parliament. In a climate of inflated claims and downright dishonesty a few fortunes were made but many more lost. The Callander to Oban Railway turned Oban into a fashionable resort although the route never made money. The line between Callander and Crianlarich closed in 1965 after a landslide in Glen Ogle.

Glen Kendrum & Glen Ogle

Glen Kendrum
Photo: Dougal Ranford

Other Activities

Lochearnhead Water Sports Centre offers waterskiing, wakesurfing, wakeboarding and kayaking for all the family. *www.lochearnhead-watersports-centre.com*

Open boat canoes, kayaks, winter walking gear and mountain bikes can be hired from Killin Outdoor Centre, a small outdoor shop at the west end of Loch Tay. *www.killinoutdoor.co.uk*

Dundee, Fife and Angus

The Fife and Angus coastlines boast mile upon mile of golden sand. Inland there are trails through wooded estates, along salmon rivers and over the hills. In west central Fife the low lying Lomond Hills give panoramic views over farmland and out to sea while the north of Angus is linked to Deeside by old droving roads over the high remote moors of the Mounth.

Largo Bay (Route 40)

Dundee from Tentsmu
(Route 39)

City Centre Running

The Green Circular cycle path forms a marathon-length loop around Scotland's fourth largest city. Lengthy sections are alongside roads but there are also miles of traffic-free paths. The best section for off-road running follows the Dighty Burn from Trottick to the sea at Monifieth. In the heart of the city, Dundee Law and Balgay Hill have small path networks and great summit views. A mainly off-road triangular circuit links these two tops with The Miley, a stretch of the disused Newtyle-Dundee railway which is now a nature reserve. Wrought iron gates on Clepington Road and Old King's Cross Road give access to this unlikely strip of urban countryside. Shore paths along the Firth of Tay give very scenic running. Head to the Riverside Park next to the airport or the Esplanade and Rock Garden east of Broughty Ferry. Head even further east on a tarmac cycle path which runs all the way to Carnoustie. On days when the red flags are down and red lights out runners are welcome to use the network of tarmac paths through Barry Buddon MOD training ground and explore the surrounding beaches.

Camperdown Park

38 Camperdown Park & Templeton Woods

Distance	7.5km (4.5 miles)	Ascent	150m (500ft)
Map	OS Landranger 54, OS Explorer 380		
Navigation •••	Follow paths around the perimeter of the country park		
Terrain •••	Gravel and earth paths, short section on pavement, several road crossings		
Wet Feet •••	Occasional puddles and shallow mud		
Start/Finish	Camperdown Park DD2 4TF NO 365 329		

A circuit through mature woodland with views of the Sidlaw Hills

This old country estate on the outskirts of Dundee is a great place to run. The sound of busy traffic on the nearby Kingsway road is quickly exchanged for birdsong and the snap of twigs underfoot. A barely perceptible climb on woodland paths leads to a road crossing and then on to one of the highlights of the route; a path along the edge of woodland with views out over farmland towards the Sidlaw Hills. Keep an eye out for the unique Camperdown Elm. Grafts from this squat, leafy mutant with drooping branches flourish in botanical gardens all over the world.

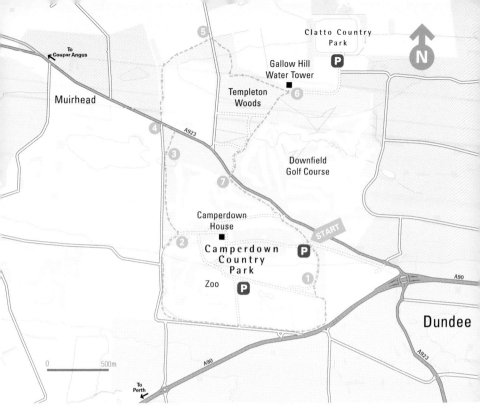

Head down a gravel path to the left of playing fields until the path curves to the right. ① Turn off left through the woods, then continue around the park's perimeter for just over 2km. Early sections can be muddy and the path improves after a second road crossing. Climb gradually to reach a road and house. ② Turn onto a signposted path between the house drive and the path onto the golf course. Follow this through trees until it approaches the A923 and curves to the right. ③ Turn off towards the road on an earth path which leads to a gate. Turn left along the road and take the first street on the right. ④ Follow Braidlaw Road for a short distance then head right into woodland. Continue through the trees and turn right onto a good gravel path which runs along the northern edge of the woods to reach a road. ⑤ Cross the road and go around the barrier into Templeton Woods. After a few hundred metres the path forks near a car park. Head left to join a wide gravel track and follow this for 500m to a junction near the water tower. ⑥ Turn right onto a track and head downhill past the golf course. After crossing a stream continue left onto a dirt road which reaches the A923 after another few hundred metres. ⑦ Cross the road into the park and turn left onto a gravel path. Cross a park road and continue following the waymarked blue trail back to the start of the route.

Trip Planning

🚌 Camperdown, Faraday St at the main park entrance. 🚗 Turn off the Kingsway (A90) onto the A923 towards Coupar Angus. Turn left at the next roundabout then first right into the park. After less than one mile park in the first car park on the right hand side of the road. **WC** Play park or Camperdown House 🍴 Camperdown Wildlife Centre or kiosk at the play park.

Other Routes

Extend the route to 10km (6 miles) by continuing straight on at **5** to run a loop around Clatto Reservoir.

Monikie and Crombie Country Park a few miles north-east of Dundee both have woodland and waterside trails. These two small country parks can be linked by short stretches of road.

Clatto Reservoir

Camperdown Park & Templeton Woods

Camperdown trail

The Sidlaw Hills offer a range of off-road running routes. From Balkello Community Woodland (364 384) follow paths north-west to join a track west of Auchterhouse Hill. The track continues through the hills to Denoon but a 6.5km (4 miles) circuit returns over Auchterhouse Hill, down to Windy Gates and up to the viewpoint on Balkello Hill. Heathery paths lead out and back to the masts on top of Craigowl Hill or simply return down good tracks to the Community Woodland.

Events

Camperdown Park hosts Dundee's annual Race for Life each June. These women-only runs are held all over the country to raise funds for Cancer Research UK. *www.raceforlife.org*

Monikie Country Park hosts several running events including a 10k and half marathon.

Forfar Road Runners organise an entertaining Multi Terrain Race which circles Forfar by linking off-road paths and tracks. The route takes in a wide range of terrain from tarmac to challenging bogs. *www.forfarroadrunners.co.uk*

Sands and forest

39 Tentsmuir

Distance	9km (5.5 miles)	Ascent	25m (100ft)
Map	OS Landranger 54 or 59, OS Explorer 371		
Navigation •••	Out by a signed path then back along the beach and waymarked trail		
Terrain •••	Earth and sand paths, forest road, sandy beach		
Wet Feet •••	Dry and sandy		
Start/Finish	Tentsmuir Forest KY16 0DR NO 498 242		

Sand, sea, seals, solitude and sunshine

Tentsmuir is impossible not to love. It is simply a great landscape for all activities – running, walking, horse riding or cycling. Although the trails through the trees make an easy trot the real joy of running here is discovered by heading out onto the beach. Golden sands stretch temptingly on for miles, and are growing even larger. Since the 1940s the dunes have expanded into the sea by an average of five metres per year. A line of WWII tank defence blocks is now stranded hundreds of metres inland. Just offshore is a long sand bar which is a favourite low tide haul out for seals. In wintertime the seals compete for space with Britain's largest population of eider ducks. Or stop by during spring or autumn along with many thousands of migrating seabirds.

🏃 START Head towards the beach and turn left at the edge of the forest onto the waymarked Seashell trail. Follow this along the edge of the trees and into woodland. Keep straight on for 2.5km following the Seashell trail and signs for the Ice House to reach a gate in the fence on the right. ① Turn left to reach the Ice House, then right onto the forest road. Continue for 1.5km until the road bends to the left at the signed Junction 4. ② Leave the track and the woods through a gap in the fence and turn right along a grassy path. Go through a kissing gate into the Nature Reserve and follow an obvious grassy path through the dunes until it meets a line of tank defences. ③ Cross the dunes onto the beach and head along the sand to a green corrugated iron observation hut. ④ Rejoin the Seashell trail at the hut and follow it through the dunes to leave the Nature Reserve by a kissing gate. Continue along the waymarked trail, cross a stream and follow the signposted Beach Return To Car Park. ⑤ The waymarked trail avoids lagoons by turning inland. Go behind a private house then run along close cropped turf to return to the car park. Watch out for ankle-turning rabbit holes.

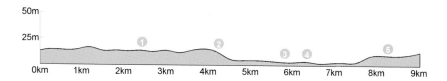

Trip Planning

Tentsmuir is a National Nature Reserve *www.tentsmuir.org* 🚗 Tentsmuir Forest is signposted from Leuchars and the B945. It is about ten miles south of Dundee. The Kinshaldy car park opens at 9am and closes at 6pm in summer, 3pm in mid-winter. An automatic pay barrier charges £1 per visit. 🚻 Kinshaldy car park (closed in winter). 🚌 Leuchars ✈ This is a popular dog walking area. Please keep dogs on lead while in the Nature Reserve or if there are seals hauled out on other parts of the beach. Cattle sometimes graze the dunes. Although the described beach route is unsuitable for buggies it is easy to construct a buggy-friendly route by linking forest roads.

Other Routes

The route is easily extended by making use of the network of forest roads. Sustrans Cycle Route 1 and the Fife Coastal Path both go through Tentsmuir Forest and on to the Tay Bridge.

Tents Moor

In the 1780s a Danish ship foundered on one of the sand bars just offshore. The ship-wrecked sailors set up a village of tents on the coastal moorland and the area became known as Tents Moor.

The Seashell Trail

Tentsmuir

Lagoon near Tentsmuir car park

Seals

Tentsmuir is one of just a few places on the east coast where both grey and common seals can be seen. Grey seals are bigger than common seals and have a distinctive 'Roman nose'. The 'grey' descriptor is misleading as both species have mottled coats varying from almost black to creamy white. Grey seals tend to have more uniform colouring than common seals.

Both species visit Tentsmuir to moult and breed. Look out for grey seal pups in autumn (October to December) and common seal pups in early summer (June and July).

Largo Bay

40 Fife Coastal Path

Distance	10km (6 miles)	Ascent	100m (300ft)
Map	OS Landranger 59, OS Explorer 370 and 371, Footprint The Fife Coastal Path		
Navigation •••	Fully waymarked coastal path		
Terrain •••	Beach, grass paths and pavement		
Wet Feet •••	Mostly sandy		
Start	Lower Largo KY8 6BT NO 425 026		
Finish	Elie KY9 1BZ NO 492 000		

One way coastal path with an optional scramble

For many centuries Fife's coastal villages were bustling ports with active fishing fleets and trading links to Holland and France. In the 17th century this coastline was so prosperous that King James VI called Fife a "beggar's mantle fringed with gold". In later centuries fortunes were reversed and it was King James' "beggar's mantle" that brought wealth in the form of coal fields and fertile farmland. From the air Fife is literally fringed with gold. Its miles of sandy beaches are a perfect playground for everyone from bucket and spade toting toddlers to kite surfers. This run follows a particularly scenic stretch of coastline. Runners with a head for heights will enjoy the optional adventure on the Elie Chain Walk near the end of the route.

Follow Coastal Path waymarkers from start to finish. 🏃 **START** Climb steps at the back of the Lower Largo car park and turn right onto a disused railway track. Follow this for just over 1.5km until level with a large house on the left. ❶ Leave the track and follow a narrow path through the dunes of a Site of Special Scientific Interest (SSSI). Tank defences mark the end of the SSSI area. From here either run along the sand or follow a narrow path through the dunes for nearly 2km to the end of the beach. ❷ Turn inland briefly, crossing two footbridges and a line of trees to reach a caravan park. Follow the tarmac road just right of the caravans to reach an information board at the far end of the site. ❸ Continue along the coast on a narrow path to climb up to mobile phone masts on top of the cliffs. Drop downhill on steep steps, turning right just in front of the golf course onto the beach. ❹ Head along the beach for about 700m then turn left onto a path to cross the golf course. After about 100m turn right onto a grassy track between stone walls which ends at a cul-de-sac. ❺ Continue onto the road and take the first opportunity to cut back down to the beach. Continue along the sand for 1km to an obvious, though half buried pipeline. ❻ Turn left and head up School Wynd. Turn right onto the High Street to reach the village green and the bus stop.

Fife Coastal Path

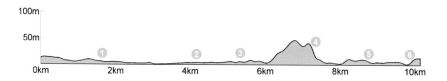

Trip Planning

The prevailing wind is from the south-west so the route is usually best run from Lower Largo to Elie. 🚌 Harbour, Lower Largo (near Railway Inn and Crusoe Hotel) and High Street, Elie (on village green) A regular service connects the two villages. 🚗 Turn off the A915 onto a minor road signed to Lower Largo. Just east of the river turn onto narrow Main Street between the Crusoe Hotel and Railway Inn. The car park is at the end of the street after a 90 degree dog leg. 🚻 Lower Largo beach car park or Stenton Row near Elie village green. 🍴 Elie Deli or the Coffee House near the bus stop on Elie High Street. Railway and real ale enthusiasts will feel at home in Lower Largo's Railway Inn. The Crusoe Hotel across the road has outdoor seating and sea views.

Other Routes

The Fife Coastal Path is fully waymarked from the Forth Bridge at North Queensferry to the Tay Bridge at Newport-on-Tay. The terrain underfoot varies from seafront promenades through sandy beaches to rough rocky coastline. There are good public transport connections all the way along the route. A 5km (3 miles) extension to the described route starts at Leven and is mostly beach running. *www.fifecoastalpath.co.uk*

Events

The Black Rock 5 Race is a sprint and splash around rocks exposed at low tide in the bay between Burntisland and Kinghorn. *www.blackrock5.org*

Other Activities

Commonsense rather than technical equipment is required for Scotland's answer to Italy's via ferrata. The Elie Chain Walk is a rocky scramble round the cliffs of Kincraig Point. It has good footholds and chains to cling to. From the west end of the beach follow a sign to the start of the chains. Or drop down a zigzag path from the top of Kincraig Point. Keeping ahead of a flood tide can be exciting so sensible folk begin their traverse about an hour after high tide. More information can be found on the Mountaineering Council of Scotland website. *www.mcofs.org.uk*

Alexander Selkirk's
birthplace, Lower Largo

The real Robinson Crusoe

In 1704 the sailor Alexander Selkirk was marooned on an uninhabited island off the coast of Chile. He had quarrelled with his captain over the seaworthiness of their ship, the *Cinque Ports*. Selkirk hoped to be picked up quickly by a passing ship but it turned out to be four years and four months before he was finally rescued. Selkirk was right about the Cinque Ports. She leaked so badly that her crew were soon forced to abandon ship. The survivors of the wreck were captured and imprisoned by the Spanish. Daniel Defoe fictionalised Selkirk's feat of survival in *The Life and Adventures of Robinson Crusoe.*

Lomond Hill Race
Photo: Chris Upson

41 The Lomond Hills

Distance	13km (8 miles)	Ascent	350m (1200ft)
Map	OS Landranger 58 and 59, OS Explorer 370		
Navigation ●●●	Follow the obvious track between the two summits		
Terrain ●●●	Stony and grassy tracks, steep path descents off the two summits		
Wet Feet ●●●	Occasional shallow mud and slippery earth paths		
Start/Finish	East Lomond NO 252 059		

Long, runnable ridge track linking two summits

These iconic Fife peaks stand proud of the low lying coastal plain. Their two tops and long linking ridge promise much and deliver. The summits are short, steep and rewarding; most of the running follows an old track along the spine of the ridge. This is easy ground with superb views over Fife and Perthshire. From the summit of West Lomond look south-west to see the top of a small crag known as the Devil's Burdens. According to legend the Devil was flying past the Lomond Hills when he was insulted by a local wifie. Being the Devil he couldn't ignore this. He dropped his burden to form the crags and unleashed a bolt of lightning which turned the witch to stone. She is still there, a tall basalt pillar on Bishop's Hill known as Carlin Maggie, "carlin" being the old Scots word for witch.

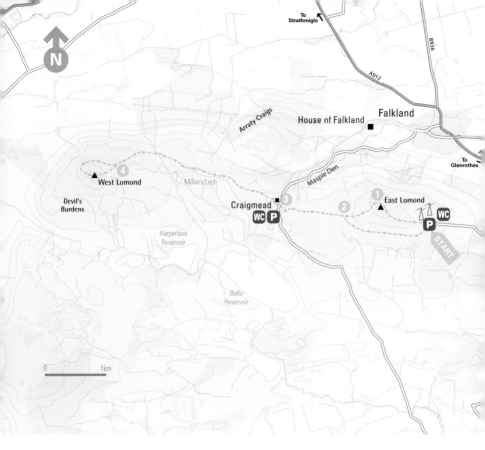

START Take the obvious path uphill from the end of the car park nearest the masts. Pass through a gate and climb to the summit of East Lomond. **1** Descend steeply on a rough path to join a good grassy track. This comes in from the left and descends to a kissing gate. **2** Go through the gate and turn right onto a wide track between stone walls. Follow this for 1km towards West Lomond and down a short stretch of rocky track to cross the road to Craigmead car park. **3** Head out the back of the car park through a small wooded valley. Leave the woodland by a gate and turn left onto a wide grass path. Continue onto a stony track and follow this to the foot of West Lomond. **4** Continue to follow the track which climbs gradually, circling the hill, then up a few gentle zigzags to the summit. This is a great runnable ascent; do not be tempted onto the more direct walking path. From the summit of West Lomond either return by the outward route or drop down the steep walkers' path. Follow the outward track back to the gate at the foot of East Lomond. **2** Do not go through the gate but continue on the limekiln track which contours around the side of the hill to finish at the car park.

Trip Planning

🚌 There is no public transport to the start of this route. Instead catch the bus to Falkland and follow paths through Maspie Den and up to the Lomonds. 🚗 The East Lomond car park is signposted from the A912 south-east of Falkland. The car park is at the end of the single track road opposite the mobile phone masts. 🚻 East Lomond and Craigmead car parks (closed in winter). 🥪 Kind Kyttock's Kitchen on Cross Wynd in Falkland (closed Mondays). On the A912 north of Falkland is the Pillars of Hercules organic farm shop and café. *www.pillars.co.uk* 🐕 Sheep graze on the track and surrounding unfenced moorland.

Other Routes

Shorter woodland trails run through the Falkland Estate below Arraty Craigs and through Maspie Den on the north side of the Lomond Hills. *www.centreforstewardship.org.uk*

West Lomond from the summit of East Lomond

The Lomond Hills

West Lomond

Two nearby Country Parks, one in Fife and the other just over the Perth and Kinross border have similar lochside trails. Loch Ore is encircled by a waymarked path of just over 5km. The Loch Leven path does not extend all the way round the loch but runs for 12.5km from Kinross Pier to Vane Farm. Both lochs have parking, toilets and other facilities. *www.fifedirect.org.uk* *www.pkct.org*

Events

The Devil's Burdens is a 31km relay race over and around the Lomond Hills organised by Fife AC. To add to the challenge the race is run in mid-winter, often in snow. *www.fifeac.co.uk*

Fife AC also organise a shorter and flatter trail race, the Falkland Flyer, which takes place in March. One of the five Tour of Fife races held in July is a trail race.

Loch Muick

42 The Capel Mounth

Distance	25km (16 miles)	Ascent	900m (3000ft)
Map	OS Landranger 44, OS Explorer 388, Harvey Cairngorms & Lochnagar		
Navigation •••	Clear paths and obvious junctions over the Mounth and round Loch Muick		
Terrain •••	Gravel and grassy paths, rough and smooth landrover tracks		
Wet Feet •••	Some boggy ground after Moulzie Farm		
Start/Finish	Glen Doll DD8 4RD NO 283 761		

A long, remote circuit on superb hill paths

There are few places in Scotland where a runner feels so small as on the Capel Mounth. The old droving road crosses high, flat, featureless moorland where the 360˚ view is simply breathtaking. The paths are well made throughout which is astounding given their remote location. Indisputably, the best view is coming over the brow of the hill to see Loch Muick laid out below. It is small wonder that Queen Victoria loved to spend her holidays here and built Glasallt Shiel on the far side of the loch. The path down to the loch is known as the 'Streak of Lightning'. Care must be taken on this fast descent as the way is narrow and it is popular with walkers. This long route saves the very best to last. The zigzagging grassy path leading down off the Capel Mounth into Glen Doll is pure joy to run.

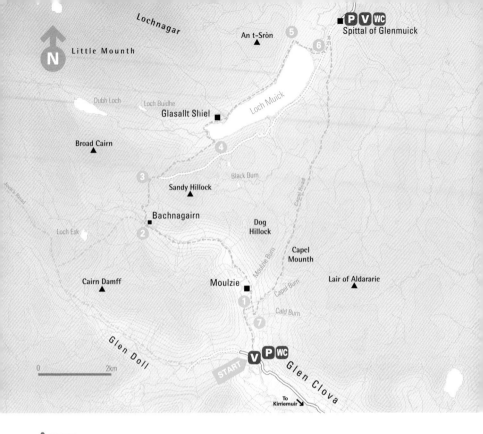

 START Head upriver through the picnic area beside the car park to join a riverside path. Continue along this for 1km then cross the river to reach a T-junction. **1** (283 774) Turn left and after about 500m take the track to the right of Moulzie Farm. Leave this track before it crosses the river and continue on a path towards a forestry plantation. A path and boardwalks run along the river side of the plantation. Soon after leaving the trees cross the river by a footbridge and rejoin the track. Continue up the glen for 2.5km to the end of the rough track. A strong path continues through the trees to the bridge at Bachnagairn. **2** (254 796) Cross the river and climb the far bank on a rocky path. Continue uphill for just over 1km to a junction just before Allan's Hut. **3** (256 808) Turn right past the hut, perhaps taking a well deserved rest on Sandy's Seat. About 100m after the hut turn left onto a good gravel path which soon drops steeply down to Loch Muick. **4** (273 818) Turn left onto the lochside path and go round the far side of Loch Muick, passing through shady pine woodland surrounding Glasallt Shiel. **5** (294 844) At the east end of the loch turn right at the boathouse and cross the outflow by a footbridge to reach a T-junction. **6** (303 841) Head away from the loch then after 500m take a

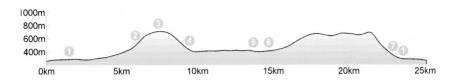

sharp right to climb above and away from the loch. As the ground levels off after nearly 3km continue straight ahead following large cairns where another track goes off left. After another 3.5km the landrover track becomes an excellent grassy path zigzagging steeply down beside the Capel Burn to reach the Moulzie Farm road. ❼ (284 771) Turn right towards the farm to return to ❶. Retrace the outward route back to the start.

Trip Planning

🚌 Clova Hotel (5km from start) 🚗 Follow the B995 through Glen Clova to the Clova Hotel and continue to Glen Doll on a minor road. The Glen Doll Ranger Base and car park (pay and display) is at the end of the public road. 🆆🅲 🆅 Glen Doll Ranger Base 🅿 🏠 The traditional watering hole in these parts is the Clova Hotel. It started off life as a drover's inn catering for travellers crossing the Mounth. Today it is popular with walkers and climbers. It has a bunkhouse and self-catering cottages as well as hotel accommodation. *www.clova.com*

Other Routes

The route can be either extended or shortened by linking it with Jock's Road – a path between Glen Doll and Glen Callater. The junction at (230 785) is not obvious. Jock's Road is an excellent path but the path east towards Loch Esk appears to be non-existent until the east side of the col where it becomes a faint line traversing the hillside above the loch. Navigation from Bachnagairn to Jock's Road is easiest.

Spittal of Glenmuick (307 850) 🆆🅲 🅿 near ❻ is an equally good start point for this route with a Visitor Centre, toilets and a pay and display car park. The 12km (7.5 miles) circuit of Loch Muick is all on good paths and makes a scenic, relatively level, trail run.

Away from the hills is a pleasant 10km (6 miles) out and back woodland trail along the bank of River North Esk. A track between Edzell Post Office and a garage leads to the riverside path. Cross the river by the road bridge at Gannochy then go through the blue door to continue along the gorge to the Rocks of Solitude.

The Capel Mounth

River South Esk

The Angus Glens

Glen Clova is one of a series of parallel valleys cutting deep into the Mounth from the south. Known collectively as the Angus Glens these valleys provide a range of routes into the hills. The five main glens, from west to east, are Glen Isla, Glen Prosen, Glen Clova, Glen Lethnot and Glen Esk. Glen Clova is the most popular with walkers and appears to have been the focus of most of the path construction work. Invermark at the head of Glen Esk is the southern start point for the most easterly Munro, Mount Keen. This is definitely runnable, even mountain bikers make it to the summit.

Aberdeen and Deeside

Geology rules in Aberdeen. Underwater oil-soaked shales fuel its economic wealth while granite tor-topped hills create short and steep off-road runs. Follow the Dee upstream towards the Cairngorms to reach Deeside - the home of classic trail running in Scotland. Miles of paths and tracks roam through Scots pine woodlands, over heather-clad hills and around idyllic lochs.

Ballochbuie, Deeside

Den Wood

City Centre Running

Aberdeen is bounded to the east by the North Sea, to the north by the River Don and to the south by the Dee. These geographical constraints define the city centre's off-road running. The northern coast has sandy beaches while the south has clifftop paths. Trails on both sides of the Don form a four-mile circuit between Grandholm Bridge and the A90 road bridge. To the south a pleasant footpath runs along the Dee and links with the Deeside Way cycle path which follows the old railway line west from Duthie Park. The River Dee path can also be linked by road to trails at Tollohill and Kincorth Hill. West of the city is Hazlehead Park. Run straight past the Queen Mother's Rose Garden to leave the manicured formal gardens and access fine trail running terrain. After crossing the golf course on a good track there are trails off to the left which return through Den Woods. Or follow signs to continue west to Countesswells Forest.

Gairnhill Wood

43 Countesswells

Distance	4.5km (3 miles)	Ascent	100m (300ft)
Map	OS Landranger 38, OS Explorer 406		
Navigation ●●●	Link waymarked trails with unmarked paths to circle Gairnhill Wood		
Terrain ●●●	Forest road, earth and gravel paths and tracks		
Wet Feet ●●●	Occasional puddles		
Start/Finish	Countesswells Forest AB15 8QD NJ 869 045		

Straightforward woodland run with views of rolling farmland

Countesswells is close to Aberdeen yet in the heart of countryside. The woodland is managed by the Forestry Commission who has marked out a range of walking trails. Combining several of these trails creates a thoroughly enjoyable run. The pleasure of running through this particular wood lies in the variety of the trees and views. At first mosses and wood sorrel are the only plants to succeed in the shade of tall conifers. Later on comes colourful mixed woodland with a thick ferny green undergrowth. Almost the whole route is run near the woodland's edge where skinny tree trunks frame views of the surrounding countryside.

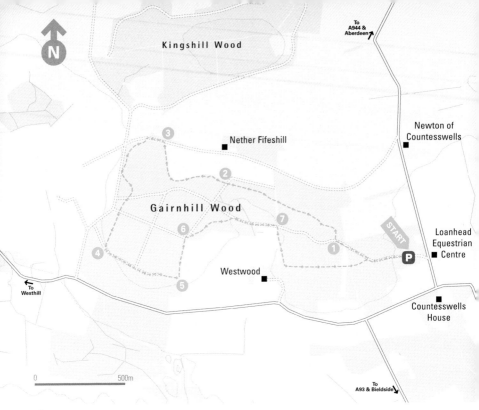

START From the information board follow the main forest road into the trees keeping right where the track forks to pass under a line of electricity pylons. ❶ Shortly after the pylons turn right onto an earth path. Run under tall dark trees for 250m then go straight ahead through a junction. After another 200m the path forks and the Green Trail goes to the left. ❷ Leave the Green Trail by taking the right fork to join a bridleway. Continue straight ahead along the side of the wood to the end of the path at a lane. ❸ Turn left down the lane for about 100m then turn left again onto an obvious path. This immediately bends right and heads into the woods. Follow it for nearly 500m crossing a broken down stone wall and a track to reach a T-junction. ❹ Turn left and head uphill. After going over the brow of the hill the path descends to a dry-stone wall. ❺ Follow the path round to the left for about 200m until the bridleway bends 90° to the left. ❻ Leave the bridleway by crossing a break in the wall and following an indistinct path through trees to the forest road. The route trends to the right and is marked by blue paint spots on the tree trunks. It can be rough and muddy. Join the forest road and continue to a crossroad. ❼ Turn right onto the waymarked Yellow Trail and follow this along the edge of woodland then left into the heart of the trees. After crossing a firebreak continue straight on to return to the car park.

Countesswells

Trip Planning

Up-to-date trail information including closures for forestry operations can be obtained from the Forestry Commission. *www.forestry.gov.uk* 🚌 Kingswells Church (2km from start).

🚗 Countesswells is on a minor road between the A93 and the A944. It is five miles west of Aberdeen city centre. From the A93 turn north at Bieldside Church, turn right at a T-junction then first left. The car park is on the left after 200m. From the A944 turn south at the Kingwells roundabout. The car park is on the right after about 1.5km.

Other Routes

Extend the route by crossing the lane at ❸ and following the bridleway around Kingshill Wood. A few miles north of Countesswells are the adjoining country parks of Brimmond Hill and Elrick Hill. A variety of interesting routes can be constructed using their well-trodden path network. North again is the Forestry Commission woodland at Kirkhill. The summit of Tyrebagger Hill makes a good objective for a run. In addition to waymarked walking and biking trails Tyrebagger is home to a permanent orienteering course and an mountain bike skills trail.

Wood sorrel

Countesswells

Countesswells Forest

Castle Island and Loch Kinord

44 Loch Kinord

Distance	6km (4 miles)	Ascent	50m (200ft)
Map	OS Landranger 37, OS Explorer 395 or 405		
Navigation •••	Fully waymarked loch circuit		
Terrain •••	Gravel and grass paths and tracks; avoidable rocky path on north side of loch		
Wet Feet •••	Occasional puddles in wet weather		
Start/Finish	Burn o' Vat Visitor Centre AB34 5NB NO 429 996		

Scenic lochside running on grassy paths

It is hard to imagine a more idyllic setting for an off-road run than Loch Kinord. This small Deeside loch is surrounded by picture perfect woodland. Birch branches dip into the water and its shores are carpeted with grass and flowers. A loch circuit is rarely a navigational challenge and this one is made even easier by full waymarking. Unsurprisingly today's visitors were not the first to love this loch. The loch was once called Loch Canmore after Malcolm III, King of Scots, who built a castle on the larger island. His devout Queen, Margaret, consecrated a chapel here in the 11th century. This was not Loch Kinord's first brush with religion. On the northern shore the route passes a well preserved Christian cross carved by 9th-century Picts. Older still is the crannog in the north-east quarter of the loch. This man-made island dates from the Iron Age when these easily defended homes were commonly built in Scottish lochs.

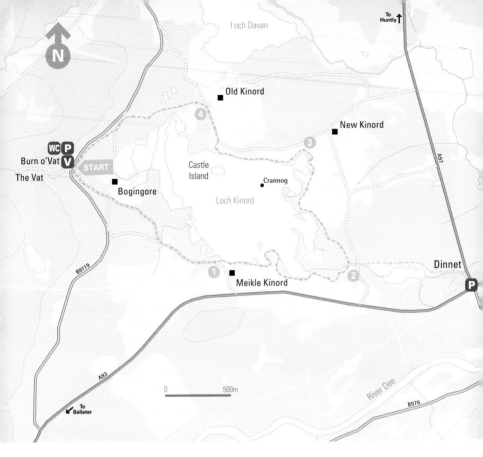

The route follows the Loch Kinord Circular Path which is well waymarked in the anti-clockwise direction only. **START** Leave the visitor centre by crossing the road into woodland and turning right onto the Loch Kinord Circular Path. The initial gravel path crosses a stony track then becomes pleasantly grassy for another 1km to reach a house and the loch. **1** Leave the track just before the house and drop down to a path along the water's edge. Follow this for nearly 1.5km along the loch, beside fields and into woodland to cross a footbridge and reach a signed path junction. **2** Turn left to continue around the loch passing between birch trees to reach a grassy field at the north-east corner of the loch. **3** Continue round to the left on a grassy path which drops down to the loch. Look offshore to see the crannog. After crossing a tumbledown stone wall continue more slowly as the path becomes rocky. Follow the path up past the Pictish Cross Stone to join a grassy track near a bench. Follow this north for about 300m to a path junction just before a fork in the track. **4** Turn left and follow the path through trees back to the Visitor Centre turnoff.

Loch Kinord

Trip Planning

Loch Kinord is part of a National Nature Reserve. *www.nnr-scotland.org.uk/muir-of-dinnet*

🚌 Dinnet (Follow a path from the back of the public car park to join the route at ❷) 🚗 Burn o' Vat Visitor Centre is on the B9119 and is signposted from both the A93 Braemar to Aberdeen road and from the B9119 at Milton of Logie. It is forty miles from Aberdeen. 🚻 Burn o' Vat Visitor Centre ☕ The Victoria Tea Room in Dinnet comes highly recommended by locals. So does the Old Station Coffee Shop a few miles down the road in Ballater. 🐕 Please keep dogs on leads or under close control. This is particularly important between April and July when ground nesting birds are raising chicks on the loch shore.

Other Routes

Extend the route to 8.5km (5.5 miles) by starting at Dinnet. A path leaves the back of the public car park at the Dinnet crossroads to join the loch circuit at ❷.

Extend the route to 10km (6 miles) by following the loch circuit to ❹ then continuing north on the track parallel with the B9119. At the road junction turn left onto a track next to a house. This rough track climbs steadily uphill to a view of Lochnagar (unfortunately framed by pylons). Turn left at the signpost to return to the Visitor Centre via a fantastic narrow path through heather and woodland.

9th-century cross

Loch Kinord

Bogingore

A longer 15km (9 miles) route links Loch Kinord with the Deeside Way and pleasant tracks through Cambus o' May Forest. This can be started at the Visitor Centre, Dinnet or Cambus o' May Forestry Commission car park. The long straight cycle path through Muir of Dinnet is somewhat tedious but the rest of the route is scenic and enjoyable to run.

Macgregors and the Vat

A visit to Loch Kinord is incomplete without scrambling into the Vat. This giant pothole was cut by glacial meltwater during the last ice age. Follow the path upstream from the visitor centre until the way is blocked. Enter the Vat by scrambling improbably over rocks in the stream bed. Once inside it no longer seems so far-fetched that a pothole could be the hideout of 18th-century outlaws. The Macgregors from Perthshire were originally hired by local crofters to protect their farms from looters. But Gilderoy Macgregor and his men quickly realised that there was more profit to be made on the wrong side of the law. From their hideout in the Vat they set up a lucrative cattle rustling business, stealing animals from Deeside crofters and driving them over the Mounth Roads to markets in Angus.

Hackley Bay
Photo: Lorne Gill/SNH

45 Forvie

Distance	8.5km (5 miles)	Ascent	75m (250ft)
Map	OS Landranger 38, OS Explorer 421		
Navigation ●●●	One tricky junction, all others waymarked		
Terrain ●●●	Gravel paths, sandy and grassy paths; slightly rough in places		
Wet Feet ●●●	Sandy rather than muddy. Localised flooding on the Heath Trail in very wet weather.		
Start/Finish	Stevenson Forvie Visitor Centre AB41 8RU NK 034 289		

Unique dunes and airy clifftop running

Forvie is a landscape like no other. Heather and lichen clad dunes stretch into the distance, a rare habitat protected by its status as a nature reserve. Before the dunes grew in size people eked out a living here and this run passes the remains of their sand covered settlement. Legend has it that three sisters cast out to sea cursed Forvie and in response to their wishes the village was buried in sand. Before reaching the buried village this run follows the route of an old track across the dunes. Little used today, this quiet path is the perfect place to fully experience the peculiar dunes landscape. The route returns along the clifftops past Hackley Bay. A well-made path underfoot allows maximum attention to be paid to Forvie's dramatic coastal scenery.

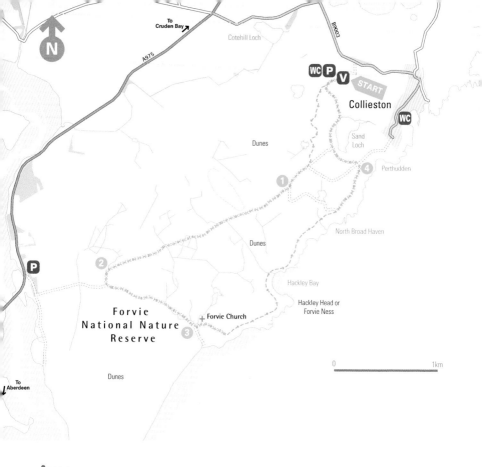

🏃 START From the Visitor Centre follow the gravel path to a kissing gate into the reserve. Continue straight on following the waymarked Heath Trail for just over 1km to reach a fork. Some care is needed to spot this junction. ① Turn right onto an old unsigned track and follow it for 2km across the dunes to an obvious hillock. Despite its age the line of the track remains reasonably straightforward to follow. It may be faint in a few places where sand has blown in. ② Follow the track left in front of the hillock and join a wide grassy track waymarked as the Dune Trail and Nave Nortrail coastal route. Follow this across the reserve to the coast. ③ A brief detour down to the beach is recommended then return to the ruined kirk. Head north on the coastal path to reach an information board near houses at Collieston. ④ Turn left onto a waymarked trail which leads back to the Visitor Centre past the Sand Loch.

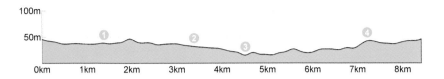

Trip Planning

V The Visitor Centre is open daily between April and October. The southern part of the reserve, which does not form part of this route, is closed between April and August to protect breeding terns. *www.nnr-scotland.org.uk/forvie* Collieston Road End (2km along a quiet country road to the Visitor Centre) The Stevenson Forvie Visitor Centre is signposted from the A975 north of Newburgh. Forvie is fifteen miles north of Aberdeen. **WC** Visitor Centre or Collieston Harbour (8am to 5pm). Newburgh Dogs must be kept on a lead or under close control at all times of year.

Other Activities

Outside tern breeding season combine this route with the Dune Trail around the southern end of the reserve to create a longer run. The Waterside car park (004 271) is an alternative access point.

The Sand Loch

Forvie

Arctic tern
Photo: Sheila Russell

The Formartine and Buchan Way is an old railway which has been converted into a cycle path. The track passes through Ellon a few miles inland of Forvie. The Way starts in Dyce and runs 40km (25 miles) north to Maud where it splits. The north branch continues to Fraserburgh (25km, 15 miles) while the east branch ends at Peterburgh (21km, 13 miles).

Forvie's terns

Sandwich, common, Arctic and little terns are summer visitors to Forvie. All four species breed on the pebbles and dunes of the southern part of the reserve. Only a fool would disturb them as terns have a natural talent for pecking unprotected scalps. Arctic terns travel the furthest of any migratory species and never experience winter. As soon as the days shorten terns take flight for the opposite hemisphere. Satellite tracking shows that Arctic terns take advantage of prevailing winds. This makes their journey much easier but also far longer. A single tern easily clocks up 70,000km in a single year. They cover an incredible 520km per day during their 40 day migration north from Antarctica.

Gordon Way

46 Bennachie

Distance	11km (6.5 miles)	Ascent	450m (1500ft)
Map	OS Landranger 38, OS Explorer 421		
Navigation •••	Waymarked Gordon Way, unmarked junctions to Oxen Craig		
Terrain •••	Gravel and earth paths, short rocky scrambles to summits of Oxen Craig and Mither Tap		
Wet Feet •••	Earth paths near Oxen Craig can be slippery		
Start/Finish	Bennachie Visitor Centre AB51 5HX NJ 698 216		

Woodland, heathery moors and an exhilarating descent

Bennachie is the most popular hill in the area and holds a special place in the hearts of Aberdonians. Bennachie is not just one hill. It is much more accurately described as a hill range or an upland plateau with several rocky tor summits. Excellent paths link these summits enabling fast running across the heathery plateau. The best bits of this run include climbing out of the trees to look across to Millstone and opening up to full speed on the final forest descent. Care is needed on the rocky scrambles to the summits of Oxen Craig and Mither Tap as well as the initial stages of the descent off Mither Tap.

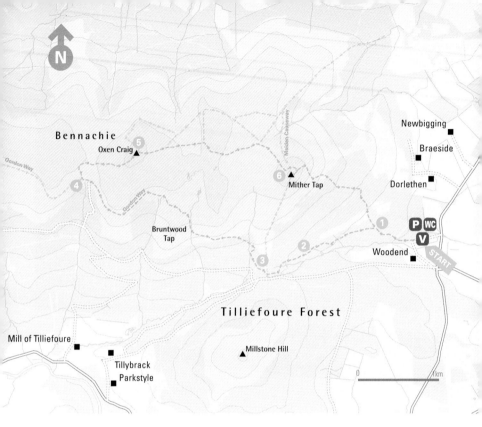

🏃 START Starting at the signpost to the left of the visitor centre follow the wide path along the edge of the woods. Continue straight ahead following the Gordon Way through two junctions and turn uphill to reach a junction near a bench. ① Head left along the Gordon Way and continue through several junctions to a forest road. ② Cross the road and continue on the Gordon Way for another 600m to reach a T-junction. ③ Turn right then almost immediately take a left-hand fork and begin to climb uphill. Continue until this track is joined by a track coming up from the valley. ④ About 100m further on leave the Gordon Way by turning right onto an unsigned narrow path through the heather. After about 250m turn right at a T-junction to head towards Oxen Craig. ⑤ Scramble over rocks to the summit and head downhill onto a good path. Keep right, following signed paths across the moorland to a path fork at rocky steps just below Mither Tap. ⑥ Take the left-hand path around the side of the hill to a signpost then up rocky steps to the summit. Return to the signpost and head down steep rocky steps signed to Bennachie Visitor Centre. After reaching the trees the running is excellent all the way back to the Visitor Centre.

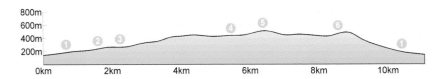

Trip Planning

Up-to-date trail information including closures for forestry operations can be obtained from the Forestry Commission. *www.forestry.gov.uk* 🚗 Bennachie is near Inverurie, about 25 miles north-west of Aberdeen. Turn off the A96 two miles north of Inverurie towards Chapel of Garioch. At Chapel of Garioch turn left, signposted to the Bennachie Centre, and continue for another two miles. **WC** Bennachie Visitor Centre (10:30am to 5pm in summer, reduced hours in winter, closed Mondays) 🚌 The Grant Arms in Monymusk is five miles south of the Visitor Centre and frequented by the Cosmic Hillbashers following club outings to Millstone and Bennachie.

Other Routes

Bennachie is accessible from four different car parks. All these access points give good runs and different perspectives on the hill. The Back o' Bennachie (660 245), Donview (673189), and Rowantree (691 243) car parks have seasonal toilets. Millstone Hill is separate to the main bulk of Bennachie and is accessible from the Donview car park.

Mither Tap

Bennachie

Bennachie plateau

Shorter runs with much less height gain can be constructed using the waymarked woodland trails at the foot of Bennachie.

Events

An annual hill race around and over Bennachie is organised by Garioch Roadrunners. The senior race is about 12.8km with 550m ascent (8.3 miles, 1150ft) and there is also a shorter race for juniors. *www.gariochroadrunners.com*

Mons Graupius?

Bennachie is one possible location of the legendary battle of Mons Graupius between the Romans and northern Britons. A band of well trained Roman legionnaires and auxiliaries dealt a mortal blow to British resistance. The 30,000 men of disparate tribes who came together to face the common Roman enemy fled or were killed. The Roman biographer Tacitus had excellent spies or perhaps simply a fertile imagination. His account of the speech given by the British leader on the eve of the battle is surprisingly detailed and eloquent. Calgacus is said to have roused his clansmen with this stirring denouncement of the Romans. "To robbery, slaughter, plunder, they give the lying name of empire; they make a desert and call it peace."

Deeside

47 Glen Tanar

Distance	16km (10 miles)	**Ascent**	400m (1300ft)
Map	OS Landranger 44, OS Explorer 395		
Navigation ●●●	Head upriver, climb uphill onto heather moorland then return by the river		
Terrain ●●●	Forest tracks, estate roads and earth paths		
Wet Feet ●●●	Occasional muddy puddles		
Start/Finish	Braeloine Visitor Centre AB34 5EU NO 480 965		

A classic trail through pine forest and over heathery hills

For most people the term 'trail running' conjures up a mental picture of consistent, well-made paths weaving through attractive woodland. Scottish trails can be a far cry from that appealing image. Except in Deeside. Glen Tanar and other estates along the Dee are home to miles and miles of well-kept tracks running through ancient Scots pine woodland. Classic trail running at its very best. This route has been chosen from a wealth of possibilities which all combine majestic pine trees, tumbling waterfalls and heathery hillsides with fine views across Deeside. This particular route circles the hill known as Baudy Meg: a name which positively invites wild speculation upon its origin. There ought to be an associated tall tale but somewhat disappointingly it appears to derive from an Anglicisation of the Gaelic for "hill of hares".

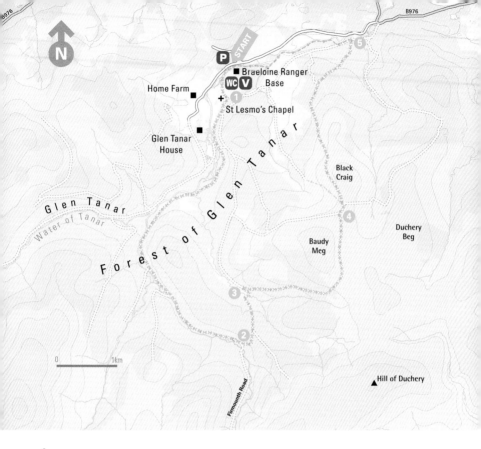

🏃 START Cross the river to the Ranger Base and toilets then follow a wide gravel track up-river to a T-junction just after St Lesmo's Chapel. ① Turn right and within 200m go right again onto a wide gravel estate road heading towards the river. Follow this riverside track upstream for 5.5km passing two bridges to reach a fork. ② Head left and uphill away from the river on a stony track. After about 400m keep left at a junction and continue for 800m to reach a junction shortly after a pond and stream. ③ Turn sharp right onto a track which leads uphill out of the forest and over heather moorland. This track goes over the shoulder of Baudy Meg to a T-junction. ④ Follow the main track right for 100m then turn left onto a track which traverses the open hillside of Black Craig. Drop down into forestry and continue on the track to reach the estate road parallel with the river. ⑤ Turn left onto the estate for 300m then right at a signpost onto a narrow gravel path. This path runs through woodland next to the river for nearly 2km to return to the bridge at Braeloine.

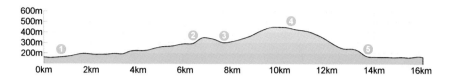

Trip Planning

This route follows tracks and paths on the Glen Tanar Estate. Access to the moors may be restricted during the shooting and stalking seasons. *www.glentanar.co.uk* 🚗 Turn off the B976 South Deeside Road at Bridge o' Ess Tower onto a minor road signed for Glen Tanar Estate and Riding Centre. Park at the pay and display Braeloine car park which is on the right 1.6 miles from Bridge o' Ess. 🚻 Next to the Ranger Office and Visitor Centre on the opposite side of the river to the car park. 🍽 Aboyne has pubs and cafés *www.theboatinnaboyne.co.uk* *www.blackfacedsheep.co.uk* Alternatively, follow the South Deeside road B976 for 8 miles towards Banchory to Finzean Estate's Farm Shop and Tearoom. *www.finzean.com* 🏠 Holiday cottages on the Glen Tanar Estate can be self-catering or the Glen Tanar housekeeper can provide oven ready dinners and freshly baked bread. *www.glentanar.co.uk*

Other Routes

All left-hand turns on the described route lead back towards Braeloine and shorten the circuit. An 8km (5 miles) riverside run through the pine woods follows the described route for just over 3.5km to a stone bridge at (466 937). Cross the river and continue straight ahead to cross a second bridge. Turn right and head downstream to recross the Water of Tanar at Knockie Bridge (477 953) and return to Braeloine.

A much longer circuit heads south and climbs into the hills by way of old droving roads. About 400m after ② turn right onto the Firmounth Road. This ancient route crosses the Mounth to Tarfside in Glen Esk. Follow the Firmounth Road to its junction with the Fungle Road at (499 853). Head north on the Fungle Road past Birse Castle to reach The Guard (519 955) and turn left to return to Braeloine. Shortcuts are possible by crossing untracked ground or faint paths to reach tracks on Hill of Duchery (504 914) or Gannoch (496 880).

Running Guiding

This route is a favourite of Running The Highlands who organise running holidays, running tours and training weekends in the Eastern Cairngorms and Royal Deeside. Their experienced guides

Glen Tanar

Forest of Glen Tanar

know the trails in this area inside out and pick the best routes for runners of all abilities and interests. *www.runningthehighlands.com*

The Mounth Roads

The long range of hills between Deeside and the Angus Glens is known as the Mounth, which simply means "mountains". The Mounth Roads are old droving routes which cross these bleak, rounded hills. Most of these ancient ways can still be followed although some sections are barely visible while others have been covered in tarmac. The Scotways guide to Scottish Hill Tracks lists and describes the condition of each of the Mounth Roads. Route descriptions and more information on these historic routes can be found on the Scotways Heritage Paths website. *www.scotways.com www.heritagepaths.co.uk*

Quoich Water and River Dee

48 Linn of Quoich & the Fairy Glen

Distance	22km (14 miles)	Ascent	350m (1200ft)
Map	OS Landranger 44, OS Explorer 404		
Navigation ●●●	Track to ford, indistinct path following Water of Quoich then obvious paths and tracks		
Terrain ●●●	Wide tracks, gravel paths, rough woodland path		
Wet Feet ●●●	Waded river crossing		
Start/Finish	Allanaquoich AB35 5YJ NO 116 910		

Quoich Water leads to the foot of remote hills and a Fairy Glen

One September day in 1715, cupped hands scooped good French brandy out of the rock pool at Linn of Quoich instead of the usual peat-stained water. The liquor was poured into a pothole by the Earl of Mar and drunk to toast the Jacobite cause. Quoich or quaich is the Gaelic for cup. In English, the pothole is known as The Punchbowl. Although the pool no longer holds brandy a drink is unlikely to disappoint after this long run. The route ventures into truly remote terrain and peeps into the long bleak glen dividing the massifs of Beinn a' Bhuird and Ben Avon. Gleann an t-Slugain "The Gullet", known as the Fairy Glen, is a scenic anomaly on the second half of the route: a real gem with a couple of lovely wild camping spots. It also hides a secret howff to be found by the knowledgeable, lucky or stubbornly persistent.

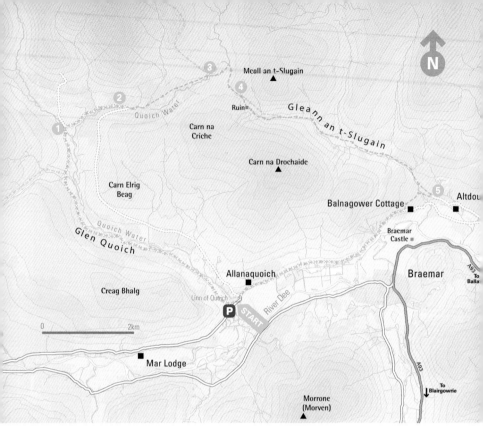

🏃 START The track starts between the parking lay-by and the river then doubles back above the lay-by. Follow this track for over 6km to a ford. ① (080 947) Wade the river then turn right onto a rough track heading east along Quoich Water to another ford. ② Do not follow the track across the river. Instead, continue on a good path, which soon ends. Multiple narrow paths, faint in places, then lead through heathery undergrowth. The general trend is a rising traverse away from the river. The paths converge on steeper ground as the glen narrows. A few hundred metres after leaving the trees and passing a ruin the route meets the obvious Beinn a' Bhuird path. ③ (111 958) Cross the river by stepping stones, climb uphill, then turn south on a good path. After 500m this path forks. ④ (117 955) Take the right-hand stony path which leads down into Gleann an t-Slugain past the ruin of Slugain Lodge. Rejoin the track at the south end of the glen and continue downhill for 3km to forestry then a further 1km to a junction. ⑤ (160 933) Turn sharp right, signposted to Linn of Quoich. Keep left soon after crossing the river to follow a track which runs parallel with the River Dee. It passes through tall trees then becomes more open with views across to Braemar. After passing several estate cottages the track reaches Allanaquoich.

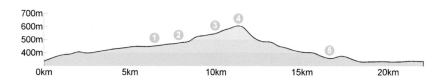

Trip Planning

After heavy rain or snowmelt the river crossings may be impassable. Access may be restricted during the stalking and shooting seasons. Invercauld Estate participates in the Hillphones and Heading for the Hills schemes. 🚗 Follow the road west of Braemar past Linn of Dee to the end of the public road at Allanaquoich. Park in a lay-by on the left before crossing the river or near an information board on the far side of the bridge. 🚻 Linn of Dee car park ☕ The Taste coffee shop is on the right soon after entering Braemar when returning from Linn of Dee. *www.taste-braemar.co.uk* There are several other cafés and hotel bars in the village. 🏠 Braemar has a range of accommodation including Invercauld Caravan Club Site, a youth hostel and several hotels.
www.syha.org.uk www.caravanclub.co.uk

Other Routes

A shorter circuit turns left off the described route just over 1km before the ford. Follow a clear path through narrow Clais Fhearnaig, turn left onto the Derry Lodge track and return by the road. This is a good alternative if the river proves to be un-crossable.
Several circular trails are waymarked from Braemar.

Linn of Quoich & the Fairy Glen

Wet feet. Who cares?

The Ballochbuie Forest is an excellent place to explore by trail running. From Invercauld Estate's Keiloch car park (188 912) cross the road and Invercauld Bridge over the Dee to access miles of paths and tracks. The Garbh Allt Falls are worth visiting. So are excellently runnable, though perennially wet, paths above the forest. This is also the most awe-inspiring approach to Lochnagar. The Allanaquoich car park, Linn of Dee car park (064 898) or Keiloch car park are all suitable starting points for long, sometimes epic, runs through the glens and over East Highland hills.

The Cairngorms and Moray

The River Spey flows through the heart of Moray, sweeping up waters from the Cairngorms on its journey to the sea. Runs range from challenging paths over remote mountain passes to sandy beaches on the Moray Firth. Running through Scotland's most ancient woodland – the Caledonian Pine Forest – is not to be missed.

Lairig Ghru (Route 54)

Culbin Forest (Route

Loch an Eilein

49 Loch an Eilein

Distance	5km (3 miles)	Ascent	50m (150ft)
Map	OS Landranger 36, OS Explorer 403, Rothiemurchus Explorer Map		
Navigation •••	Signposted loch circuit		
Terrain •••	Wide woodland paths		
Wet Feet •••	Occasional, avoidable puddles		
Start/Finish	Loch an Eilein PH22 1QT NH 897 083		

Easy-peasy lochside trail through ancient Caledonian forest

Loch an Eilein, Loch of the Island, is one of Scotland's most loved beauty spots. The best times to run here are early in the morning or as the sun sets. At these hours the lochside trail is peaceful and the reflected sky colours at their most beautiful. Nestled in ancient Scots pine woodland and overlooked by the Cairngorm Mountains it is hard to imagine a more perfect setting for a trail run. The romantic Highland landscape is completed by the ruined castle standing on the island for which the loch is named. Loch an Eilein is part of the Rothiemurchus Estate owned by the Grant family. The entire estate is criss-crossed with trails ideal for running. These paths extend past the estate's boundaries up into the mountains and through Glenmore into Nethy Forest.

START Head past the Visitor Centre and toilets to the loch shore. Cross the stream flowing out of the loch then turn right. Follow this wide path clockwise around the loch, keeping right at all junctions, to return to the start.

Trip Planning

Loch an Eilein is on the Rothiemurchus Estate. *www.rothiemurchus.net* 🚌 Loch an Eilein, B790, 1.7km from start) 🚗 Turn off the ski road at Inverdruie onto the B970 towards Insh and Feshiebridge. After a mile take a left turn signposted to Loch an Eilein. The car park and Visitor Centre is at the end of the road. The relatively steep parking charge goes towards maintenance of the Rothiemurchus Estate. 🚻 Loch an Eilein Visitor Centre 🍴 Ord Ban Restaurant Café at Inverdruie. A couple of miles south on the B970 The Potting Shed Tearoom at Inshriach Nursery has a reputation for impressive cakes. (March to October. Closed Wednesdays.) ⌂ The Rothie-murchus Estate Camp and Caravan Site at Coylumbridge has scenic pitches under tall pine trees

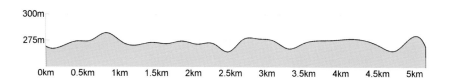

at the start of the Lairig Ghru path. Dogs are allowed around the caravans but not in the tent areas. *www.rothiemurchus.net* There is a SYHA Hostel in Glenmore and plenty of hotels, B&Bs and self-catering accommodation in the area. *www.syha.org.uk www.visitcairngorms.com* Dogs should be kept under close control, preferably on a lead, especially between April and June when ground nesting birds are raising chicks.

Other Routes

For a longer road and trail run start at the long stay Woodland (free) car park at Inverdruie (901 110). Follow the Rothiemurchus Path from (901 108) past Lochan Mor to Milton Cottage then Loch an Eilein. Return by turning off at (897 086) onto a stony track to Blackpark.

Superb paths and tracks form an extensive network throughout the Rothiemurchus Estate and the wider area. They are almost without exception perfect for trail running. Maps of the path network are available at various points on the Estate including the Loch an Eilein Visitor Centre. Extend the route by circling Loch Gamhna or heading west to 'Piccadilly' junction (916 079) and visiting Glen Einich, Loch Morlich or the Lairig Ghru.

Events

This is a justifiably popular area for events. Most are held on scenic roads or a combination of roads and forest tracks. They include the Cairngorm Charmer, Cairngorm Challenge, Aviemore Half Marathon and Abernethy 10-Mile Road Race. *www.cairngormrunners.org*

Other Activities

Rothiemurchus and Glenmore's paths and tracks are great for non-technical mountain biking as well as trail running. Mountain bikers are discouraged from cycling round Loch an Eilein. Bikes can be hired from Bothy Bikes at Inverdruie. *www.bothybikes.co.uk*

In winter the Cairngorms become a playground for lift-based and back country skiers. *www.cairngormmountain.co.uk* Back country ski mountaineering equipment can be hired from Mountain Spirit in Aviemore. *www.mountainspirit.co.uk*

Loch an Eilein

The ruined island stronghold
on Loch an Eilein

Glenmore Lodge is Scotland's National Outdoor Training Centre and runs courses in everything from open boating to winter mountaineering. Many independent mountain instructors and guides also operate in and around the Cairngorms. *www.glenmorelodge.org.uk www.mlta.co.uk www.ami.org.uk www.bmg.org.uk*

The castle on the island

The ruined castle was once the stronghold of the Red Comyns and later re-built by Alexander Stewart, Earl of Buchan, known as the Wolf of Badenoch. Folklore tells of a zigzag underwater causeway whose secret was only ever known by three living clansmen. Other, more prosaic, sources speak of the causeway being submerged when the water level of the loch was raised in the 18th century. Over the years the castle has been a home and a prison, a refuge for Grants and besieged by MacDonalds. Now in ruins, the castle is one of the most romantic places to get married in all of Scotland.

Link trail from Kingussie

50 The Wildcat Trail, Newtonmore

Distance	10km (6 miles)	**Ascent**	100m (350ft)
Map	OS Landranger 35, OS Explorer 402, Wildcat Trail Map		
Navigation •••	Follow distinctive black cat waymarkers		
Terrain •••	Earth and grass paths, pavements, quiet road, many gates and stiles.		
Wet Feet •••	Occasional puddles and slippery earth path		
Start/Finish	Near Highland Folk Museum PH20 1AY NN 724 995		

Follow the cat along the Spey and over the moors

Clan Chattan is a confederation of Scottish families including Macintoshes, Macphersons and Farquharsons. Their coat of arms features a wildcat and the motto 'touch not the cat bot [without] a glove'. Excellent advice, but of little practical use as every single one of Scotland's small wildcat population is an expert at skulking. They are rarely seen far less handled. Some are known to live near Newtonmore so there is a remote chance of spotting one on this run. Even if the real thing proves elusive there are plenty of opportunities to spot cats of many (freakish) colours throughout the village. The orbital route is well waymarked through a range of landscapes from meandering riverbank to open moorland. The traverse above the River Calder and the view towards Glen Banchor are highlights.

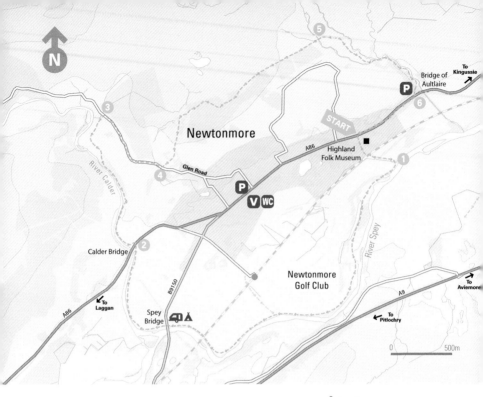

The route follows distinctive black cat waymarkers throughout. 🏃 START Turn down a lane signed to the River Spey between a tall white house and a bungalow on the north edge of Newtonmore. Go straight ahead between Highland Folk Museum buildings to cross the railway then continue onto a sometimes overgrown path leading through woodland to the river. ① Continue along the riverbank for 4km crossing several stiles and going under the railway and the Spey Bridge to reach the A86. ② Cross the road and turn left through a gate. After passing the cemetery a short uphill leads to a scenic path above the River Calder. Continue through a gate and follow the grassy track uphill to the road. ③ Follow the single track road back towards Newtonmore. (The Wildcat Trail takes a short, not particularly worthwhile, detour through the trees on the left.) ④ At the first houses turn left onto a rough track signed to Upper Knock. Continue onto a grassy track through stunted birch woodland. Running along the woodland's edge is impeded by an over-abundance of kissing gates. Just left of the fence is open moorland and a good view of the Monadhliath. 2km after leaving the road the path crosses a track and footbridge. ⑤ After crossing the bridge, join a track briefly then head right across grass to a gate. Drop down to the burn through more gates then follow it down to the road. ⑥ Return to the start of the route and Newtonmore by the tarmac cycle path on the opposite side of the road.

The Wildcat Trail, Newtonmore

Trip Planning

Maps and further information about the trail can be found at The Wildcat Centre on Newtonmore's Main Street. *http://sites.google.com/site/thewildcattrailnewtonmore* 🚂 Newtonmore (300m on a signed footpath through fields to river). 🚐 Waltzing Waters, Newtonmore. 🚌 Newtonmore is on the A86 just west of the A9. Park in a lay-by on the west side of the A86 just north of the 30mph zone at ⑥. Alternatively, there is a free public car park in the village centre just off Glen Road. 🚻 Near the Wildcat Centre. 🍺 The Glen Hotel at the fork of the Perth and Laggan roads. Arrive early as it gets packed most Friday and Saturday nights. *www.theglenhotel.co.uk* Or try the Letterbox Restaurant *www.letterboxrestaurant.co.uk* or The Pantry Tearoom. 🏠 Creag Meagaidh B&B in the centre of Newtonmore is owned by keen runners Geoff and Alison. *www.creag-meagaidh.co.uk* 🐕 Sheep graze in adjoining fields. Some of the stiles are not dog friendly.

Other Routes

Nearby Kingussie has a network of waymarked paths which include the summit of Creag Bheag and a link to the Wildcat Trail. Maps are displayed at Kingussie's public car park (755 007).
Above Newtonmore a hill track circuit goes up Carn an Fhreiceadain and over Beinn Bhreac. Another hill track known as the Burma Road climbs up into the Monadhliath from Lynwilg near Aviemore (874 110). The best Burma Road route is a long one way to Carrbridge via Sluggan and General Wade's military road.

Events

The Newtonmore 10 Mile Road Race is held in March. A Pasta Party on Friday night begins a weekend of running and ceilidh dancing culminating in a Hangover Mile on Sunday morning. *www.newtonmore.com*

Other Activities

Newtonmore is a popular place to start an open boat paddling expedition down the River Spey. Northern Xposure are one of many providers who organise expeditions down the Spey. *www.woolly-mammoth.co.uk*

The Wildcat Trail, Newtonmore

WildcatTrail sign

Ten miles south-west of Newtonmore on the A86 are the Laggan Wolftrax purpose-built mountain bike trails. *www.forestry.gov.uk/wolftrax* Bikes can hired on-site at BaseCamp MountainBikes. *www.basecampmtb.com*

The Scottish Wildcat

Wildcats are Britain's largest remaining land-based predator. As recently as the 1950s these animals were thought to be man-killers and hunted down. Bears, wolves and lynx were all hunted into extinction hundreds of years ago. Wildcats are larger and more muscular than domestic cats with a thick coat and distinctively bushy tail. Less than four hundred are thought to remain in the wild and they are under threat from habitat change and interbreeding with domestic cats. Their admirers rate the cats' intelligence, resourcefulness and fearlessness. *www.scottishwildcats.co.uk*

Ben Rinnes from Carn Daimh summit

51 Carn Daimh, Glenlivet

Distance	10km (6.5 miles)	Ascent	350m (1200ft)
Map	OS Landranger 36, OS Explorer 404		
Navigation •••	Waymarked as Walk 5: the Carn Daimh Circuit		
Terrain •••	Farm track, rough grass and hill paths, particularly rough after Tomnavoulin turn-off		
Wet Feet •••	Muddy junction in Ellick Wood and boggy after Tomnavoulin turn-off		
Start/Finish	Clash Wood, Tomnavoulin AB37 9JE NJ 208 265		

Follow smuggler's footsteps on this Whisky Country hill circuit

One run over these rough hills clearly illustrates why crofters found illicit whisky distilling to be more lucrative than farming. War was waged here over many generations between folk whose livelihood depended on the 'sma stills' and the hated excise men or 'gaugers'. Robbie Macpherson was a legendary Glenrinnes distiller who smuggled liquor to ports on the Moray coast. His seemingly innocent pony convoys concealed vast quantities of illegal spirits buried in sacks of wool or grain. This route follows the least rough and muddy hill paths in the area. It gives the merest hint of the challenge facing 18th-century smugglers and gaugers as they chased each other round these hills.

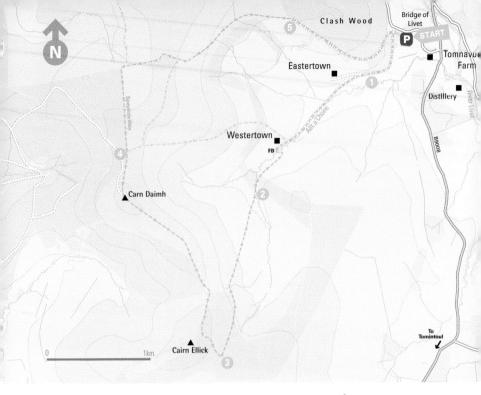

This route follows Glenlivet Estate's waymarked Carn Daimh Circuit. 🏃 **START** Head uphill on the forest road for a short distance then turn left onto a waymarked woodland path. This runs along the edge of woodland to stiles and a track junction. **1** Continue towards the hills on the lower of the two farm tracks. After passing Westertown Farm the track crosses a stream and goes round a hairpin bend. Continue for another 500m past forestry and over a second stream. **2** Where the track turns left continue uphill on a rough path between fences. Go through a gate and onto a track through the woods which becomes increasingly muddy as it nears a junction. **3** Turn right onto the Speyside Way and follow this out of the woods and over Carn Daimh to a signed junction. On a clear day the summit has a fantastic 360° panorama with Ben Rinnes to the north and the Cairngorms Mountains to the south. **4** The waymarked route continues straight on over very rough tussocky ground to a fence, turns right along the fence and then heads left above the forest as the trail descends the hill. (The worst tussocks can be avoided by following the Robbie Macpherson trail for a short distance then heading left on faint paths to contour along the top of the slope and rejoin the Carn Daimh Circuit.) Continue traversing the hillside on grassy sheep paths above the trees then cross to the far wood. **5** Follow the forest road downhill back to the start.

Carn Daimh, Glenlivet

Trip Planning

The route is waymarked by the Glenlivet Estate which is part of the Crown Estate. *www.glenlivetestate.co.uk* 🚌 Post Office, Tomnavoulin (750m from start) 🚗 Turn off the B9008 just north of Tomnavoulin village at a small signpost to the Clash Wood car park. The car park is on the left after about 500m. 🚾 Tomintoul village centre and at the Glenlivet Estate Office during office hours. 🏪 Tomnavoulin has a small post office and shop. Tomintoul options include The Old Fire Station Tearoom, The Clock House restaurant and the Glen Avon Hotel. 🏠 Wild Farm Cottage is a self-catering cottage at the foot of Carn Daimh with a hot tub, sauna and plunge pool. Its owners, Tilly and Alan Smith, are both keen runners. The Wild Farm is home to part of the Cairngorm Reindeer Herd. *www.wildfarmcottages.co.uk*

Other Routes

Shorten the route by turning towards Tomnavoulin at ④ and joining the Robbie Macpherson Smuggler's Trail. Descend on a good path, go through a firebreak then cross fields to the left of the farmhouse to rejoin the outward route.

A longer road and hill path circuit follows the road from Clash Wood to Blairfindy then returns over the hills on the waymarked Speyside Way Spur.

The Glenlivet Estate has waymarked a range of routes for walkers and mountain bikers. The walking routes tend to have rough and muddy sections. Leaflets and information can be obtained from the Estate Office in Tomintoul.

Events

The Glenlivet 10k is a road race with proceeds going to the charity Chest Heart and Stroke Scotland. *www.theglenlivet10k.com*

Other Activities

At the time of writing The Glenlivet Estate had started to construct a mountain bike centre and trails at Glenconglass on the west side of Carn Daimh.

Carn Daimh, Glenlivet

Speyside Way and
Glenlivet Trail markers

Forested sand dunes

52 Culbin

Distance	12km (8 miles)	Ascent	50m (200ft)
Map	OS Landranger 27, OS Explorer 422		
Navigation •••	Head east ticking off numbered junctions then follow the beach west to Buckie Loch		
Terrain •••	Forest tracks, sandy beach		
Mud •••	Good grip even in wet weather		
Start/Finish	Wellhill NH 997 614		

Forested sand dunes, a colourful harbour and endless beach

Culbin is quite an incredible place. Its sand dunes are the largest of their type in all of Europe. But this was not always the case. Until the 17th century Culbin was an estate of fruitful orchards and farmland. Violent storms blew in ever-increasing volumes of sand and the farms were finally abandoned in 1694. Culbin's dunes continued to expand and the inhospitable, shifting, un-navigable sands became notorious. In the 19th century conifers were planted to stabilise the dunes. Today, Culbin's forest tracks are peaceful places to run, walk or cycle. The sandy forest floor supports an unusual and attractive carpet of multi-coloured lichens. A highlight of the route is emerging from beneath shady trees to a view of colourful harbour cottages across Findhorn Bay.

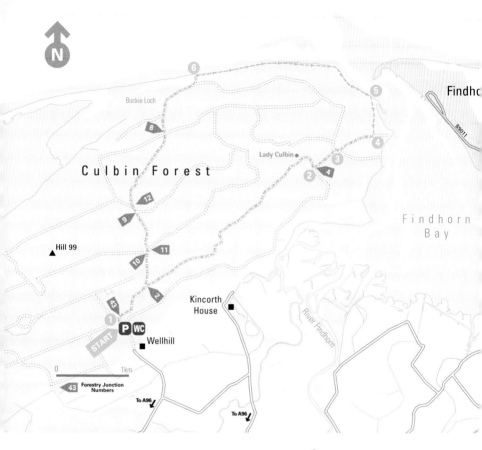

Most of the track junctions are marked by numbered posts. 🏃 **START** Head past the barrier into the forest to reach Junction 43. **①** Turn right and continue straight on through Junction 2 to arrive at Lady Culbin's buried trees after about 2km. Soon after passing these trees the track curves round to the right to reach Junction 4. **②** Turn left and follow the track for about 250m to an unmarked fork. Take the right-hand fork which quickly leads to another junction. **③** Head right and almost immediately turn off left onto a track signed for Findhorn Bay. Follow this for 400m to an unmarked track on the left. **④** Turn left and follow the track to the edge of the forest and a viewpoint overlooking Findhorn Bay. **⑤** Follow the beach for nearly 2km and turn inland at the end of the forest. This area of dunes and salt marsh is known as Buckie Loch. **⑥** Follow a grassy track inland through Buckie Loch (an area of grassland which was a seasonal loch over 100 years ago). Turn right onto a forest track and follow it for nearly 2km heading inland through several crossroads to return to Junction 2. Veer right to return to Junction 43 then left back to the car park at Wellhill.

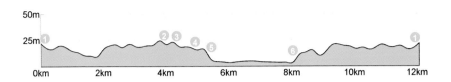

Trip Planning

All of the key track junctions at Culbin are numbered. The map leaflet available at the car park is an indispensable aid to navigation. *www.forestry.gov.uk/culbin* 🚐 Culbin Forest is ten miles east of Nairn by road and a couple of miles north-west of Forres. The Wellhill car park is signed from the A96. 🚻 Wellhill 🍴 🏠 Nairn for conventional options or the Findhorn Foundation for an alternative way of life. *www.findhorn.org* 🚲 Culbin's wide forest tracks are recommended for family friendly cycling and buggy walks or runs.

Other Routes

Culbin's numbered junctions and extensive network of forest tracks make a wide range of runs possible. The only waymarked trail is 5.5km (3.5 miles) long and goes to a viewpoint on top of Culbin's highest dune (99ft).

The Moray Coast Trail runs along the firth and can be linked into many circular runs. An excellent 6.5km (4 miles) run between Cullen and Portknockie combines an old railway viaduct with clifftop paths and beach. It passes impressive rock arches – the Bow Fiddle Rock and the Whale's Moo – and seeing dolphins is a high possibility.

Before reaching the sea the River Findhorn flows through a dramatic gorge and magnificent old trees of the Darnaway Forest. Quiet woodland paths and tracks can be explored from the Dunearn Burn car park on the west side of the gorge or from more popular Sluie on the east.

Events

The Moray Forest Runs are a popular series of four/five mile runs. The series visits Monaughty, Quarrelwood and Roseisle Forests as well as Culbin. *www.forresharriers.org.uk*

www.moravianorienteering.org   *www.walkjogrunmoray.org.uk*

Other Activities

Culbin's intricate dune landscape and exceptionally runnable forest floor make Culbin a world class orienteering venue for local, national and world events. *www.moravianorienteering.org*

Wet feet
Photo: Dougal Ranford

Moray Cetaceans

Dolphins are regularly spotted in the Moray Firth. It is home to the most northerly population of bottlenose dolphins in the world. Around two hundred live here and lots of other species are frequently spotted including common dolphins, Risso's dolphins, harbour porpoises and minke whales. If no dolphins interrupt the run consider heading to the Black Isle on the far side of the firth. Chanonry Point between Fortrose and Rosemarkie is said to be the best on-land dolphin spotting location in the world. Learn more at the World Dolphin Conservation Society Centre in Spey Bay. *www.wdcs.org*

River Spey at Aberlour

53 Speyside Way Circuit

Distance	18km (11 miles)	Ascent	275m (900ft)
Map	OS Landranger 28, OS Explorer 424		
Navigation •••	Follow the Spey and the Fiddich then return over the hill		
Terrain •••	Gravel path, grassy track, forest road, quiet tarmac road		
Wet Feet •••	A boggy firebreak lets down an otherwise dry route		
Start/Finish	Victoria Bridge (Penny Bridge), Alice Littler Park AB38 9NY NJ 262 428		

A runners tour of Speyside Malts

Fifteen kilometres of this route is on excellent off-road tracks and paths. The Speyside Way is by definition linear and presents limited opportunities for circular trail runs. So the last couple of kilometres of this route head downhill on quiet tarmac roads. But only the most pedantic purist will object as the previous fifteen kilometres are on excellent disused railway tracks and an easy to follow hill path. The train journey along the Spey and the Fiddich would have been a memorable experience. With sleepers and rails long gone, these level tracks now provide easy running in beautiful surroundings. The last leg of the route goes over The Gownie. Pause on the ascent to admire the panoramic view back over Dufftown and lose count of the numerous pagoda-shaped distillery roofs. The fast descent towards Aberlour is sure to raise a grin.

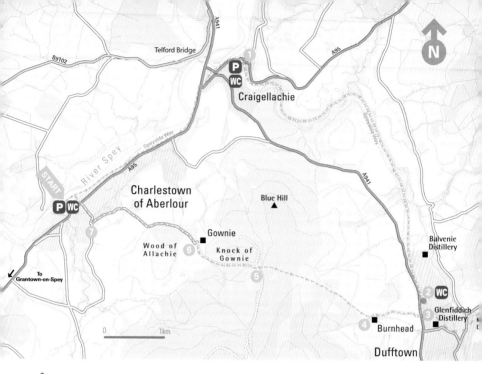

🏃 START Head downstream on the riverside path and after passing the old railway station veer right at a Speyside Way marker onto the old railway track. Continue along this for 4km to reach the Fiddich car park and toilets at Craigellachie. ① Continue on the railway path for another 5km beside the Fiddich towards Dufftown. (This footpath has been affected by landslips but at the time of writing these were easy to step around.) As it nears Dufftown the path crosses the road into Balvenie Distillery and continues through a gate to reach Dufftown Station. ② Go along the platform and turn right after the station building following Isla Way signs to Dufftown. Continue towards Dufftown on the pavement next to the A941 for about 300m to reach the 30mph speed limit signs. ③ Cross the A941 and go up a stony track to the right of distillery buildings. Keep right and follow this track straight uphill for 800m past a building to a crossroad with a grassy track. ④ Turn right and climb through young woodland to a gate at the corner of plantation forest. Continue on a clear, though sometimes muddy, path through gorse, trees and heather moorland. After climbing over a stile the route goes down 250m of wet and muddy firebreak then continues downhill on track to reach a forest road junction. ⑤ Continue downhill with smooth and easy to run forest road underfoot. After less than 1km there are good views left to Ben Rinnes. The track then goes through a gate to end at a tarmac road. ⑥ Head left and downhill for 2km to a T-junction. ⑦ Turn right to continue downhill. Cross the High Street (A95) and continue straight ahead past the church and old station to return to the Spey.

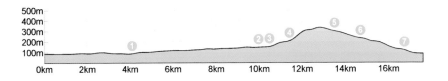

Trip Planning

🚌 Aberlour Square 🚗 Turn off the A95 at Aberlour Square towards the Speyside Way Visitor Centre and Alice Littler Park. Follow the road left to a large car park next to the river. 🚾 Speyside Way Visitor Centre (Old Aberlour Railway Station), Fiddich car park, Dufftown Railway Station. 🍴 Aberlour has several cafés, a good deli and the original Walkers Shortbread bakery. 🏠 The Mash Tun on Aberlour Square offers beer, bar meals and accommodation. Naturally, it also boasts an extensive whisky selection. *www.mashtun-aberlour.com*

Other Routes

A level 8km (5 miles) run goes along the Speyside Way from Aberlour to Craigellachie and back. By turning off the railway track towards the Spey on the eastern side of both the A95 tunnels it is possible to loop round past the Telford Bridge to rejoin the outward path.

Speyside Way

Speyside Way Circuit

Keith &
Dufftown
Heritage
Railway

Events

The most northerly race in the Scottish Ultra-Marathon Series follows the Speyside Way for 36.5 miles from Ballindalloch to Buckie. Good tracks, relative flatness and the fact that it is one of the shortest of the SUMS series all contribute to its popularity. *www.sumschampionship.org*

Other Activities

A distillery tour is practically obligatory for visitors to Speyside. Aberlour Distillery offers tours as do several of the distilleries in Glen Fiddich.

The Spey and the nearby Findhorn are both popular rivers for rafting. Depending on taste this can vary from a leisurely float downstream to a white-knuckle ride with thrills and spills.

Whisky Facts

The word whisky derives from the Gaelic uisge beatha (oosh-keh bay-aa) meaning "water of life".

The toast slàinte (slaan-ch) "health" or slàinte mhath (slaan-ch vaa) "good health" should be responded to with do dheagh slàinte (dough yo hlaan-ch) "your good health".

A wee dram – the size of this whisky measure depends on the host's generosity and their liking for the recipient

The Angel's Share – the portion of whisky that evaporates from the cask as it matures.

The southernmost distillery in Scotland is Bladnoch in Galloway. The most northerly is Highland Park on the Orkney Mainland, (Scapa misses out on this title by a mere half mile).

Lairig Ghru

54 Lairig Ghru & Lairig an Laoigh

Distance	48km (30 miles)	Ascent	1300m (4200ft)
Map	OS Landranger 36, OS Explorer 403, Harvey Cairngorms & Lochnagar		
Navigation •••	Clear paths over Bynack More and through the glens. Map and compass required		
Terrain •••	Forest tracks, smooth, rough and rocky paths. Several hundred metres of boulder field		
Wet Feet •••	Boggy over Bynack More. Stepping stones at Fords of Avon may not be crossable.		
Start/Finish	Forestry Commission Allt Mor car park, Glenmore PH22 1RB NH 976 097		

A classic and almost entirely runnable Cairngorms circuit

The geography of the Cairngorms lends itself to epic adventures. Mere hill walking does not do the place justice and quite frankly, long walk-ins and rounded slopes make these hills fairly dull to walk up one at a time. The passes linking Rothiemurchus with Deeside are clearly ripe for linking into long circumnavigations. This route is far more runnable than can reasonably be expected given its location. All the ascents are gradual enough to be run with relative ease. The top of the Lairig Ghru is a boulder field but this does not detract from the overall quality of the run. An even less runnable obstacle lies ahead, the boulder choked Chalamain Gap. The Gap is a bizarre geological feature but this is not the reason for the route choice. On its far side is the best running trail in the whole of the Cairngorms.

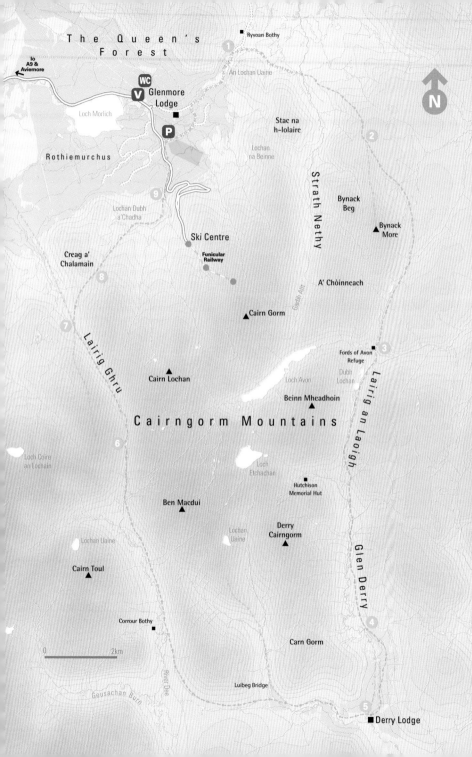

The Queen's Forest

Ryvoan Bothy

1

To A9 & Aviemore

An Lochan Uaine

WC
V Glenmore Lodge

P

Loch Morlich

Rothiemurchus

Stac na h-Iolaire

Lochan na Beinne

2

Strath Nethy

Bynack Beg

Bynack More

Lochan Dubh a'Chadha

9

Ski Centre

Funicular Railway

A' Chòinneach

Garbh Allt

Creag a' Chalamain

8

Cairn Gorm

7

Lairig Ghru

Cairn Lochan

Loch Avon

Fords of Avon Refuge

3

Dubh Lochan

Beinn Mheadhoin

Cairngorm Mountains

Lairig an Laoigh

Loch Coire an Lochain

6

Loch Etchachan

Hutchison Memorial Hut

Ben Macdui

Lochan Uaine

Derry Cairngorm

Cairn Toul

Glen Derry

Corrour Bothy

4

Carn Gorm

0   2km

River Dee

Luibeg Bridge

Geusachan Burn

5

Derry Lodge

N

This is a remote trail with no easy escape routes. Map, compass and the ability to use both competently are essential. The Fords of Avon may be uncrossable, particularly after heavy rain or snow melt. Snow lingers in the Cairngorms so this route may not be runnable until late spring or early summer. **START** Cross the Allt Mor and follow a forest road straight ahead to a T-junction, ignoring all side-tracks and crossing a shallow stream on the way. Turn right towards Ryvoan Pass and continue past An Lochan Uaine (The Green Lochan) to a fork. ① (003 110) Head right towards Braemar, cross the Nethy and head up onto the shoulder of Bynack More to a fork on level ground. ② (039 087) Take the left branch around the side of the hill and follow a boggier and rougher path down to Fords of Avon. ③ (042 031) Cross by stepping stones and continue on an obvious, rocky path over Lairig an Laoigh. The descent is more easily runnable and continues through Glen Derry to a fork at a footbridge. ④ (039 957) Take either fork to reach the bridge at Derry Lodge. The right bank path is slightly shorter and easy to run though it has a few more tree roots than the left. ⑤ (040 935) Cross boggy ground then continue along the river on a wide well-made gravel path. Descend into a fenced-off enclosure and cross Luibeg Burn by stepping stones or the footbridge further upstream. Climb uphill and contour around the side of Carn a' Mhaim then descend into the Lairig Ghru. The path is clear and runnable as it follows the east side of the glen then climbs to the Pools of Dee. ⑥ (973 006) Pick a way through 600m of rocks to the cairn at the top of the pass then descend on a rocky, tricky to run path to the boulder choked stream crossing where the Braeriach path joins from the left. ⑦ (959 036) Cross the stream and after 100m climb steeply up the bank to head north-east, taking either branch where the path forks, to reach the Chalamain Gap. ⑧ (964 051) Pick a way over the boulders to reach easy running on the trail past the reindeer enclosure. Enjoy the view of the Northern Corries, Meall a' Bhuachaille and the Ryvoan Pass where this run began. ⑨ (983 071) Drop down zigzags to cross the Allt Mor and head downstream on the easy to run Allt Mor Trail to cross the ski road and return through woods to the start.

Trip Planning

This route goes through the Cairngorms National Park. *www.cairngorms.co.uk* 🚌 Glenmore. 🚗 Follow the ski road through Glenmore and continue for a further half mile towards Cairn-

Lairig Ghru & Lairig an Laoigh

gorm. The Forestry Commission Allt Mor car park is on the left. **WC** Glenmore 🍴 Fish and chips at Glenmore SYHA Hostel, bar meals at Glenmore Lodge. Active Cafaidh, Café Mambo or the Mountain Café above Cairngorm Mountain Sports are all good options in Aviemore. 🏠 The hot tub and sauna at self-catering Reindeer Cottage come into their own after this route. It is owned by runners Tilly and Alan Smith who have a second self-catering cottage near Tomintoul. *www.wildfarmcottages.co.uk* Glenmore has an SYHA Hostel and a large camp and caravan site beside Loch Morlich. The Rothiemurchus Estate Camp and Caravan site at Coylumbridge is smaller and under tall Scots pines. *www.rothiemurchus.net*

Other Routes

A much shorter route continues towards Nethy Bridge at ❶. Follow the track through the ancient pines of Nethy Forest to Forest Lodge then return by the track past Rynettin. This red roofed house has one of the best views in the Cairngorms. Rejoin the Ryvoan Pass track and retrace the outward route. If a drop off and pick up can be arranged try the one way run from Nethy Bridge to Glenmore.

Red or blue?

Cairngorm is the unremarkable looking hill whose slopes become a winter playground for hardy skiers. Its summit weather station is rimed in foot thick ice for a considerable part of the year. In 1986 it recorded the UK's highest ever wind speed – 173 mph. Cairn gorm is Gaelic for "blue hill". This name has come to apply to the whole mountain range – the Cairngorms, the Blue Hills. Except the old Gaelic name for this range is Am Monadh Ruadh which means "The Red Mountains". There is plenty of time to consider which name is more appropriate when carefully boulder hopping over the distinctively coloured rocks at the top of the Lairig Ghru.

Inverness and Ross

The Moray, Beauly, Cromarty and Dornoch Firths cut deep into Scotland's north-east coast giving sea views to many Easter Ross runs. To the west are rugged mountains, wild glens, remote lochs and the intricate, island-strewn shore of Wester Ross. Running trails range from easy lochside and woodland paths near Loch Ness to a long one way trail through the remote Letterewe and Fisherfield Deer Forests.

Loch Croisg, Wester Ross

Craig Dunain overlooks Inverness City Centre

City Centre Running

Two waterways cut through the heart of Inverness and the city has its very own hill in wooded Craig Dunain. An excellent place to begin off-road running is along the banks of the River Ness and across the string of Ness Islands joined one to another by footbridges. This short run links up with Bught Park and can be lengthened by running out and back along the riverside walkway. Following the Caledonian Canal to Muirtown Basin and South Kessock results in lovely views north across the Beauly Firth. Craig Dunain has narrow earthy single track, lovely woodland paths and grassy tracks which make it a great play-ground for runners and mountain bikers. The Great Glen Way skirts round the side of Craig Dunain providing excellent longer distance running on a well-made path through mixed woodland. The footpath is fully waymarked all the way to Fort William (117km, 73 miles).

Loch Ness, Tor Point
and Dores Beach

55 Aldourie & Loch Ness

Distance	7km (4.5 miles)	Ascent	50m (200ft)
Map	OS Landranger 26, OS Explorer 416		
Navigation •••	Through Torr Wood to Aldourie Castle and back by the loch shore		
Terrain •••	Grass or gravel tracks and paths		
Wet Feet •••	Occasional muddy puddles		
Start/Finish	The Dores Inn IV2 6TS NH 598 349		

A gentle run through woodland by the shore of Loch Ness

Only one short stretch of Loch Ness shoreline does not have a road running alongside. At Dores the land kinks out into the loch while the road continues straight and true towards Inverness. Courtesy of this kink the pebble beach at Dores has an impressive outlook down the length of the loch. The wooded promontory behind the beach contains wide tracks and paths that link together to form this pleasant circuit. Most of Torr Wood was planted in the 1760s so the run passes under branches of mature beech and Scots pine. Some of the trees are much older, such as the coppiced beeches on the high point of An Torr, a short detour off the described route. Further on another short detour leads to a picture perfect view of Aldourie Castle. At the time Torr Wood was planted Aldourie was a plain rectangular residence. Its fanciful turrets and crenulations were added by the Victorians.

🏃 START   Go up steps at the back of the car park and turn left past the play park onto a track. This runs parallel with the beach and forks soon after entering the woods. ① Take the right-hand fork to climb up to and continue on a level grassy forest track. After about 600m this curves round to the left and reaches a T-junction. ② Turn right onto a wide grassy track to continue for another 1km along the edge of the woods to reach houses. ③ Turn sharp left and follow the dead end road down to reach the shore of Loch Ness at Aldourie Pier. ④ Turn right and follow the narrow shore path through overgrown vegetation to peek at Aldourie Castle. Return to the pier and continue along the shore by an obvious path through the woods which goes around the point and returns to the junction at ①. Return to Dores Inn by the outward path or along the pebble beach.

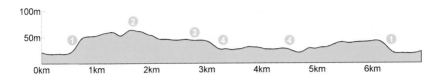

Trip Planning

The music festival Rockness is held at Aldourie Farm in June. Access to Torr Wood is not restricted but the area is very busy for the duration of the festival. 🚐 Dores Inn 🚗 Dores is eight miles south-west of Inverness on the B862. Park in the public car park next to The Dores Inn. 🍴 The Dores Inn's patio and beer garden are very popular on sunny summer days. *www.thedoresinn.co.uk* 🏠 The whole of Aldourie Castle can be let for holidays or events, as can several self-catering cottages on the estate. *www.aldouriecastle.co.uk*

Other Routes

The 45km (28 miles) South Loch Ness Trail follows paths, tracks and minor roads from Loch Tarff near Fort Augustus to the outskirts of Inverness. Much of the waymarked trail is away from the loch with small climbs gaining good loch views. *www.visitlochness.com*

Torr Wood

Aldourie and Loch Ness

Aldourie Castle

Also south of Loch Ness is The Trail of the Seven Lochs. This 80km (50 miles) circuit can be split into shorter loops using minor roads. The trail passes through wild, remote country on surfaces varying from knee-deep heather to tarmac road. Some of the best paths and scenery are found at Inverfarigaig. *www.southlochnessaccess.org.uk*

World Record Attempt, 1952

On 29th September 1952 the hydroplane turbojet *Crusader* sped down Loch Ness at an average speed of 206.89mph to travel a mile in just 17.4 seconds. At that time the recently set world record was 178.497mph. Observers saw the boat begin to porpoise as it finished the measured mile. On the return journey pilot John Cobb was soon in trouble. Three wayward ripples disturbed the mill pond surface of the loch and their impact with *Crusader* was fatal. The boat disintegrated and Cobb was killed instantly. Without a complete return journey the record could not be officially ratified. However, there is no doubt that *Crusader's* top speed was around 240mph. John Cobb's memorial stone is at Drumnadrochit. The current water speed record is 317.60mph set in 1978 by Ken Warby in the *Spirit of Australia*.

Clava Estate track
Photo: Fran Williams

56 Beinn Bhuidhe

Distance	10km (6 miles)	Ascent	375m (1200ft)
Map	OS Landranger 27, OS Explorer 422		
Navigation •••	Clava Estate information boards display maps at the key junctions		
Terrain •••	Forest and estate roads and tracks, gates and stiles		
Wet Feet •••	Estate roads may be muddy in places		
Start/Finish	Lay-by near Finglack Farm road end IV2 5EN NH 767 444		

Straightforward running on moor and hill tracks

In 1745 the Jacobite supporters of Bonnie Prince Charlie were soundly beaten by the troops of the Duke of Cumberland at Culloden. According to military historians the slopes of Beinn Bhuidhe were considered as a possible battleground before the lower moor was settled upon. This route follows estate roads across heathery moorland then climbs gradually to the summit of Beinn Bhuidhe Beag. Claiming the summit of Beinn Bhuidhe Mhor is an optional extra. These tracks feel surprisingly remote considering how close Beinn Bhuidhe is to Inverness. Good wide tracks, runnable gradients and views over the Beauly Firth make this a great route whether heading out for a solitary leg stretch or a sociable trot with a bunch of friends.

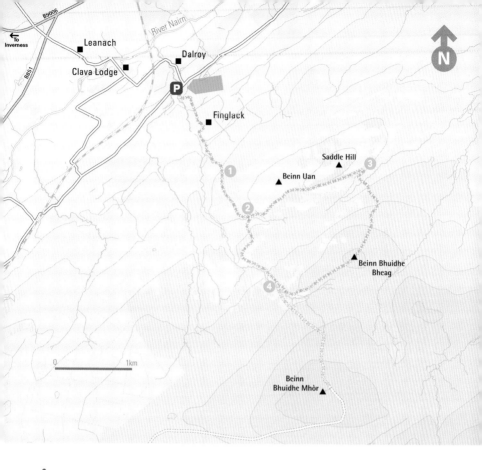

🏃 **START** Cross the river then turn right up a dirt road. Follow this uphill for 750m and round to the right where a left-hand turn leads to Finglack Farm. Continue through a gate and climb uphill through forestry plantation and over a stile onto the Clava Estate. ❶ Continue across the open moor for 750m to a track junction. ❷ Take the track on the left for 1.5km past Saddle Hill to reach the next junction. ❸ Turn right to drop down into the valley and climb up to the summit of Beinn Bhuidhe Beag. The track continues down the east side of the hill to a junction. (Turn sharp left here to go out and back to Beinn Bhuidhe Mhor. This adds 3.5km (2 miles) and 200m (600ft) ascent to the basic circuit.) ❹ Continue north-east to rejoin the outward route at ❷ and return to the start.

Beinn Bhuidhe

Trip Planning

Access to the hill may be restricted during the shooting season. 🚗 Turn off the B9006 near Culloden Battlefield at a sign to Clava Cairns. Continue straight on past Leanach Farm and follow the road left under the viaduct to reach a T-junction. Turn right and park in a lay-by behind a tree island just after crossing the river. Beinn Bhuidhe is a six mile drive west of Inverness and the A9. 🚻 ♿ Culloden Visitor Centre 🐕 A sign at the Clava Estate boundary requests that dogs are kept on lead. This is particularly important during the ground bird nesting season.

Events

Runners and walkers taking part in the Heartbeat Challenge cross Clava and Moy Estates then return by cycling along the old A9. The Challenge raises funds to help treat cardiac and cardiovascular diseases in the Highlands and Islands. *www.heartbeatchallenge.co.uk*

The Moray Firth
Photo: Fran Williams

Beinn Bhuidhe

Hilltop folly

57 Fyrish

Distance	13km (8 miles)	Ascent	475m (1500ft)
Map	OS Landranger 21, OS Explorer 438		
Navigation ●●●	Turn left on the first loop of this figure of eight and right on the second loop		
Terrain ●●●	Forest roads and tracks, gravel path, rocky up to the summit		
Wet Feet ●●●	Occasional puddles		
Start/Finish	Novar Estate Jubilee Path car park IV17 0XJ NH 627 715		

Forest tracks lead to an impressive hilltop folly

The distinctive 'ruin' on the skyline was built for Sir Hector Munro during an 18th-century eco-nomic recession. The design is said to be modelled on the gates of Negapatam, an Indian city captured by Sir Hector from the Dutch. Some claim that Sir Hector trundled the building blocks downhill under cover of darkness in order to prolong his employment of local labourers during the recession. Sir Hector's folly enjoys panoramic views down the Cromarty Firth and over the Black Isle. The route follows excellent tracks which climb gradually through the forest and loop around the hill with views in all directions. Runners looking for an additional challenge should seek out Fyrish's sister follies on Creag Ruadh and Meann Chnoc.

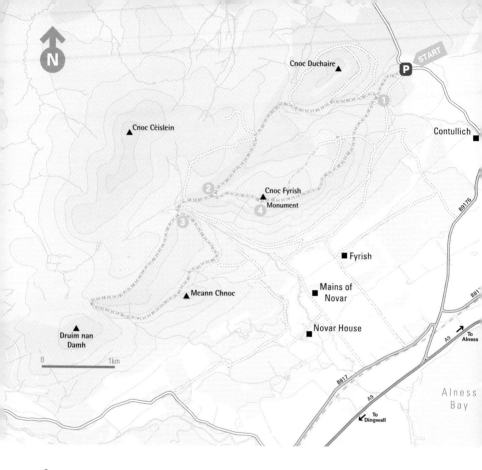

START Follow the Jubilee Path for a short distance to crossroads with a forest road.
❶ Turn right onto this road then keep left at all junctions; follow good tracks for 3.5km to a
junction on the ridge west of the summit of Fyrish. ❷ Turn right and head downhill on a stony
track to cross two streams and then climb up to a junction. ❸ Take the left-hand track and head
downhill with good views across to Fyrish. Stay on good forest roads and keep right at junctions
to return to ❸. The only exception to this right-hand rule is the junction near Meann Chnoc
where the route continues straight ahead following the main forest road. Return to junction ❷
and take the rough track uphill to the monument on the summit of Fyrish. ❹ Continue past the
folly and follow the Jubilee Path straight downhill back to the car park.

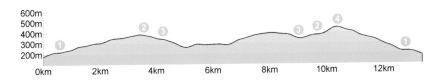

600m
500m
400m
300m
200m

0km   2km   4km   6km   8km   10km   12km

Trip Planning

🚗 Turn off the B9176 north-west of Alness onto a minor road signed to Boath. The Novar Estate woodland car park is on the left after one mile. **WC** Alness, next to the Mitchell Lane public car park. 🍽 Three miles east of Alness on the A9 is the Tomich Café which serves a straightforward selection of savouries as well as impressive traybakes. Five miles towards Inverness is the Storehouse of Foulis farm shop and café. *www.storehouseoffoulis.com*

Other Routes

Strath Rory and Scotsburn Wood to the west of Tain have good running on paths and tracks. The short waymarked trails at Aldie Burn near Tain are scenic and can be extended by following tracks and forest roads deeper into the trees.

Russula, Aldie Burn

Fyrish

Fyrish from Meann Chnoc

Events

The Tain Hill Trail Race circumnavigates Tain Hill on undulating forest tracks.

www.tainrunners.co.uk

Easan Dorcha and Coire Lair

58 The Coulin Pass & Coire Lair

Distance	15km (9 miles)	Ascent	500m (1700ft)
Map	OS Landranger 25, OS Explorer 429		
Navigation ●●●	Signposted forest road, obvious paths and path junctions		
Terrain ●●●	Forest road, estate roads, gravel and stony paths		
Wet Feet ●●●	Occasional puddles		
Start/Finish	Achnashellach Station NH 003 484		

Unbeatable combination of stalker paths and mountain scenery

The Coulin Forest hills lack the height of their Torridonian neighbours and so are happily neglected by Munro baggers. The network of excellent stalkers' paths that criss-cross these hills is a perfect trail-running playground. This route just touches on the eastern end of the range leaving plenty of paths for future exploration. The undoubted highlight is the superb panorama of hills surrounding Coire Lair. The Coulin Pass is a very old droving road which appears on the earliest maps of Scotland. The traditional route follows the Old Pony Track which zigzags directly uphill from Craig. Today the Pony Track is rough and boggy: the best running route follows a modern forest road.

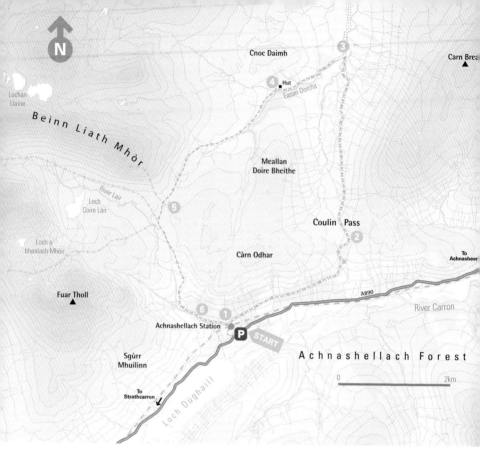

🏃 **START** Cross the level crossing at Achnashellach Station to reach a junction of forest roads. ① Take the higher of the two roads on the right, signposted to the Coulin Pass. Follow this uphill, keeping left at a fork after nearly 2km to climb out of the forest. ② Continue following the track over the Coulin Pass and down towards Glen Torridon. ③ Cross the Easan Dorcha Bridge and turn left onto an estate track which follows the river upstream to end at an estate hut. ④ Cross the footbridge and continue on a good stalkers' path to climb up into Coire Lair. ⑤ Keep left at three cairned junctions and follow another good stalkers' path downhill beside the stream. ⑥ Follow the path through an unusual circular gate and turn right onto the forest road to return to the junction at ①. Turn right to return to the station.

Trip Planning

Access may be restricted during the stalking season. Between 15th September and 20th October contact the Achnashellach Estate Stalker on 01520 766266 for advice. The route also crosses the Coulin Estate where runners should stick to the main paths during the stalking season (Head Stalker 01445 760383). 🚂 Achnashellach (by request) 🚙 Achnashellach Station is signposted off the A890 at a red telephone box. Park in the lay-by on the opposite side of the road as there is no parking at the station. 🚻 Lochcarron 🍽 🏠 Lochcarron. A couple of miles east at Craig is the oldest independent hostel in Scotland. *www.gerryshostel-achnashellach.co.uk* On the north side of the Coulin is Torridon with an SYHA Hostel and a campsite. *www.syha.org.uk* The Coulin Estate has a couple of self-catering cottages on the shore of Loch Coulin with spectacular views of Torridon. *www.coulin.co.uk*

The Coulin Pass & Coire Lair

Fuar Tholl

Other Routes

Consistently good paths, incredible scenery and range of routes make the Coulin Forest one of the best areas for mountain trail running in all of Scotland. Accommodation on both sides of the hills at Torridon and at Lochcarron or Craig gives scope for multi-day running adventures. The paths shown on the Ordnance Survery map exist and are generally in good condition.

Maddened by midges

In 1940 the Commandos were formed to support the regular troops of the British Army. Where better to train for clandestine missions than remote North West Scotland? But even the hardiest troops were driven to madness by that notorious scourge of the Highlands, the midge. The Midge Control Unit was set up by the government in 1952 to find out how midges could be eradicated. The Unit based many of its trials near Achnashellach. Although no way of exterminating the species was identified scientists learnt a lot about these tiny flies. Midges have the fastest wing beat of the insect world at 62,670 beats per minute. Less than 10% of the population sucks blood – only females laying a second batch of eggs require a blood meal. Multiple empirical tests prove that midges are easily outpaced by simply running faster.

High trail north of Loch Affric

59 Loch Affric

Distance	17km (11 miles)	Ascent	250m (800ft)
Map	OS Landranger 25, OS Explorer 414 and 415		
Navigation ●●●	Straightforward track and junctions around the loch		
Terrain ●●●	Stony track and dirt estate road		
Wet Feet ●●●	Stepping stones across streams		
Start/Finish	River Affric Forestry Commission car park IV4 7NB NH 200 233		

A classic loch circuit through Highland scenery

Glen Affric is the most famously beautiful Scottish glen and rightly so. Its rivers, lochs, mountains and ancient woodland live up to every stereotyped preconception of wild Highland scenery. Unusually for a loch circuit this trail traverses the hillside high above the water; a great vantage point from which to view the landscape. Blue water fringed by gnarled pines lies far below while the upper reaches of the glens and hills beyond the loch present tempting opportunities for future forays. The track around the loch is straightforward to navigate and superb running terrain. Although Glen Affric is a great place to visit at any time it is particularly special in autumn when the bracken carpeting the hillsides is bright rust-orange and the trees by the river turn brilliant yellow and red.

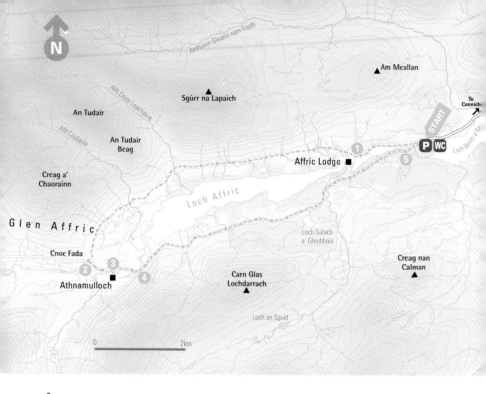

🏃 **START** Follow the road to Affric Lodge. ① Take the right-hand path around its grounds signposted to the loch and Kintail. This path quickly joins a wide rough track which continues for about 7km to the far end of the loch. There are several stream crossings some of which may be difficult or even impassable after heavy rain. ② Turn left onto a dirt road and cross a bridge to reach Athnamulloch bothy. ③ Turn left at the building to cross a tributary river by stepping stones and continue along the main riverbank to a T-junction with an estate road. ④ Turn left onto the road and follow it for 7km back to the east end of the loch. ⑤ Turn left to cross the bridge over the river then turn right up a steep path to return to the car park.

Trip Planning

Glen Affric is a National Nature Reserve. *www.forestry.gov.uk/glenaffric* This route is partly on Forestry Commission land and partly on the Affric Estate. 🚗 Glen Affric is just under forty miles south-west of Inverness. Turn off the A82 Inverness to Fort William road at Drumnadrochit onto the A831 signed for Milton, Cannich and Beauly. At Cannich turn left at the T-junction and follow the minor road for ten miles to the River Affric car park at the end of the public road. **WC** River Affric car park 🏠 Glen Affric (Alltbeithe) Youth Hostel **(079 202)** is 13km (8 miles) by foot

or mountain bike from the River Affric car park. 📧 🏠 The Slaters Arms in Cannich offers real ales and bar meals as well as accommodation in a couple of self-catering log cabins. The Bog Cotton café at Cannich Caravan and Camping Park is open all year round and welcomes non-residents. *www.syha.org.uk www.slatersarms.com www.highlandcamping.co.uk*

Other Routes

A 30km (18 miles) route goes through Glen Affric to Kintail on the west coast. Follow the described route to the far end of Loch Affric then continue past Alltbeithe and Camban MBA Bothy into Glen Licht to reach the road at Morvich. Alternatively, a 23km (14 miles) route turns south at Alltbeithe and meets the A87 just east of Cluanie Inn.

A more challenging 30km (19 miles) circuit starts in Kintail at Morvich Countryside Centre and circles Beinn Fhada. It is easiest to navigate in a clockwise direction. Climb on a good path through the Gates of Affric and follow an indistinct, boggy though runnable path past remote

Glen Affric

Loch Affric

Loch Affric

Loch a' Bhealaich to near Alltbeithe Glen Affric Youth Hostel. Return past Camban Bothy and through Glen Licht.

Events

The Highland Cross is a 50 mile duathlon which starts at Kintail on the west coast and runs through Glen Licht and Glen Affric to Beauly in the east. *www.highlandcross.co.uk*

The Glen Affric Duathlon was a shorter running and biking event held annually between 2004 and 2009. At the time of writing there were plans to resurrect this event.

Monarch of the Glen

The Glen Affric deer are the many-times great grandchildren of the stag painted by Sir Edwin Landseer in 'Monarch of the Glen'. The proud stag against a misty mountain backdrop is one of the most familiar 19th-century images. The painting was commissioned by the House of Lords but the House of Commons refused to authorise the purchase. Dewars, the whisky distillers, bought the reproduction rights for the image and deliberately used it to alter the public perception of whisky. At the time whisky was considered a rough, low class drink. Dewars turned whisky into a high society tipple by playing on Victorian associations of the Highlands with romance, adventure and the landed gentry. Today, a single dram can cost up to £20,000 (from a bottle of Dalmore 64 Trinitas sold in 2010). Landseer's Glen Affric stag played a crucial role in this meteoric rise in public opinion.

Dubh and
Fionn Lochs

60 Poolewe to Corrie Hallie

Distance	43km (26 miles)	Ascent	1000m (3500ft)
Map	OS Landranger 19, OS Explorer 435, Harvey Torridon & Fisherfield		
Navigation •••	Obvious tracks and paths past Kernsary, Carnmore and Shenavall		
Terrain •••	Excellent stalkers' paths and estate roads, rough ground at river crossing		
Wet Feet •••	The river into Loch na Sealga must be waded		
Start	Poolewe IV22 2LA NG 858 808		
Finish	Corrie Hallie IV23 2QN NH 114 849		

An epic one way run through the heart of Fisherfield

Its remoteness, dramatic mountain scenery and excellent paths make this one of the best long distance journeys in the North West Highlands. With no escape routes and a sometimes problematic river crossing it is not a route to attempt in poor weather. While the route can be easily run in either direction it is described from west to east in order to finish with a fantastic downhill blast to the road at Corrie Hallie. Two bothies are passed en route at Carnmore and Shenavall. These provide basic shelter and are maintained by the Mountain Bothies Association. Shenavall is particularly popular with walkers attempting the numerous Munros in the area including the distinctive rocky pinnacles of An Teallach. The more basic Carnmore bothy is at the foot of some of the longest mountain rock climbs in the whole of the British Isles.

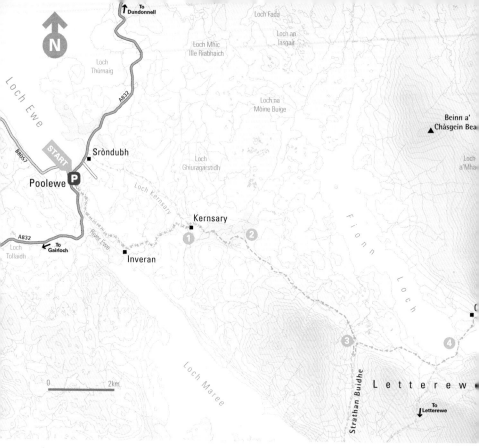

🏃 **START** Follow the track along the River Ewe for nearly 3km to Inveran then cross moorland to Kernsary. ① (893 793) Cross the river and turn right after the houses. Continue to the end of the track as it enters the forest and swings north-east. ② Head right on a path leading out of the trees and across 4.5km of moorland to a larger stream. ③ Cross if possible, or follow the path upstream to cross near (943 756). Then continue towards Fionn Loch and the causeway that separates it from Dubh Loch. ④ Cross the causeway and follow the path past Carnmore to climb diagonally uphill above Dubh Loch. After the path levels out continue straight ahead at a cairn to pass a couple of lochans. The path zigzags down into Gleann na Muice Beag to reach the river flowing through Gleann na Muice. ⑤ Follow the riverbank path downstream to the head of Loch na Sealga. ⑥ The river which flows into the loch is usually easily waded but can be impassable after heavy rain or snow melt. After reaching Shenavall bothy (066 810) continue up Strath na Sealga on an improving landrover track. (A steeper, rougher and wetter shortcut goes up the hill directly behind the bothy.) Just over 1km past Achneigie House follow the landrover track left over the col to the fast descent into Corrie Hallie.

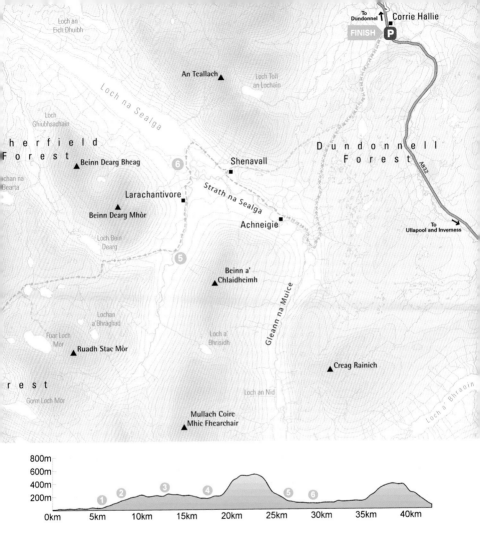

Trip Planning

Access may be restricted during the shooting and stalking seasons. After heavy rain or snow melt the river into Loch na Sealga may be impassable. An early morning bus service runs from Poolewe Post Office to Inverness and stops at Corrie Hallie on request. The bus returns from Inverness in early evening. This timing makes it easiest to run from Corrie Hallie to Poolewe. Local taxis can be contacted through the Tourist Information Centre at Gairloch (01445 712071). Turn off the A832 at Poolewe onto the road along the east side of the River Ewe. The car park is almost immediately on the left. Parking at Corrie Hallie is in a sometimes crowded lay-by at the side of the road. WC Poolewe The Bridge Cottage Café in Poolewe (daily during summer and

Poolewe to Corrie Hallie

An Teallach

weekends in winter). North of Corrie Hallie is the Dundonnell Hotel and Maggie's Tea Room at Camusnagaul. ⌂ The Dundonnell Hotel. *www.dundonnellhotel.com* Independent hostel, B&B, caravan and self-catering accommodation at Camusnagaul. *www.sailmhor.co.uk www.camusnagaul.com* Poolewe has B&Bs and a Camping and Caravanning Club site (01445 781249) (NG 862 812). A few miles north of Poolewe on the B8057 camping is tolerated at Firemore beach (NG 817 880). There are no toilet facilities and campers are asked to pay a nominal charge by honesty box. The MBA maintained bothies at Shenavall and Carnmore can be used to split the route. *www.mountainbothiesassociation.org.uk*

Other Routes

Start at Incheril near Kinlochewe (NH 038 624) for a longer 44km (27 miles) run. The path along the shore of Loch Maree is less runnable than the described route. After passing the Slioch turn-off the path becomes indistinct as it traverses just above woodland. An excellent stalkers' path climbs over the hill behind Letterewe Lodge and down to Fionn Loch.

A 10km (6 miles) alternative circuit starts from Poolewe. Follow the A832 to Srondubh then run along the shore of Loch Kernsary, returning to Poolewe by the River Ewe track.

Events

The Great Wilderness Challenge for walkers and runners raises funds for the Highland Hospice and a number of other charities. The original twenty-five mile route between Dundonnell and Poolewe is now accompanied by shorter thirteen and seven mile routes. The event is extremely popular and usually fully subscribed within weeks of opening for applications. *www.greatwildernesschallenge.info*

Caithness and Sutherland

The landscape of the far north of Scotland changes markedly from east to west; from the wide open expanses of Flow Country to the rugged, rocky outcrops of North West Sutherland. Running away from the crowds is never a problem in this part of the world. Some of its best runs explore the spectacular coastline, treading lightly on airy clifftop paths or running barefoot on golden sand.

Duncansby Head, John o' Groats

Big Burn

Dunrobin Castle

61 Big Burn & Dunrobin Castle

Distance	10km (6 miles)	Ascent	100m (350ft)
Map	OS Landranger 17, OS Explorer 441		
Navigation ●●●	Up and down the burn then weave through woods to the castle and on to the shore		
Terrain ●●●	Gravel, earth and grass paths, estate road		
Wet Feet ●●●	Earth paths may be slippery in wet weather		
Start/Finish	The Big Burn, Golspie KW10 6RS NC 839 006		

Woodland, river gorge and a coastal castle

Sheltered woodland and windswept shore: this is a run of contrasts. Each half can be run independently or extended over flat or hilly ground. At the north end of Golspie the Big Burn has carved a picturesque gorge into the lower slopes of Ben Bhraggie. After following the river through its dark rocky gorge and sun-dappled hazel trees the route crosses the A9 into the Dunrobin Estate. These paths are less well used with surprises including an overgrown memorial to a former Duchess and sudden emergence onto the drive in front of the impressive facade of Dunrobin Castle. The best view of the castle is from the shore. Its imposing walls and turrets nestle in woodland beneath the watchful eye of the Duke of Sutherland's statue on Ben Bhraggie.

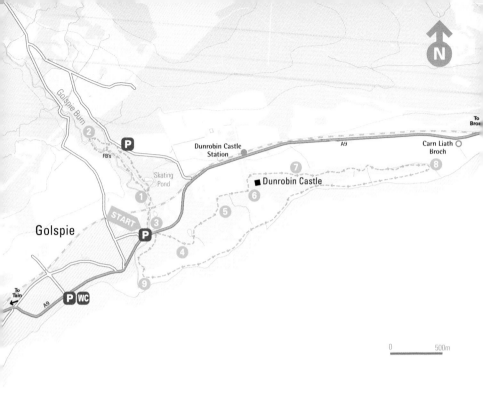

Golspie

Dunrobin Castle Station

Skating Pond

START

Dunrobin Castle

Carn Liath Broch

To Bro

A9

To Tain

A9

0   500m

🏃 START Follow the path upstream from the car park to cross a footbridge, go under the viaduct and continue to a fork. ① Keep left, continuing upstream to cross and recross the river on
a series of bridges. Towards the head of the gorge turn right to go out and back along a boardwalk
to visit the waterfall then climb steps to the top of the gorge. ② Cross the river then take the
first right turn to head downstream. Just before the path descends to rejoin the outward route it
is possible to take a short detour around the skating pond. ③ After returning to the car park
cross the A9 and turn left following the pavement to a walker's gate. Take the left-hand path into
the wood and follow it for about 300m to an indistinct fork under mature beech trees. ④ Take
the left-hand path marked by a blue waymarker. Continue through an avenue of younger trees
and past the overgrown memorial to Harriet, Duchess of Sutherland to reach a tarmac road.
⑤ Turn left and then right at the T-junction to reach the main drive. ⑥ Head away from the
castle and take the second of two tracks on the right. ⑦ At the cemetery gates turn left following the red waymarked trail along an embankment. After 600m the red trail turns right. Do not
take this, instead, continue straight on to the end of the embankment. ⑧ Climb over the stile and
descend to a grassy track heading back towards the castle. Go through a gate into woodland then

keep left to follow a succession of paths and tracks along the shore past the castle. ⑨ On reaching houses go through a gate and turn right just before the bridge into Golspie. Climb a few steps to a T-junction then turn left to follow a woodland path back to the A9.

Trip Planning

🚌 Golspie Post Office (500m to start) 🚗 The Big Burn car park is signed off the A9 at the north end of Golspie. Follow a lane past Sutherland Stonework to reach the car park. 🚾 Golspie Main Street/Fountain Road public car park 💺 🏠 Coffee Bothy at the public car park or one of the hotels on the A9, the Golspie Inn or Ben Bhraggie Hotel.

Other Routes

Climb up to the Duke's Monument on Ben Bhraggie by road and forest tracks from the top of the Big Burn at ②. A path descends directly to Golspie from the summit or continue exploring the trail network shared with mountain bikers.

A flat alternative extends north from ⑧ along the grassy shore track to Brora. The out and back path passes close to the Carn Liath broch, a well preserved iron age stone tower.

Events

Thurso-based North Highland Harriers organise a series of trail runs over the winter months. This run is a shortened version of one of their routes. *www.northhighlandharriers.co.uk*

Other Activities

Ben Bhraggie boasts the longest purpose-built single track mountain bike descent in the UK. Over 18km of bike trail have been developed by the community-led company Highland Wildcat. Red and black trails start at the Main Street/Fountain Road car park. Blue routes are accessed from above the Big Burn. Maps and guides are available online or from local shops. *www.highlandwildcat.com*

Big Burn & Dunrobin Castle

Speckled wood butterfly

Highland Clearances

The names of the Duke of Sutherland and his factor Patrick Sellar will forever be associated with the Clearances. Their method of evicting tenant farmers was notoriously brutal. Hillsides and houses were set on fire with little regard for human safety. Sellar was brought to court, but acquitted, for the murder of an old woman who burnt to death in her home. All over the Highlands people were cleared off the land to make way for large sheep farms. Thirty miles from Golspie the windows of Croick Church near Ardgay carry tragic messages scratched by Glencalvie evictees in 1845. The Glencalvie Clearance was witnessed by a newspaper reporter. The graphic article he wrote after returning to London brought the plight of the Highlanders to the notice of wider British society for the first time.

Towards Cape Wrath

62 Sandwood Bay

Distance	15km (9 miles)	Ascent	250m (800ft)
Map	OS Landranger 9, OS Explorer 446		
Navigation ●●●	Track to Sandwood Bay then by clifftops to a stream valley and back to the track		
Terrain ●●●	Stony track, earth and rocky paths, sandy beach		
Wet Feet ●●●	Wet feet likely on the return by Loch a' Mhuillinn		
Start/Finish	Blairmore IV27 4RU NC 194 600		

Adventurous clifftop running with superb views

Am Buachaille guards the southern end of Sandwood Bay. This impressive rock pinnacle was first climbed in 1967 by Tom Patey, Ian Clough and John Cleare, the pioneers of Scottish sea stack climbing. An exciting path hugs the cliff edge overlooking the stack. There are few views which can rival the one from this path whether looking out to Am Buachaille or back across the golden crescent of Sandwood Bay. Far in the distance is the white dot of the lighthouse at Cape Wrath. Although the beauty of Sandwood Bay is well known the bay remains a place of splendid isolation. The dunes possess an astonishing capacity for absorbing human visitors and it is easy to feel completely alone here. Allow extra time for this run as Sandwood Bay is hard to leave. In fact, why not take a tent and stay the night?

Am Balg

Sandwood Bay

Am Buachaille

Rubha nan
Cùl Gheodhachan

Càrn an Righ
▲

Loch Clais
nan Coinneal

Loch
Mheadhonach

Rubh an Fhir Leith

Loch a'
Mhuilinn

Allt Briste

Lochain
nan Sac

Cnoc Poll
a' Mhurain
▲

Loch na
Gainimh

Na Stacain

Sheigra

Loch Aisir

P **Blairmore**

Loch Deibheadh

Loch Mòr a'
Chraisg

START

Loch Aisir Mòr

Eilean an Ròin Mòr

To
Kinlochbervie

Sandwood Loch

Làn Mòr

Strath Shinary

0   2km

START Follow the track signposted to Sandwood for 1.5km to reach Loch na Gainimh. ❶ A well-used shortcut avoids a bend in the track just beyond the loch. After this shortcut stick to the main track which becomes a wide and runnable path. After passing Loch a' Mhuillinn the route climbs gradually for 1km then traverses the lower slopes of Druim na Buainn. ❷ As the path heads round the side of the hill a view of Sandwood Bay suddenly appears. Follow the main path towards the bay and as it heads down into the dunes keep slightly to the right, staying on a strong path, for the easiest route to the beach. ❸ At the southern end of the bay an obvious though rough path climbs steeply up to the right. Once on top of the cliffs the running is good although care is required as the path is very close to the edge in places. Continue along the clifftop until the ground begins to drop away into a stream valley. ❹ Turn inland and follow a reasonable path across the shoulder of Càrn an Righ towards the stream. Follow the north bank of the stream to reach Loch a' Mhuillinn and continue along its boggy shore to rejoin the main track. Turn right and retrace the outward route back to Blairmore.

Sandwood Bay

Trip Planning

The John Muir Trust owns Sandwood Estate. They provide free parking, toilets and a freshwater tap at Blairmore as well as maintain the trail to Sandwood. There is a donations box in the car park. *www.jmt.org* 🚗 Follow the B801 through Kinlochbervie and turn off towards Oldshoremore and Sheigra. A large car park is on the left in Blairmore. 🚻 Blairmore 🅿 For self-caterers there is a viewpoint and picnic table overlooking Loch Inchard at Achriesgill. 🏠 The Kinlochbervie Hotel, The Old School Restaurant and Rooms or the Rhiconich Hotel are on the road back from Blairmore. All serve food and drink to non-residents. 🐕 Unfenced sheep grazing particularly near Blairmore and Sandwood.

Other Routes

Cape Wrath, the most north-westerly point of the British mainland is seven miles from Sandwood Bay. There is no path across the heathery moorland but the round trip makes a good tramp in a truly remote setting. Be warned that tourist-filled minibuses regularly arrive at the lighthouse. On the return make a short detour to Strathchailleach bothy to the north-east of Sandwood Bay. This isolated bothy was the home of James MacRory Smith (Sandy) for 32 years and his murals still adorn its walls.

Events

Durness is the home of the Cape Wrath Challenge: a series of races held over six days culminating in the Cape Wrath Marathon. A jam-packed social programme complements the running activities and ends with a traditional Scottish ceilidh. The Cape Wrath Challenge is a small and friendly event with strict limits on the number of entrants. *www.capewrathchallenge.co.uk*

Other Activities

Scotland's north coast is a top destination for surfers. In contrast to crowded beaches further south, surfers here often ride their wave alone with perhaps a seal or two for company. There is a reason for this solitude – bring a thick wetsuit and flask of hot chocolate. Surf Wrath in Durness teach surfing, run coasteering trips and hire out equipment. *www.surfwrath.co.uk*

Sandwood Bay

Am Buachaille

John Muir

John Muir was a 19th-century American (Scottish-born) naturalist and conservationist. He spent many years living in Canadian and American wilderness areas, undertaking epic journeys on foot and publishing descriptions of his explorations. Muir co-founded the Sierra Club and his writings continue to shape global attitudes to conservation. The John Muir Trust is a UK charity dedicated to the protection of wild land for nature and people. Founded in 1983, the organisation now owns over 25,000 hectares of land including Ben Nevis, Knoydart and parts of Skye. Sandwood is the Trust's most northerly estate.

Loch na Gainmhich
and Quinag

63 Inchnadamph

Distance	22km (14 miles)	Ascent	900m (3000ft)
Map	OS Landranger 15, OS Explorer 442		
Navigation •••	Indistinct path. Cairned descent to Loch na Gainmhich is easily missed.		
Terrain •••	Gravel and rough, rocky paths		
Wet Feet •••	Boggy at Loch Fleodach Coire and descent to Ardvreck		
Start/Finish	Inchnadamph IV27 4HN NC 250 216		

A remote path through the barren yet beautiful Assynt landscape

In the late 1800s Peach and Horne mapped the geology of Assynt using stocky hill ponies to transport both themselves and their samples over the rough ground. There are no such luxuries for today's runner. In most other respects there has been little change since the time of Peach and Horne. The Assynt landscape is the most distinctive in all of Scotland. In places a skimming of vegetation covers gray-white quartzite while elsewhere jumbled rocky shards lie bare. Surprisingly good paths cross this barren ground and form a highly runnable route. Time is of little importance on such a wilderness run so take the opportunity to detour to the top of Britain's highest waterfall, the Eas a' Chùal Aluinn. Its 200m (658ft) drop is over three times higher than Niagara Falls.

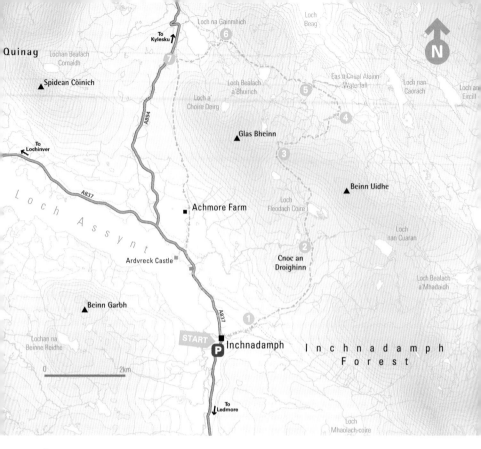

🏃 START Cross River Traligill by the road bridge and turn right towards Inchnadamph Lodge.
① Before the track recrosses the river turn off left onto a cairned hill path. Climb uphill for 3km to reach a small shelter and path junction. ② (273 239) Turn left and descend gradually to the west side of Loch Fleodach Coire. Cross its boggy outflow to a faint path on the far hillside. Climb north-west up to the bealach on an increasingly obvious path. ③ (265 262) Zigzag down the far side of the bealach past a lochan. The path becomes indistinct and care is needed to stay on route. After 2km it reaches an obvious feature – a narrow neck of land between two lochans. ④ (280 270) Turn left on the far side of the lochans at a cairn and follow the path north-west for 1km to a river crossing. (Detour right to visit the Eas a' Chùal Aluinn waterfall. Badly eroded, muddy paths lead down both sides of the river to precipitous viewpoints.) ⑤ (273 277) A good path leads north-west from the river crossing over the Bealach a' Bhuirich. Descend for about 2km from the bealach to the first levelling out of the path. There is a cairn on the right and a flat boggy area and hillock to the left. In clear weather watch for the first time Quinag disappears

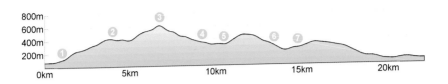

behind a hillock. ❽ (251 288) Turn sharp left across untracked flat boggy ground. After a stream is crossed the path down to Loch na Gainmhich becomes more obvious. Once past the loch the path climbs up to a track junction near the A894. ❼ (239 284) Turn left onto the stony track and climb over the shoulder of the hill to a wet descent. Go through gateposts to the right of the track onto a fine grassy path which joins a farm road leading to the A837. Turn left and follow the grass verge for 2km past the ruins of Ardvreck Castle and Calda House to return to Inchnadamph.

Trip Planning

Access may be restricted during the shooting and stalking seasons. 🚌 Inchnadamph, Hotel Road End 🚗 Inchnadamph is twenty three miles north of Ullapool on the A837. The public car park is just south of the River Traligill at the Inchnadamph Hotel turn-off. 🅿 🏠 The Inchnadamph Hotel bar serves food and is open to non-residents. *www.inchnadamphhotel.com* On the far side of the river the Inchnadamph Lodge has dormitories and private rooms with self-catering facilities. *www.inch-lodge.co.uk*

Other Routes

There are many miles of estate roads and stalkers' paths to explore in the north of Scotland with potential for extremely remote, challenging and invariably long trail routes. The Reay Forest has runnable paths east and west of Loch Stack (NC 296 402). This wilderness area is rarely visited and is best avoided during the first months of the stalking season.

Other Activities

Visit the Bone Caves just south of Inchnadamph by following the Allt nan Uamh. Pieces of animal bone were found by Peach and Horn in 1889. Later excavations uncovered bones from bears, wildcats, humans and over 1000 fragments of reindeer. Assynt is part of the North West Highlands Geopark. *www.northwest-highlands-geopark.org.uk*

Inchnadamph

Above Fleodach Coire

The Highlands Controversy

In the 19th-century Inchnadamph was the epicentre of a vitriolic scientific debate. It began when the Geological Survey's Director, Roderick Murchison, and his successor, Archibald Geikie, mapped the North West Highlands as simple layers of younger rocks deposited on top of older ones. Their view was challenged by James Nicol who hypothesised a major fault with older rocks forced on top of younger ones. Murchison and Geikie dismissed Nicol's theory but it refused to go away. Detailed mapping by two dedicated amateur geologists, Charles Lapworth and Charles Callaway, independently supported Nicol's ideas. Eventually, Geikie sent the Survey's best two geologists, Peach and Horn, to investigate. They swiftly confirmed Nicol's theory and Geikie, knowing the argument was lost, switched sides and rushed a paper into Nature. Four hundred million years ago the Moine Thrust pushed west for over 100km, stretching and folding rocks as though they were putty. It is one of the most important geological sites in the world.

Loch More

64 Loch More

Distance	26km (16 miles)	Ascent	125m (400ft)
Map	OS Landranger 12, OS Explorer 450		
Navigation •••	Signposted and obvious junctions through the forest and across the moors		
Terrain •••	Forest and estate roads		
Wet Feet •••	Occasional puddles		
Start/Finish	Loch More KW12 6UP ND 090 471		

Long, level tracks through remote forest and moorland

This route strikes deep into the heart of Caithness Flow Country. Even travelling to the start is a journey into the middle of nowhere. Shadows chase patches of colour-changing sunshine across grass and heather moorland. The nearest hills are on the horizon and only a few stands of plantation forest block the wind's passage. Full advantage of this is taken by the gently turning giants of Causeymire wind farm. A significant part of this route follows a wide road through plantation woodland. There is little variety or prettiness in the scenery. It is the remoteness of this route that makes it special: the isolated train station, the desolate hunting lodge and the subtle hues of the empty landscape on either side of the meandering River Thurso.

🏃 **START**   Follow a dirt road through forest and along the side of Loch More to a fork on the far side of the loch. ① Take the right-hand track and pass through gates into forestry. Continue through the trees and past a lochan for 8km to meet the railway line. ② The track turns south-west and follows the railway for a further 2km to Altnabreac Station. ③ Continue past the station for 100m then take the left-hand fork across the river. After the bridge keep left and head uphill to pass the turreted Lochdhu Lodge after about 2km. Soon after the track leaves the forest and crosses moorland for 3km to a T-junction at Dalnawillan. ④ Turn left and go through a working farm with barking, kennelled dogs. The track follows the River Thurso to Loch More and back to ①. Turn right onto the outward track to return to the car park.

Trip Planning

Access may be restricted during the shooting and stalking seasons. 🚂 Altnabreac (request stop at ③) 🚗 Loch More is a few miles off the A9 between Wick and Thurso. Turn off the A9 onto the B870 at Mybster following signs to Westerdale and Achanarras Quarry. Continue straight ahead where the B870 turns right towards Glengolly and Scotscalder. After passing Strathmore

Lodge continue for nearly another mile to a fork. Park on the right next to an information board. There are no toilet facilities. 🖵 🏠 East of the A9 is the Brown Trout Hotel at Watten which serves bar meals and has accommodation. Halkirk, Thurso and Wick have a wider range of food and accommodation.

Other Routes

Spectacular coastal scenery is the reason for running at John o' Groats. Leave the unattractive tourist centre by the shore path and follow it up to the lighthouse. Continue out and back along the clifftops overlooking three impressive sea stacks.

Events

Thurso-based North Highland Harriers organise a series of trail runs over the winter which start at 4.5 miles and culminate in a run round Loch More. *www.northhighlandharriers.co.uk*

Dalnawillan Lodge

Loch More

Flow Country

The Castle of Mey 10k is run on tarmac paths and roads through the scenic castle grounds.
www.mey10k.co.uk

Other Activities

Look for fossil fish at Achanarras Quarry on the B870 near the A9. Or explore relatively modern human remains at the Grey Cairns of Camster near Wick, east of Loch More. These are some of the best preserved Neolithic chambered cairns in Britain.

Blanket Bog

Caithness and Sutherland are home to the largest and most diverse peat bog in Europe. It is three times bigger than any other UK or Irish peat bog and has unusually extensive carpets of sphagnum moss. Such large bogs are called blanket bogs. Most of the UK's blanket bogs began to form 5000–6000 years ago and depths of over 5m are quite common. Peat forms when wet, acidic conditions prevent the complete decay of vegetation. Drainage and changes in land use are leading to the loss of Britain's bogs. Even so, peat still covers approximately 13% of Scotland. To find out more about peat bogs visit the Forsinard Flows RSPB reserve. It is on the A897 or can be reached by train from Altnabreac.
www.rspb.org.uk

Islands

Getting to Scotland's islands is often half the adventure. Despite their relative inaccessibility these islands have well-trod, easy trails as well as more challenging part-trail, part-hill routes. All are unforgettable places to run.

Skye's Cuillin from Raasay

Port Dubh
Photo: Keri Page

65 Kerrera

Distance	10km (6 miles)	Ascent	250m (800ft)
Map	OS Landranger 49, OS Explorer 359		
Navigation •••	Circle the southern half of the island		
Terrain •••	Stony tracks and rough tarmac road		
Wet Feet •••	Good grip even in wet weather		
Start/Finish	Kerrera Ferry Jetty PA34 4PE NM 830 286		

Track circuit on an easily accessible traffic-free island

Kerrera is only five hundred metres from the mainland but feels a whole world apart. This route follows tracks and rough tarmac road in a loop around the southern half of the island. The short detour to ruined Gylen Castle is a must. Despite its aesthetic clifftop setting the MacDougall chieftain who built the castle was more concerned with its suitability as a lookout post. His worry was justified. In 1642 the castle was besieged and its occupants massacred. A young boy survived to become the next clan chief. The seascape from this old lookout is well worth the detour even though there are stunning views all the way round the trail. Stopping at the Tea Garden is a convenient excuse to delay the return to the mainland.

🏃 **START**   Step off the ferry and follow the road along the shore. After 150m the road forks and the route takes the right-hand branch to head uphill towards the middle of the island. Continue past the second set of houses (Bailliemore) to a gate on the left with a faded slate sign. ❶ Turn left through the gate and follow the track over the hill and down to Barnabuck House. ❷ Avoid the house by going to the right of the triangular walled garden then climb left up a grassy verge to join a higher track. Continue along this for 2km past Ardmore to reach Gylen Castle Tea Garden and Bunkhouse. ❸ Soon after the Tea Garden follow a signpost right through a gate to follow a grassy track out and back to Gylen Castle. This detour adds 1km to the route. After returning to the main track, which becomes a rough tarmac road, climb to Upper Gylen then descend to follow the east shore 2km back to the ferry slip. Climbers will be unable to resist the temptation to scramble up a triangular fin of dyke passed along the way.

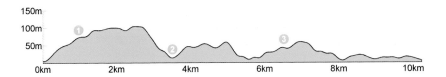

Trip Planning

The Kerrera ferry runs all year round. *www.kerrera-ferry.co.uk* 🚌 Oban Kerrera Ferry 🚗 Follow signs to Gallanach past Oban's main ferry terminal onto a narrow coastal road. Continue for around two miles and park on the right just before the ferry slip. 🛟 🏠 🚻 The Tea Garden and Bunkhouse at Lower Gylen is open during the summer (April to September, closed on Mondays and Tuesdays). Winter opening is more limited. (Customer toilets only.) *www.kerrerabunkhouse.co.uk* 🐕 Unfenced grazing all the way round, particularly along the eastern shore.

Other Routes

Oban is the main ferry port for the Inner Hebrides. The closest of the Inner Hebrides islands is Mull which has beautiful coastal scenery and white sand beaches. It also has good trail running on coastal paths and forest tracks. These can be combined in the north of the island near Glengorm Castle. Although many trails are out and back a circuit from Ensay goes round the Treshnish peninsula on grassy paths, tracks and road. An outstanding out and back run goes along the south side of Ulva, a private island off Mull's west coast.

Events

Forget the ferry. Competitors in the Craggy Island Triathlon swim from Gallanach to Kerrera before cycling and running around the island. *www.craggyislandtriathlon.com*

Mull and Coll host half marathons and shorter races followed by energetic ceilidhs. The Coll course is partly on road and partly on grassy tracks through the dunes. *www.mullrunners.com* *www.collhalfmarathon.co.uk*

Oban is the start point for a long distance sailing and hill running event. The Scottish Islands Peaks Race sees teams of sailors and hill runners battling their way across the waves and over the hills of Mull, Jura and Arran to reach Troon on the Ayrshire coast.

www.scottishislandspeaksrace.com

Kerrcra

Gylen Castle

Newton Point

66 The Cock of Arran

Distance	12km (8 miles)	Ascent	275m (900ft)
Map	OS Landranger 69, OS Explorer 361		
Navigation •••	Signposted paths onto the hill then follow the coast		
Terrain •••	Tracks, grassy hill and shore paths. Part of the shore path is too rocky to run		
Wet Feet •••	Boggy patches along the shore		
Start/Finish	Lochranza KA27 8JF NR 937 506		

A mixed bag of sublime running and coastal scrambling

Part of this route is unrunnable – the rest is exceptional. Raving about an ascent is unusual but the rising traverse up the side of Glen Chalmadale is easily runnable and has a superb view of Arran's high jagged peaks. The grassy path down to Laggan Cottage is one of the best descents in Scotland. Pure dead brilliant by any rating system. The next section is testing, but worthwhile. Be prepared for slow going as the coastal path is rough and rocky. Admire the view of Bute, watch out for seals and stop to inspect the fossilised footprints of an unsettlingly large millipede. The intermittently runnable section culminates in the unrunnable rubble of an old landslide. The difficulties end after scrambling over and around these sandstone boulders. The remainder of the route follows a level grassy path around the coastline and into Lochranza.

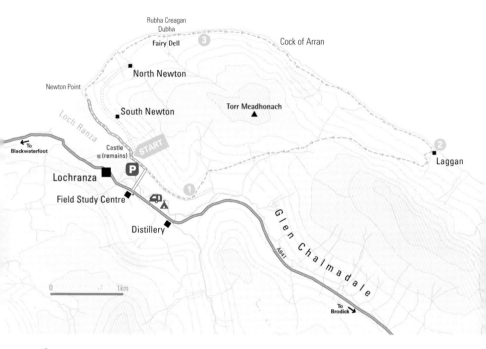

🏃 **START**   Head inland along a minor road. This becomes an unsurfaced lane climbing uphill past houses to an information board and path signed to Laggan. ① Turn left onto the Laggan path and follow a rising traverse up the line of an old stony track to the col between Torr Meadhonach and Creag Ghlas Cuithe. Continue over the col and down to the white cottage at Laggan. ② Turn left at the cottage and follow the shore path. Although the route is clear the path is too rough and rocky to run in many places. After nearly 5km of intermittently runnable terrain the path disappears into the boulders of an old landslide. ③ A few hundred metres of scrambling over and around rocks leads to a shingle beach then a level grassy path which gives easy running back round Newton Point to the start of the route.

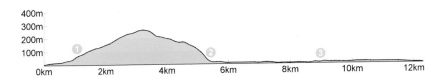

Trip Planning

🚌 Lochranza, Newton Road at the Field Studies Centre 🚗 Turn off the A841 opposite the Field Studies Centre and follow Newton Road round left to a small grassy parking area at the head of Loch Ranza. 🚾 Lochranza Pier 🍽 Lochranza Hotel or the tiny Sandwich Station opposite Lochranza Pier (seven days, 9am to 6pm). *www.thesandwichstation.com* 🏠 Lochranza has a youth hostel, hotel, campsite and B&B accommodation. *www.syha.org.uk www.lochranza.co.uk www.arran-campsite.com* 🐕 Unfenced grazing.

Other Routes

More consistently runnable trails can be found near Brodick Castle, out and back through Glen Sannox or Glen Rosa and through the Forestry Commission's Glenrickard Forest near Lamlash.

Above Laggan

The Cock of Arran

Red Deer, Loch Ranza

Events

Arran hosts several events including the Isle of Arran Half Marathon, the Goatfell Hill Race and the Round Arran Relay.

Fossil Footprints

A few hundred metres after joining the shore path at Laggan the route passes a ruin next to a square-sided natural harbour. Look on the right hand wall of the harbour to see a very rare trace fossil. Between two parallel scratches are the three hundred million year-old tracks of a giant arthropod – a relative of today's centipedes and millipedes. Arthropleura was the largest invertebrate ever to walk on Earth. The creature that made the tracks at Laggan would have been about one metre long but palaeontologists have found evidence of Arthropleura which grew up to three metres.

Dùn Caan from Bealach Ruadh

67 Dùn Caan, Raasay

Distance	16km (10 miles)	Ascent	550m (1800ft)
Map	OS Landranger 24, OS Explorer 409		
Navigation •••	Faint path at start of descent but otherwise paths and junctions are clear		
Terrain •••	Grassy shore path, tarmac road, stony path, rougher descent, forest roads and paths		
Wet Feet •••	Boggy and muddy descent		
Start/Finish	Raasay Ferry Terminal IV48 8TD NG 545 362		

Trail, road and hill running with superb sea views

The distinctive flat-topped summit of Dùn Caan has one of the best views in the whole of the Highlands. Take a camera and be prepared to shoot a 360° panorama from the trig point taking in Skye's Red and Black Cuillin, the Trotternish Ridge and across the Inner Sound to Applecross and Kintail. Easy running on quiet roads and a stony path make light work of the ascent of Dùn Caan. The descent path is wetter, rougher and muddier but runnable with care. It has a distractingly good view of Skye. Raasay is often overlooked despite the short and frequent ferry service connecting it to its bigger and more famous neighbour. Although this run can easily be done as a day trip Raasay merits a longer stay and further exploration.

🏃 **START** Head left at the top of the ferry slip past old boats and cars to pick up the way-marked shore path. Follow waymarkers around the headland, through rhododendrons, a gate and down to the shore for 700m. ① Follow waymarkers inland and up the right hand side of a field to the road. Turn left along the road for nearly 1km to a passing place just before a left-hand bend. ② Take a grassy path which climbs up from the passing place, through a gate and onto a track which leads to the upper road. ③ Turn left onto this road for 1km then continue uphill to the summit of the main road just before the Balmeanach sign. ④ Turn onto the stony path signed to Dùn Caan and climb gradually over moorland to a lochan at the top of an escarpment. Descend steeply, cross boggy ground and climb a zigzag path to the summit. ⑤ Retrace steps down the zigzags. Do not recross the boggy ground, but instead follow an equally boggy track line along the side of the valley. As the old track line curves round the hillside head downhill to the lochan. ⑥ Cross the stream as it enters the lochan and follow a clear narrow path on the

right-hand side of the water. Veer right up a small escarpment, cross a stile and follow the right hand side of the stream down to the forest. The path is clear with stretches of excellent runnable terrain interspersed with rough and boggy sections. ⑦ Go through a gate and descend steeply through trees to the forest road. Cross the closest bridge, signed "Burma Road 1.5km", and continue for 500m to a waymarked path junction. ⑧ Head right and uphill on the footpath to cross slightly boggy ground then descend on a soft pine needled path through conifers. Cross the road and continue straight ahead on the path then turn right onto the Temptation Hill track which heads downhill past Loch a' Mhuillin to the main island road. ⑨ Head right and downhill to return to the ferry.

Trip Planning

🚌 Frequent daytime sailings from Sconser to Raasay. *www.calmac.co.uk* 🚍 Sconser Ferry Terminal 🚗 The ferry terminal is on the A87 just over twenty miles from the Skye Bridge. 🚾 Sconser and Raasay Ferry Terminals. 🛏 🏠 Raasay House provides overnight accommodation and a café/restaurant/bar for residents and day trippers. *www.raasay-house.co.uk* 🐕 Signs request that dogs are kept on leads while on Raasay.

Other Routes

Raasay Forest has a variety of waymarked and signposted routes. An information leaflet available on the ferry or at Raasay House describes paths through the forest and around the island. These vary from easily runnable terrain to rough, boggy moorland or rocky shoreline paths.

Other Activities

Raasay House offer a wide range of water and land-based outdoor activities including sea kayaking, coasteering and gorge walking. *www.raasay-house.co.uk*

Dùn Caan, Raasay

Black Cuillin from Dùn Caan

Calum's Road

In recent centuries a combination of forced and natural emigration has emptied the Highlands and Islands. The inhabitants of Arnish, a North Raasay crofting village, knew that
their settlement would be deserted too if it remained without a road. In 1964, after de-
cades of unsuccessful lobbying of the local council, Calum MacLeod decided to build the
road himself. Armed with a pick, shovel and wheelbarrow it took him over ten years to
build the one and three quarter miles of single track road which connects Arnish with Bro-
chel Castle. An understated plaque by the side of the road fails to convey just how quixotic
this idea was. Stand by the cairn, look at the rough peat bogs and marvel at the strength
in mind and body of the man who set out to build this road single-handed.

Camas Malag
and Blaven

68 Boreraig & Suisnish, Skye

Distance	17km (11 miles)	Ascent	325m (1000ft)
Map	OS Landranger 32, OS Explorer 412		
Navigation •••	Signed from the road then clear path over the hill and along the coast		
Terrain •••	Tarmac road, stony and grassy tracks and paths		
Wet Feet •••	A few puddles, bits of soft ground and stepping stones across small streams		
Start/Finish	Camas Malag IV49 9BB NG 582 193		

Sea and mountain views from road, track and coastal path

Most potential trail runs on Skye begin promisingly but degenerate into bog and boulders. This one is different. A stretch of scenic road running is followed by excellent, consistently runnable tracks and paths. Skye is renowned for its incredible scenery and in this respect the route does conform; singling out just one highlight is tough. The grassy descent into the clearance village of Boreraig? The smooth shore path with its colourful rock flowers and views of the Small Isles? Or the impressively spiky ridge of Blaven which dominates the skyline for the final leg of the route?

START Head away from the sea along the tarmac road. Barking dogs are likely to run out while passing the cluster of houses just before reaching the Broadford to Elgol road. ① Continue straight ahead onto this road. It is fairly quiet and although it has no pavement it is easy to escape onto the verge when cars go past. Watch out for fast moving lorries travelling to and from the nearby marble quarry. Follow the road past the loch, church and stand of trees to a gate on the right before houses. ② Turn right through the gate and climb uphill on a gravel track. After about 250m go right at the T-junction onto the Marble Line track. At the circular base of the old winding wheel continue uphill on a rougher path through the old marble quarry, a Site of Special Scientific Interest (SSSI) for its geology. Go through a gate onto a grassy track which becomes a stony path leading over the hill and down to the standing stone in the centre of Boreraig. ③ Continue on grassy paths just to the right of the ruins then follow a clear path along the shore and up to the top of the cliff. The path levels out with views of the Small Isles as well as the Black and the Red Cuillin mountains. It then descends towards ruins and a modern farm building at Suisnish. ④ Follow a rough track on the right-hand (uphill side) of the fence to join the farm track leading back to Camas Malag.

Boreraig & Suisnish, Skye

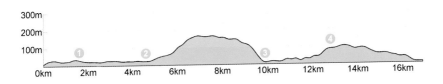

Trip Planning

🚌 Broadford, Suardal Houses near ② or Torrin, Kilbride Road End at ①. 🚗 Drive south from Broadford on the B8083 towards Elgol. Before reaching Torrin turn left towards Kilbride and park on grassy turf at the end of the tarmac road. 🚻 Broadford, opposite the car park next to the garage. ☕ Two miles towards Elgol is the Blue Shed Café at Torrin. *www.theblueshedcafé.co.uk* 🏠 Torrin or Broadford. Camas Malag is occasionally used for wild camping. This should be done in very small numbers and for one or two nights only. Bring water as the area is heavily grazed. Ensure all rubbish is taken away and the hay left pristine for its next visitors. 🐑 Unfenced sheep and cattle grazing, particularly around Boreraig and at Camas Malag

Other Routes

The best view of the Cuillin is from the otherwise unnotable summit of Sgurr Hain (503 207). An excellent trail runs through Glen Sligachan from the old road bridge then a rockier path climbs up to a low ridge just north of the summit. The path down to and around Loch Coruisk is not runnable.

The Trotternish Ridge offers 27.5km of grassy clifftop hill running and is described in Steven Fallon's *Classic Hill Runs and Races in Scotland*. Experience its weird rock architecture on 10km of well-trod paths around the Quiraing. Start at a lay-by near Flodigarry (463 710).

Other Activities

Turn the route into a mini triathlon by cycling the road section and leaving bikes at Suardal for pickup on the drive out. Deep water off smooth pink granite bedrock at Camas Malag is perfect for swimming although quite seaweedy at low tide.

Skye's mountains are unlike any other UK hills. The Black Cuillin boast the only Munro which requires a rock climb to reach its summit – the aptly named Inaccessible Pinnacle. The full ridge traverse is a challenge for experienced mountaineers who take around fourteen hours to walk between its first and last summits. The ridge has been run in an impressive 3 hours 17 minutes by Es Tresidder. Hiring a qualified guide is recommended for non-climbers who wish to explore the

Boreraig & Suisnish, Skye

Loch Eishort

ridge's trickier summits. Try High Mountain Guides *www.highmountainguides.com* or Skye Guides *www.skyeguides.co.uk*.

Island Industry

After leaving the road at Suardal the route follows an old railway track built over one hundred years ago to carry marble quarried in the Strath to the pier at Broadford. Some say Skye's attractive grey-white marble was used to build Iona Abbey, the Vatican and the Palace of Versailles. When the quarry first opened experienced Belgian quarrymen were brought over to train local workers. Despite substantial initial investment the enterprise closed after only a few years. Parts of the quarry buildings can still be seen including the circular base of the winding wheel used to pull the train up the hill. The modern quarry, further towards Blaven, produces some decorative stone but most of the rock is crushed onsite to make pebbledash or lime.

Harris from Berneray

69 Reinigeadal, Harris

Distance	19km (12 miles)	Ascent	675m (2200ft)
Map	OS Landranger 14, OS Explorer 456		
Navigation ●●●	Lochside track to road, signed return from Reinigeadal		
Terrain ●●●	Stony track, tarmac road and grassy path		
Wet Feet ●●●	Occasional puddles and soft spots		
Start/Finish	Lay-by near Urgha NB 184 004		

Old track and quiet road lead to a dramatic coastal path

North Harris is the hilliest part of the low lying chain of islands known as the Western Isles or Outer Hebrides. Intricate sea inlets and rocky, rugged hills characterise their eastern coastline and form the backdrop to this run. A good lochside track up Gleann Lacasdail climbs over a pass to join a single track road by Loch Seaforth. This road was built in 1989, making Reinigeadal the last Scottish settlement to be connected to the public road network. The route continues on a scenic path high above the shore which used to be Reinigeadal's only land connection to the outside world. The islands out to sea are the Shiants and the Scottish mainland is a barely visible line on the horizon. After descending to the head of Loch Trolamaraig the path climbs steeply over the hill to a fast final descent down to Urgha.

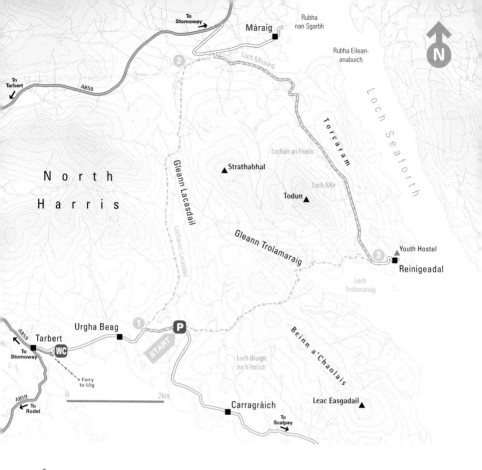

🏃 START Follow the road towards Tarbert for 500m and climb uphill to a lay-by. ① Turn right onto a track and follow it downhill, along the shore of the loch then up over the col at the head of the glen. Descend into the next valley to a junction just before the main track descends to and crosses the river. ② Turn right and go through a couple of gates to reach the road. Follow this along the sea loch then steeply uphill over the pass and down to Reinigeadal. ③ Just before the first house turn right onto a grassy coastal path signed to Urgha. Follow this obvious path as it contours around the bay then climbs over a low hill to reach the head of Loch Trolamaraig. Cross the footbridge and zigzag steeply up over the col. Continue straight ahead to descend to the start.

Trip Planning

🚢 Caledonian MacBrayne operates ferries from Uig on Skye to Tarbert on North Harris.
🚗 The parking lay-by is on the Tarbert to Scalpay road about two miles east of Tarbert. The path

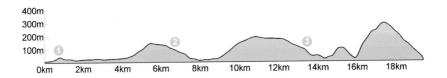

to Reinigeadal is signed from the lay-by. 🚾 Tarbert Tourist Information Centre 🍵 First Fruits Tearoom opposite the Tourist Information Centre in Tarbert or the Harris Hotel on the Stornoway road. 🏠 The Gatliff Trust operates several Hebridean hostels including Rhenigidale. A stay at any of these bothy-style hostels is recommended. *www.gatliff.org.uk*

Other Routes

The Reinigeadal Path is part of the Harris Walkway, a twenty five mile linear route. Another part of the Walkway follows the Scholar's Path between Grosabhay (151 927) and Kyles Stockinish. Road running is needed to complete the circuit or continue along the Coffin Path through Bealach Eorabhat to Seilebost before joining the road. There are some boggy sections.

The Bogha Glas (186 115) to Miabhaig (100 062) track makes an excellent 17km (10 miles) one way run. Joining the two ends by roads creates a 37km (23 miles) circuit including an off-road shortcut on the old postman's path just north of Maraig (194 069).

Events

The Harris Half held in early July is the last in the series of Western Isles Half Marathons. These popular races are renowned for their great social atmosphere as well as particularly scenic road running. The first run takes place during late May in Stornoway on the Isle of Lewis. This is followed by runs on Benbecula, Skye, Barra and finally Harris. *www.srac.org.uk/heb3.htm*

Other Activities

The west side of the Outer Hebrides is utterly different to the east. No island visit is complete without a walk along one of the spectacular white sand beaches and through the machair. These Hebridean flower meadows are a riot of colour during June, July and August.

Bikes travel for free on Calmac ferries and road cycling tours of the Western Isles are a popular way of seeing these islands.

The shallow Sound of Harris is perfect for sea kayaking. Adventure Hebrides offer guided kayak trips and a range of other water and land-based adventures. *www.adventurehebrides.com*

Reinigeadal, Harris

Loch Trolamaraig

Gaelic

The Outer Isles are the stronghold of the Gaelic language in Scotland. A basic understanding of some Gaelic words helps interpret place names throughout the Highlands and Islands. The Ordnance Survey publish a useful glossary online *www.ordnancesurvey.co.uk* For more detail consult Peter Drummond's comprehensive *Scottish Hill Names: Their Origin and Meaning*.

Basic landforms
Lairig, Bealach, Cadha (narrow) – Pass
Beinn, Monadh, Meall (rounded) – Hill
Gleann, Srath (wide) – Valley

Useful descriptions
Beag – Little
Mor – Big
Cas – Steep
Bogach – Bog
Tioram – Dry
Leacach – Stony

Colours
Buidhe – Yellow
Dearg – Red
Liath – Grey
Odhar – Dun-coloured
Ruadh – Red or brown
Uaine – Green

The Old Man of Hoy

70 The Old Man of Hoy

Distance	21km (13 miles)	Ascent	625m (2000ft)
Map	OS Landranger 7, OS Explorer 462		
Navigation •••	Map and compass for untracked moorland, otherwise obvious paths and features		
Terrain •••	Good paths and runnable untracked moorland with short springy heather		
Wet Feet •••	Moorland is boggy in places		
Start/Finish	Moaness Ferry Pier HY 245 039		

An adventurous trail and hill run past dramatic coastal scenery

A superbly constructed path crosses the moor from Rackwick Bay to the clifftop viewpoint overlooking the Old Man of Hoy. At 137m this is Britain's highest sea stack. Many rock climbers aspire to climb the Old Man and while most are content to abseil back down to sea level a few take a faster route. In 2008 the stack was base jumped by Tim Emmett, Roger Holmes and Gus Hutchinson Brown. Sea cliff climbers are accustomed to bird attack but runners are not. During the summer months this run is not recommended for the ornithophobic. Hoy's upland moors are the breeding grounds for 17% of the world's population of great skuas. Known as bonxies, these large brown sea birds attack at eye level. They (probably) will not connect if deterred by rapidly windmilling arms. In clear, dry weather the untracked moorland is fairly easy to run and the view from the summit of Cuilags is superb.

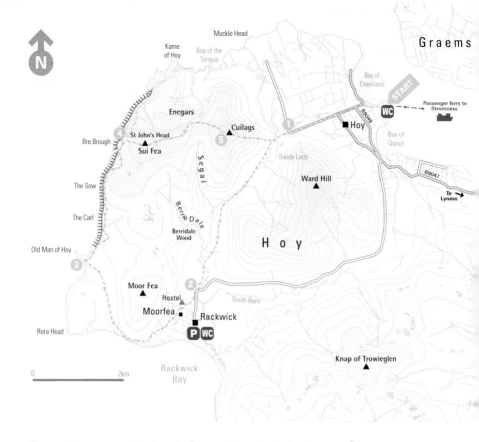

Shorten the route to 16km (10 miles) by starting at Rackwick Bay, near ❷, if staying on Hoy or run the route as a day trip from Stromness as described. 🏃 START Step off the ferry at Moaness and head straight up the road for over 2km to a right-hand bend beneath Cuilags. ❶ Continue straight ahead onto a track signed to Rackwick which goes past Sandy Loch and continues as a clear, signed path through the glen. The 4km path is rough, narrow and consistently runnable to the road on the far side of the island. ❷ Turn right and head uphill on the road, then follow signs for the Old Man of Hoy to continue uphill past the front of the youth hostel. Keep climbing on grassy track and then path to leave Rackwick Bay. The path then descends across moorland to cliffs above the Old Man of Hoy. ❸ Continue along the clifftop to St John's Head where a large section of cliff has clear intentions of becoming the next sea stack. ❹ Turn inland on one of several faint paths. All of these soon disappear. Continue over gradually rising untracked moorland to reach the trig point near the summit of Sui Fea. Head left of the lochan, then follow high ground round the head of the valley to climb Cuilags. ❺ Descend very steep, tussocky hillside westwards towards the Moaness Ferry Pier.

The Old Man of Hoy

Trip Planning

Hoy is an RSPB Reserve and care should be taken to avoid disturbing the birds, particularly during spring and summer. If attacked, wave hands above head height and move away as quickly as possible. 🚌 🚢 Graemsay passenger ferry from Stromness to Moaness, North Hoy. *www.orkneyferries.co.uk* 🚗 🚢 A car ferry runs from Houton, eight miles south-east of Stromness, to Lyness on Hoy. *www.orkneyferries.co.uk* Drive twelve miles to park at Rackwick Bay and follow signs for the Old Man of Hoy to join the route near ②. 🚾 Rackwick Bay and Moaness Pier 🍴 Beneth'ill Café is a few hundred metres from the Moaness Ferry Pier. (Summer only. Closes with the last ferry.) 🏠 Rackwick Hostel has a great location overlooking the bay. Hoy Centre is near the Moaness Ferry Pier. *www.hostelsorkney.co.uk* Stromness has a range of accommodation including hostels. *www.brownsorkney.com* It is possible to sleep on board the ferry if catching the early morning boat to Scrabster. *www.northlinkferries.co.uk* 🐕 Dogs should be kept on a short lead or under close control while on the RSPB Reserve. This applies to the whole route except for Rackwick Bay and near Moaness.

Machair

The Old Man of Hoy

Bonxie on Cuilags

Other Routes

To omit Cuilags descend south down Berrie Dale or Segal and join the Rackwick Path. Continuing north along the cliffs from St John's Head is not recommended. The path becomes thickly vegetated and unrunnable with steep sea cliffs and crags which are tricky to navigate in poor weather.

TV Wars

In the mid-1960s the BBC and ITV engaged in a 'war' of increasingly audacious outdoor broadcasts that stretched the limits of television technology. This culminated in 1967 when army landing craft deposited sixteen tons of equipment on the beach at Rackwick Bay. Giant sledges were used to haul the kit three miles across the moor to the cliffs overlooking the Old Man of Hoy. This set the stage for the live broadcast of six of Britain's best rock climbers tackling three different routes on the sea stack. In the words of producer Alan Chivers, filming the climbers was "a bigger headache than anything I've ever done before". In spite of its complex logistics the live broadcast was a triumphant success.

Resources

Public Transport

Traveline Scotland – timetables and journey planner for all bus, rail, coach, air and ferry services in Scotland *www.travelinescotland.com* 0871 200 22 33 (24 hours)

ScotRail – train services throughout Scotland *www.scotrail.co.uk*

Citylink – coach services throughout Scotland *www.citylink.co.uk*

Car Journey Planning

Google Maps *www.google.com/maps*

Bing Maps *www.bing.com/maps*

Traffic Scotland – up-to-date information on closures, roadworks and traffic jams *www.trafficscotland.org*

Weather

Mountain Weather Information Service - mountain area forecasts in Scotland, England and Wales *www.mwis.org.uk*

UK Met Office – general and mountain forecasts *www.metoffice.gov.uk*

MetCheck – general forecasts *www.metcheck.com*

Live Eye Views from Traffic Scotland – particularly useful for checking roadside snow conditions *www.trafficscotland.org/lev/*

Accommodation

Visit Scotland – national tourist information organisation with information on travel, accommodation and places to visit *www.visitscotland.com* 0845 22 55 121

Tourist Information Centres – contact information *www.visitscotland.com/guide/where-to-find-us*

Undiscovered Scotland – visitor guide with accommodation and local business listings *www.undiscoveredscotland.co.uk*

Many regions and communities have their own websites with information on local accommodation and businesses.

The Mountain Bothies Association (MBA) is a member-funded organisation which maintains around 100 bothies in remote parts of the UK. The owners of these shelters have made them available for free public use and they are maintained by work parties of MBA volunteers. Follow the bothy code by only using bothies for short stays in groups of less than six people, leaving the

Resources

bothy clean and tidy with dry kindling, carrying out all litter, burying human waste and obeying restrictions during the stalking and lambing seasons *www.mountainbothies.org.uk*

Wild camping is permitted everywhere access rights apply except for seasonal restrictions along the East shore of Loch Lomond. Wild camping is lightweight, done in small numbers and only for a few nights in any one place. Avoid buildings, farmland and stalking or grouse-shooting land during the season. Bury human waste and carry out toilet paper and sanitary items as these take a long time to biodegrade. Carrying out human waste is required in popular wild camping areas such as the Cairngorms National Park. For more information contact The Mountaineering Council of Scotland *www.mcofs.org.uk*

Mapping

Paper Maps

Ordnance Survey – 1:50,000 Landranger and 1:25,000 Explorer maps *www.ordnancesurvey.co.uk*
Harvey Maps – 1:40,000 British Mountain Maps, 1:25,000 Superwalker maps for popular areas and National Trail maps *www.harveymaps.co.uk*

Mapping Software

Software such as Memory Map or Anquet Maps allows users to look at Ordnance Survey maps and plot routes on their home computers. Runners with GPS devices can download plotted routes to their devices or upload recorded routes *www.memory-map.co.uk www.anquet.co.uk*

There are also many similar online-only applications; *www.bikehike.co.uk* or *www.gmap-pedometer.com* provide simple interfaces which enable users to plot and download their own routes. Online communities store large databases of public routes uploaded by their members. These include Ordnance Survey getamap *www.getamap.ordnancesurveyleisure.co.uk* Garmin Connect *http://connect.garmin.com/* WalkJogRun *www.walkjogrun.net* and MapMyRUN *www.mapmyrun.com*

Online grid conversion tools convert grid references into post codes for use with sat navs *www.streetmap.co.uk/gridconvert.html*

Access and Representation

Scottish Natural Heritage's outdoor access website gives detailed guidance on access legislation *www.outdooraccess-scotland.com*

Scotways, the Scottish Rights of Way and Access Society *www.scotways.com* 0131 558 1222

The Mountaineering Council of Scotland *www.mcofs.org.uk* 01738 493942

Scottish Hill Runners *www.shr.uk.com*

Running Clubs

There are running clubs all over Scotland packed with enthusiasts of all abilities. Joining a club is a great way to become a better runner while also making friends and discovering new routes. Find a local club through the searchable map on the membership pages of the Scottish Athletics website *www.scottishathletics.org.uk* or by calling them on 0131 539 7320. Every club is different so it is worth finding out about the running speed of club runs, coaching sessions and the club's emphasis on road, off-road and social activities.

jogscotland is the recreational arm of Scottish Athletics and has groups all over the country. jogscotland makes walking and jogging accessible to everyone including absolute beginners *www.jogscotland.org.uk* 0131 273 3003.

Specialist running shops often organise group runs or can provide contact details for local clubs. Orienteering combines running with navigation and is a good way to develop the skills needed for more remote off-road runs. Find a club or local events by contacting the Scottish Orienteering Association *www.scottish-orienteering.org* 01479 861374.

Racing

Trail races are increasing in number although there are relatively few pure trail races compared to the number of road and hill events. Most events are listed in the Scottish Running Guide which is available free from many sports centres and running shops. The list is also available online at *www.scottishrunningguide.com*

The Scottish Hill Racing website is an independent website providing details on races, results, runners and clubs for hill races *www.scottishhillracing.co.uk*

Mountain marathons are two day events which combine hill running, orienteering and camping. Most events have a range of courses to suit different levels of physical ability and navigational skill. The Lowe Alpine Mountain Marathon (LAMM) and the Highlander Mountain Marathon are both held in Scotland *www.lamm.co.uk* *www.highlandermountainmarathon.org.uk*

Resources

Some adventure races, triathlons and duathlons combine trail and/or hill running with other activities. The Sleepmonsters website has a comprehensive listing of multi-sport events *www.sleepmonsters.co.uk*

Training, Coaching and Guiding

Most clubs organise training sessions as well as social runs. These usually include activities such as hill reps or fartleks. Many coaches work with clubs and it is also possible to hire personal coaches for individuals or small groups.

Confident and accurate navigation only comes through practice but the basic techniques can be taught on courses intended for orienteers or hill walkers. Suitable courses are run by Glenmore Lodge, Scotland's National Outdoor Training Centre as well as by many other providers *www.glenmorelodge.org.uk* 01479 861 256

An increasing number of companies offer coaching and guided running. In Scotland these include: Running The Highlands who organise running holidays in Deeside and the Cairngorms *www.runningthehighlands* and the Perthshire company Wild Outdoors which offers training and guided running as well as slower paced wildlife holidays *www.wildoutdoors.info*

New Route Ideas

Books and magazines

Scottish Hill Tracks published by Scotways, the Scottish Rights of Way and Access Society, is the definitive list of Scotland's ancient rights of way. These old routes vary in quality from excellent tracks to untracked rough ground and bog.

Steven Fallon's *Classic Hill Runs and Races in Scotland* is the essential reference book for Scottish hill runners. It describes 35 hill races and 35 other hill routes in the Southern Uplands, Highlands and Islands.

Trail Running is published quarterly and is the only UK magazine dedicated to off-road running. Information aimed at walkers and mountain bikers can be adapted to running.

Outdoor shops, bookshops and tourist information centres usually sell a range of guidebooks.

Land owners

Many land owners waymark or signpost routes on their land. Information can be found on their websites, by contacting estate offices or on boards located at access points. Some national organisations are listed below but there are many smaller private estates all over the country which encourage public access.

The Forestry Commission *www.forestry.gov.uk*

Scottish Natural Heritage *www.snh.gov.uk*

John Muir Trust *www.jmt.org*

National Trust for Scotland *www.nts.org.uk*

Online communities and databases

Online communities (see Mapping) can provide ideas of where other people go running in particular areas. Many online communities or route databases intended for walkers and mountain bikers are also useful for trail and hill runners. New websites for runners, walkers and bikers appear all the time so an internet search is the best way of finding suitable sites.

Regional and local information

Tourist information centres often have free leaflets describing local walking routes. Many of these are also available online through local or national websites. *http://walking.visitscotland.com*

Many running clubs write up regular training runs on their websites and post route maps.

Acknowledgements

The quotation at the start of the book is from a poem by Charles Hamilton Sorley called "The Song of the Ungirt Runners". Sorley was born in Aberdeen in 1895 and educated at Marlborough College where his favourite activity was cross-country running. War broke out soon after Sorley left school and he died, aged twenty, at Loos. Robert Graves described Charles Sorley as one of the three most important poets killed during the Great War.

A great many people have helped me research this book by suggesting routes, welcoming me on club runs, showing me favourites, accompanying or accommodating me on my travels and even running back and forth for photographs. Mere words are inadequate thanks. This project has benefited enormously from the support and advice of the following clubs and individuals, any remaining inaccuracies and errors are mine alone and apologies to anyone I have inadvertently missed. Ayr Seaforth (Laurence Baker), Cairngorm Runners (Steve Wall), Carnethy (Adrian Davis, Konrad Rawlik), Cosmic Hill Bashers (Simon Peachey, Colin Russell), Dumfries Running Club (Susan Graham), Dundee Road Runners (Andrew Llanwarne), Forfar Road Runners (Mark Melnyk), Galloway Harriers (David Beattie, Grant Morrow, Rick Williams), Greenock Glenpark Harriers (Stevie McLoone), Harmeny Pentland Runners (Iain Morrice, Frank Tooley), Highland Hill Runners (Roxy and Ross Bannerman, Eilidh and Paul Raistrick), Hunters Bog Trotters (Dan Gay, Ian Harkness, Kate Jenkins, Alison Johnston, Don Naylor, Geoff Simpson), Inveraray jogscotland (Fiona Corner), Lochaber (Peter Duggan, Keri Page, Bruce Poll, Ben Wallace), Isle of Mull Cycling Club (Jim Keenan), Moorfoot Runners (Marion Blackwood, Ruth Noble), North Highland Harriers (Colin Earnshaw, Dave Hall), Shettleston (David Jamieson), Strathearn Harriers (Liz and Phil Mestecky), Tain Runners (Anne Mackay), WalkJogRunMoray (Nick Brown, Angela Reid, Marie Third), Westerlands (Elizabeth and Neil Adams, John Donnelly, Manny, Brenda and Maisy Gorman, Cat Miller, Graeme Orr, Johnston Orr, Hamilton Semple, Tilly Smith, Chris Upson), Jenn West and Jo Armstrong, Simon Bates, Elspeth and Raph Bleakley, Gail and Chris Born, Jo Boyd, Tim Burton, Diana and Tom Challands, Nancy Chambers, Liz and David Culshaw, Vicki and Ben Dodman (Rockhopper Sea Kayaking), Annabel Drysdale and Lorne Gill (SNH), Pat and Mike Duguid, Di Gilbert and Derek Boggan, Jen and Andy Edwards, Shirley Singh and John Goldsworthy, Robbie Gordon (PKCT), Lisa Handcock, Katie and Sam Hawkins, Rik Higham, Vicky Hilton (Glenlivet Estate), Will Huckerby and Ruari Watt (Forestry Commission), Rob Jarvis (High Mountain Guides), Matt Jenneson (Invergarry Lodge Hostel), Willie Johnstone (Speyside Runner), Matt Jones (Cannich Campsite), Scott Kennedy and Colin Hastie (Run 4 It), Gavin McCutcheon, Angus McKellar, Colin Meek and Paul Tattersall (Go Further Scotland), Erica Niven (Scottish Borders Ranger Service), Tim Pickering (Adventure

Thanks for making it fun

Hebrides), Viv Scott, Neil Stewart (Running the Highlands), Robert Sanderson (Adventure Zone Scotland), Neil Smith, Tom Thorpe, Charlie Watt, Emily and Fran Williams, Nigel Williams (Glenmore Lodge), Chris Wolfe (Argyll Guided). Huge thanks to Franco and the team at Pesda Press for turning raw text into a thing of beauty. Friends met through BSES, UBMC, EUMC and SAC have inspired and continue to inspire my outdoor adventures. Special thanks go to Alison Culshaw, Ellie Homewood, Dougal Ranford and my fantastic family for their unswerving and enthusiastic support throughout.

Index

Index

Index